The Transformation of the State

Also by Georg Sørensen

DEMOCRACY AND DEMOCRATIZATION:
Processes and Prospects in a Changing World

DEMOCRACY, DICTATORSHIP AND DEVELOPMENT:
Economic Development in Selected Regimes of the Third World

CHANGES IN STATEHOOD:
The Transformation of International Relations

INTRODUCTION TO INTERNATIONAL RELATIONS:
Theories and Approaches (2nd edn) (*with Robert Jackson*)

POLITICAL CONDITIONALITY (*editor*)

WHOSE WORLD ORDER?
Uneven Globalization and the End of the Cold War (*editor with Hans-Henrik Holm*)

The Transformation of the State

Beyond the Myth of Retreat

Georg Sørensen

palgrave
macmillan

First published 2004 by
PALGRAVE MACMILLAN
Houndmills, Basingstoke, Hampshire RG21 6XS and
175 Fifth Avenue, New York, N.Y. 10010
Companies and representatives throughout the world

PALGRAVE MACMILLAN is the global academic imprint of the Palgrave Macmillan division of St. Martin's Press, LLC and of Palgrave Macmillan Ltd. Macmillan® is a registered trademark in the United States, United Kingdom and other countries. Palgrave is a registered trademark in the European Union and other countries.

ISBN 0–333–98204–5 hardback
ISBN 0–333–98205–3 paperback

This book is printed on paper suitable for recycling and made from fully managed and sustained forest sources.

A catalogue record for this book is available from the British Library.

Library of Congress Cataloging-in-Publication Data
Sørensen, Georg, 1948–
    The transformation of the state : beyond the myth of retreat / Georg Sørensen.
        p. cm.
    Includes bibliographical references and index.
    ISBN 0–333–98204–5 (cloth)—ISBN 0–333–98205–3 (paper)
        1. State, The. 2. Political development. 3. Globalization. I. Title.

JC11.S58 2004
320.1—dc22   2003055876

10   9   8   7   6   5   4   3   2   1
13   12   11   10   09   08   07   06   05   04

Printed and bound in Great Britain by
Creative Print & Design (Wales), Ebbw Vale

For
Birgit Kanstrup, Jonna Kjær,
Inge Rasmussen and Elin Tveskov

Contents

List of Figures, Tables and Boxes

Figures

Tables

Boxes

Preface

Scholars in all major areas of social science have always focused on sovereign states. They are the basic units of the international system/society; they create the rules that other actors (companies, organizations, movements, individuals) play by; they provide security, freedom, order, justice and welfare for their citizens. But the state is challenged from many quarters and this is reflected in the scholarly debate. Titles such as *The End of the Nation State* (Ohmae 1996), *The Retreat of the State* (Strange 1996), *The End of Sovereignty?* (Camilleri and Falk 1992) or *Governance without Government* (Rosenau and Czempiel 1993) have all helped create the impression that the state is seriously under attack and that a new system 'beyond' the sovereign state is in the making.

This book is first and foremost an introduction to the major debates about how the state is being transformed; it highlights the nature of and evidence about that transformation as seen through those debates. The first chapter sets out the broad contours of debate between those who argue that the state is in retreat and state-centric scholars who argue that it retains its distinctive importance. Subsequent chapters cover the major areas that have provoked the debate between the 'retreat' and the 'state-centric' positions. It is argued that both views provide new insights but also have shortcomings. The relevant insights concern the fact that whereas states have lost influence and autonomy in some areas, as indicated by the 'retreat' argument, they have also been strengthened in various respects identified by the 'state-centric' argument. The shortcomings are connected to narrow definitions and lack of comprehensive analysis. Both views overly downplay the general process of *change* in sovereign statehood over time, leading to new strength in some areas and new weaknesses in others. I use the term 'state transformation' as a general heading under which to summarize these changes in both directions.

The debate about the state is connected to different theoretical views on states and power. Three such views will be presented: the realist, the liberal and the critical. The theoretical views are not neutral: they load the dice in favour of different beliefs. Realists most often think states remain strong; liberals most often think states are growing weaker; critical theorists are more ready to talk about a complex process of state transformation.

In order to assess what has happened to the state, history is important. A baseline idea of what existed before is needed in order to understand the changes that have taken place. The ideal type of the 'modern state', set forth in Chapter 1, is such a baseline. It defines the major features of the modern, Westphalian state as it had developed mainly in Western Europe and North America by around 1950. A further necessary baseline is a broad starting definition of the state sufficient to provide a basis for the comprehensive analysis of state transformation. The conventional view of the state is a suitable starting point: we are dealing with sovereign, territorial entities with a population and a government. But we need to elaborate further on what are the main aspects of statehood in relation to which to contrast the different views on the transformation of the state.

Robert Cox's notion of 'historical structures' is helpful in this regard (Cox 1996). A historical structure is a picture of a particular configuration of forces. It consists of material capabilities, ideas and institutions. Applying this to sovereign states, they can be seen as historical structures made up of material capabilities, ideas and institutions.

In terms of material capabilities, the focus is on the economy. We especially want to know how economic globalization affects states: are they put under pressure in new ways and are they less able to provide social welfare for their citizens? An answer to this question requires a clarification of the elusive concept of globalization. We also need to evaluate the extent to which the economies and state–market relations of the advanced capitalist countries have or have not been transformed as a result of economic globalization. I argue that welfare policies have been upheld and sometimes even expanded in the face of globalization; but they have also faced new challenges as a result of economic change.

In terms of institutions, the focus is on the political-administrative institutions of the state; that is, the government and the state apparatus. We need to discover whether this political level or realm of the state has been transformed and how any changes should be interpreted in context of the 'retreat' versus 'state-centric' debate. Many scholars observe a growth of interstate, transgovernmental and transnational relations but there has been substantial debate about both its extent and its consequences, especially for politics and accountability. Those who think that the changes taking place are a threat to democracy are generally highly sceptical of the prospects for democracy outside the realm of the sovereign state. Others are much more optimistic on democracy's behalf, arguing that democracy can be extended to international institutions as well. A key theme of this book is that there has been a transformation away from governance in the context of national government towards multilevel governance at overlapping national, local and international levels. I see no reason why democracy should not be possible under these new conditions but the challenges for democracy and democratization in the new context have only just started to be examined and explored.

Finally, in terms of ideas, the focus is on nationhood and identity. Nationhood means that a people within a territory makes up a community. The community is based on citizenship (including political, social and economic rights and obligations), and on nationality or 'sentiment' (meaning a common language and a common cultural and historical identity based on literature, myths, symbols, music and art). We shall see that both the community of citizens and the community of sentiment are challenged by several new developments. Has this led to a transformation of citizenship and of collective identity and, if so, in what specific ways? My argument is that communities are being transformed increasingly to include supranational elements.

Having addressed the core substantial aspects of state transformation, we are ready to take on the problem of sovereignty. Sovereignty contains the rules that define the locus of political authority and set the context for relations between states. What happens to sovereignty as a consequence of the substantial changes in statehood? It will be argued that there is a juridical core of sovereignty – constitutional independence – which remains in place. But at the level of regulative rules, meaning the rules by which actors actually play the sovereignty 'game', sovereignty has developed in new ways. This is evidenced in the context of supranational governance (for example, the European Union), where member states allow for comprehensive and systematic interference in each other's 'domestic' affairs. It is also manifested in the way weak, less developed states have had to accept a high degree of external intervention in order to qualify for international aid. The institution of sovereignty will surely survive, but its content has changed considerably. I argue that a new sovereignty game has emerged among the advanced states, especially in the European Union areas of Europe. I also argue that the least developed Third World countries have a sovereignty game with special features.

With the transformation of the state, what are the prospects for violent conflict or for war? Since the Cold War ended, there have been very few interstate wars; we live in the longest period since the Roman Empire of peace between the great powers. Has interstate war become obsolete? In some ways it has: war between consolidated democracies is next to impossible. But violent conflict has certainly not disappeared. Domestic conflict (intrastate war) is sharply increasing in the very weak states, most of which are located in sub-Saharan Africa. And mass-murder terrorism is a new item on the agenda after the attacks of 11 September 2001.

Most of the debate about the state is focused on the advanced capitalist states in the triad, by which I mean Western Europe, North America and Japan/East Asia. This book attempts a more comprehensive analysis by including, on the one hand, the least developed states in the Third World, and, on the other hand, the modernizing states in Asia, Latin America, the Middle East and Eastern Europe. Three of those modernizing states are singled out for further scrutiny: China, India and Russia. It will be demonstrated how the security problem, the state–market relationship, and the relationship to international order play out in context of the various processes of modernization that are taking place.

The final chapters draw together the results of the analysis and discuss the theoretical ramifications. We began with the debate between 'retreat' and 'state-centric' scholars about what is happening to the sovereign state. Both of these positions go too far in the direction of a zero-sum view where the state is either 'losing' (retreat scholars) or 'winning' (state-centric scholars) in a contest with other actors. The appropriate view is that of 'state transformation'. The questions of transformation to what, and why, will both be addressed.

As regards the advanced states, I diagnose that they are in a process of transition from modern to what I call postmodern statehood. I define a postmodern ideal type of state and explain its characteristics in major areas: government, nationhood and economy. I also define an ideal type called the weak, postcolonial state; the claim is that this type helps us understand the current make-up of statehood in significant parts of the Third World. I argue that together with the concept of 'modernizing states', these provide appropriate tools for grasping the major variations in sovereign statehood at the beginning of the new millennium.

The conclusion considers the theoretical ramifications of the analysis and outlines the substantial challenges to analysis that emerge from a system of different types of state undertaking various processes of transformation in the five key areas of democracy, sovereignty, state power, security and economic globalization.

GEORG SØRENSEN

Acknowledgements

The idea for this book emerged from discussions with my publisher, Steven Kennedy. I wanted to do something else at first; he helped me get focused on a book about the transformation of the state. His advice, and his reviewers' on my initial draft typescript, together with a set of detailed and insightful observations that I solicited from Linda Weiss, helped me produce a much improved final version. I am really grateful to them all for their suggestions and counsel.

Stine Bælum and Eva Dyrberg have been excellent research assistants. Stine traced much of the material for several chapters; Eva carefully proof-read the manuscript and came up with many suggestions for better formulations; she also compiled the index.

Colleagues at the Department of Political Science in Aarhus once again provided a stimulating and encouraging research environment; special thanks to Ole Nørgaard for his careful reading of the manuscript. I began working on the project in 2001; it was completed in the summer of 2003. During that period, I also served as Head of Department. Department heads are not normally expected to have time to write books; it has only been possible for me because I have had the best administrative and secretarial assistance that anyone could ask for, in particular from Birgit Kanstrup, Inge Rasmussen, Jonna Kjær and Elin Tveskov. The book is dedicated to them, with my deepest appreciation.

GEORG SØRENSEN

List of Abbreviations

APEC	Asia-Pacific Economic Cooperation
ASEAN	Association of Southeast Asian Nations
BJP	Bharatiya Janata Party
CCP	Chinese Communist Party
CIA	Central Intelligence Agency
ECOWAS	Economic Community of West African States
EU	European Union
FDI	foreign direct investment
G3	Group of Three (Europe, Japan and North America)
G7	Group of Seven (the USA, Canada, Britain, Germany, France, Italy and Japan)
G8	Group of Eight (the USA, Canada, Britain, Germany, France, Italy, Japan and Russia)
GATT	General Agreement on Tariffs and Trade
GDP	gross domestic product
GNP	gross national product
GRI	Global Reporting Initiative
IFI	international financial institution
IGO	intergovernmental organization
IMF	International Monetary Fund
INC	Indian National Congress
INGO	international non-governmental organization
IPE	international political economy
IR	international relations
Mercosur	Mercado Commún del Sur
NAFTA	North American Free Trade Agreement
NGO	non-governmental organization
NMD	National Missile Defense
OAS	Organization of American States
OAU	Organization of African Unity
OECD	Organisation for Economic Co-operation and Development
OPEC	Organization of Petroleum Exporting Countries
PPP	purchasing power parity
RMA	revolution in military affairs
SADC	Southern African Development Community
SAP	Structural Adjustment Programme
SWPR	Schumpeterian Workfare Postnational Regime

TNC	transnational corporation
UN	United Nations
UNITA	União Nacional para a Independência Total de Angola
WTO	World Trade Organization

Chapter 1

The Debate: Context, History and Concepts

Background
The importance of history
The importance of concepts and theories
Conclusion

Background

We live in turbulent times. The most dramatic political change since the end of the Second World War took place more than a decade ago when the Berlin Wall came down, the Cold War ended, and the Soviet Union was dissolved. The competitive struggle between a Western and an Eastern bloc, which had been the major framework for global politics for more than 40 years, came to an end. The tenth anniversary of the end of the Cold War has been celebrated and the USA has been struck by the mass-murder terrorism of 11 September 2001; a coalition led by the USA and the UK has removed Saddam Hussein from power in Iraq. But we still really do not know what came after the Cold War. Is it American supremacy, a unipolar world? Is it a much more complex pattern of cooperation and conflict between a multipolarity of countries and regions? Or is it something else entirely? It is because we do not know for sure that we speak of the 'post-Cold War' period. The 'post-' prefix is a reliable indicator that we are not clear about what kind of political world we have. As a commentator once quipped: 'If Marx had not precisely analysed capitalism we would still call it post-feudalism.' A post-Cold War era indeed; but how much change is there, and what is really going on?

The most dramatic social change is often labelled 'globalization'; many observers focus on the economic aspects of this phenomenon. And sure enough, economic exchange across borders is an increasingly important occurrence. As a recent study of globalization documented (Scholte 2000: 86), the exceptional growth of foreign investment stock, foreign exchange turnover, transborder companies, receipts from international travel and export processing zones combine with a host of other, similar indicators to present a picture of a world dominated by one unified marketplace. Yet sceptics maintain that world exports were as high (as a percentage of gross national product, or GNP) during the decades up to the First World War as they are today. Other economic indicators, such as total foreign investment and international bank transfers, were also at very high levels in the early twentieth century. Economic globalization indeed; but how much change is there and what is really going on?

It is in the wake of these bewildering political and economic changes that a debate about the fate of the sovereign state has emerged anew. Big changes invite stocktaking and assessment of larger developments. When the world is locked in a fixed pattern we tend to take that pattern for granted; when the fixed pattern breaks up, all sorts of questions concerning past and future events and realities come into sight. We used to think that we knew precisely what a state was. J.D.B. Miller expressed that view in no uncertain terms: 'Just as we know a camel or a chair when we see one, so we know a sovereign state. It is a political entity which is treated as a sovereign state by other sovereign states' (Miller 1981: 16). Today, we are much less certain because the entity known as the sovereign state appears to evolve in radically different directions in Western Europe compared to Southeast Asia or sub-Saharan Africa as against North America. In many ways, the sovereign state continues to look formidably strong: it is the prevailing form of political organization: nearly everybody on earth lives in a sovereign state and is a citizen of one. In other ways, the sovereign state appears to be under attack from global market forces, regional institutions, international organizations, popular movements, and many other entities. It is these seemingly contradictory developments that have opened a new debate about what happens to the state. The fate of the state is the subject of the present book.

The most dramatic version of the 'retreat of the state' argument foresees a veritable end of the state as we know it. Ernst-Otto Czempiel writes that 'we have to give up the notion and the concept of the state as well as the terminology that is traditionally connected to it … There are no "states" acting in the transitional world; there is no use preserving in terminology what can no longer be found in reality' (Czempiel 1989: 132). For Kenichi Ohmae, 'traditional nation-states have become unnatural, even impossible business units in a global economy' (Ohmae 1996: 5); instead, Ohmae diagnoses the emergence of a borderless economy of 'regional states': that is, 'an area (often cross-border) developed around a regional economic centre with a population of a few to 10–20 million' (ibid.: 143). Regional states are the likely organizational units of this globalized world; in any case, power over economic activity will devolve from nation-states to 'the borderless network of countless individual market decisions' (ibid.: 39). John Naisbitt claims that democratization and economic globalization lead to smaller and smaller countries: 'The nation-state is dead. Not because states were subsumed by super-states, but because they are breaking up into smaller, more efficient parts – just like big companies ... As we move toward linking up millions of host computer networks, countries will become irrelevant and begin to fade away' (Naisbitt 1994: 43, 58). Jean-Marie Guehenno finds that 'The spatial solidarity of territorial communities is disappearing, to be replaced by temporary interest groups ... If solidarity can no longer be locked into geography, if there is no longer a city, if there is no longer a nation, can there still be politics?' (Guehenno 1995: 17).

Another group of scholars pursue the idea of a 'retreat of the state', but the developments they foresee are somewhat less dramatic than the 'Endists' portrayed above. The gist of this group's argument is that the position of the sovereign state is threatened by a number of different trends; in effect, the power and autonomy of the state compared to a host of other actors is in a process of decline. According to Deanne Julius, 'nearly all those writing on globalization agree that it erodes the power of states' (Julius 1997: 454). Martin Albrow observes that the global age poses a social transformation which 'threatens the nation-state in a more extensive way than anything since the inter-national working-class movement of the nineteenth century' (Albrow 1996: 5). He is echoed by Mathew Horsman and Andrew Marshall: 'The traditional nation-state, the fruit of centuries of political, social and economic evolution, is under threat. Changes in the structure of the international economy, technological advance, and the end of the Cold War together will force – indeed are already forcing – a realignment of the relations among states, citizens and the international economy' (Horsman and Marshall 1994: ix).

Susan Strange makes the point that 'the domain of state authority in society and economy is shrinking ... what were once domains of authority exclusive to state authority are now being shared with other loci or sources of authority' (Strange 1996: 82). The state is becoming 'just one source of authority among several, with limited powers and resources' (ibid.: 73); indeed, 'where states were once masters of markets, now it is the markets which, on many crucial issues, are the masters over the governments of states' (ibid.: 4). These claims are backed by a review of ten areas where states used to play a strong or even dominant role. They include: the defence of society against violence; maintaining the value of the currency; choosing the appropriate form of capitalist development; correcting cyclical booms and slumps; providing a safety-net for the old and the young, the sick and disabled, and the unemployed; taking responsibility for taxation; controlling foreign trade; taking charge of setting up domestic infrastructures; protecting national champions of economic development; and taking control of the use of violence. In overall conclusion, Strange asserts that 'the world market economy has outgrown the authority of the state' (ibid.: 190). A further consequence of this is increased power for the major actors in the global market-place, the large corporations; structural change is 'thrusting multi-nationals more squarely [on] centre-stage in world affairs' (Stopford and Strange 1993: 65). And states are forced to not 'merely negotiate among themselves; they now must also negotiate – if not as supplicants then certainly as suitors seeking a marriage settlement – with foreign firms' (ibid.: 2).

Several of the scholars cited above welcome what they see as a retreat of the state in the face of economic globalization. Another group of scholars inspired by neo-Marxist world systems analysis (Wallerstein 1974) endorse the empirical claims about a retreat of the state, but they are critical of what they identify as the state's submission to the logic of capital accumulation on a global scale. In 1984, Hugo Radice argued that 'the *national* economy is nothing more than a Keynesian myth' (Radice 1984: 119); his claim is that 'the capitalist world economy is now so thoroughly integrated across national boundaries that an autonomous national capitalist strategy is no longer possible ...' (ibid.: 113; see also Coates 1999, 2000; Radice 1999).

The International Political Economy (IPE) scholars who diagnose a 'retreat of the state' focus their argument on economic and technological change. There are developments in production, distribution and finance, in themselves tied in with much more rapid technological innovation, that put states under pressure. Other scholars are more prone to focus on broader social and political trends. James Rosenau argues that the present system is changing from a 'state-centric, anarchical system' to a 'multi-centric world composed of diverse "sovereignty-free" collectivities': that is, 'non-state actors, most importantly individuals, who increasingly challenge the old "state-centric" system' (Rosenau 1993: 282). Individuals are of increasing importance according to Rosenau, because they have greatly extended their activities owing to better education and access to electronic means of communication as well as foreign travel. Mark Zacher notes how ecological as well as economic interdependence increases the need for international cooperation. As a result, the number of both intergovernmental organizations (IGOs) and nongovernmental organizations (NGOs) has increased dramatically (Zacher 1992). The argument is that a dense network of international organizations erodes, or at least circumscribes, the external autonomy of states.

'State-centric' scholars make three basic types of argument against the 'retreat of the state' view. The first concerns the extent to which the challenges to the state recorded by the 'retreat' view are really something novel. The second argument is that to the extent the challenges are novel, the state remains firmly in control of what is going on. Finally, there are several indicators that states have grown much stronger rather than weaker in recent decades. Let us look at the first argument.

Was it not always the case that economic interdependencies, financial flows, the network of international institutions and so on acted as more or less critical constraints on states? Take world exports; as a percentage of world GNP, world exports in 1970 were below the 1880–1910 level. In other words, the rapid increase in world trade between 1950 and 1975 can be seen as a recovery 'from the disruption caused by the two world wars' (Thomson and Krasner 1989: 199). Paul Hirst and Grahame Thompson find that:

> the level of integration, interdependence, openness, or however one wishes to describe it, of national economies in the present era is not unprecedented. Indeed, the level of autonomy under the Gold Standard in the period up to the First World War was much lower for the advanced economies than it is today. (Hirst and Thompson 2000: 60)

As a result, the present situation is very much business as usual. There has not been 'any golden age of state control. States, conceived of as central administrative apparatuses, have never been able to free themselves from concerns about external and internal challenges' (Thomson and Krasner 1989: 198).

The second argument of the 'state-centric' view emphasizes the high degree of control that states exercise over market forces as well as over other actors, including corporations, individuals and groups in civil society. States are by no means overwhelmed by economic globalization; they have themselves actively created the regulatory framework which makes that whole process possible. Economic actors look to states in order to 'gain market access and to "level the playing field" of international competition' (Kapstein 1994: 6). States enforce rules and supervise the players in the marketplace and they intervene in order to achieve order and stability; 'nation-states have created a regulatory structure for international economic activity in order to provide the global economy with its safety net' (ibid.: v).

Finally, 'state-centric' scholars maintain that even if there may be new challenges to the state, its capacities for responding have increased immensely. Technological innovation has been put at the service of the state; today, the state's ability to obtain and accumulate information about citizens and groups is better developed than it ever was; the same is true of the state's capacity for regulation, surveillance and extraction of resources (Krasner 1993a: 314). Finally, the sovereign state remains the preferred form of political organization. No serious competitor has emerged; in fact, the number of sovereign states in the world has gone up from 74 immediately after the Second World War to 192 by the turn of the century.

The debate between 'retreat' and 'state-centric' scholars is not easily settled (for additional contributions to it, see Held and McGrew 2003). It would appear that both groups make valid points. Even if it seems somewhat premature to declare that the nation-state is dead – this is obviously not the case – it is true that something important is happening to the state in the context of economic globalization and new social developments. And it is absolutely plausible that this may in several ways have led to the shrinking of 'the domain of state authority in society and the economy' (Strange 1996: 82). At the same time, state capacity has undoubtedly expanded on a number of dimensions in recent decades and that has enhanced the abilities of states for regulation and surveillance, amongst other things. In sum, the problem is not so much the isolated observation of this or that trend, made by scholars in the two groups; the problem is rather that these observations are misleadingly generalized into a single picture of the state growing either stronger or weaker. Misleading generalization is then connected to an equally misleading idea of the state either 'winning' or 'losing' in its contest with other actors. The changes that take place in states are seldom part of a zero-sum game. Increased power and influence on the part of individuals, groups and corporations does not necessarily mean that the power and influence of states is generally in decline. Furthermore, the power and influence of individual actors, including states, can only be accurately assessed in relation to specific issues or arenas. For example, a state's ability to wage war is not the same as its ability to demand loyalty or its capacity for extracting resources. A precise assessment of capacity must always be tied to specific arenas and contexts (cf. Weiss 1998: 4).

It follows from this that the general claims about states growing either much weaker or much stronger must be viewed with reservation. But how do we avoid the trap of 'winning versus losing' while simultaneously holding on to the important insights presented by several retreat as well as state-centric scholars? Simply, I would argue, by accepting that both types of changes can take place at the same time. This means moving away from a zero-sum view of 'winning' or 'losing' and accepting instead a more theoretically open view of transformation. Starting from the idea of 'transformation' makes it possible to study the changes which states undergo, both in their internal make-up and in their relations with other actors, without making the false assumption that this is a game of only 'winning' or only 'losing'. It is a game of change, of transformation, which is almost always more complex. Take the relationship between states and markets. States regulate markets; they create the rules markets play by and thus to a significant extent *control* markets. Furthermore, states are *empowered* by markets because markets produce vital revenue for states. But states are also highly *dependent* on properly-functioning markets and can be severely *constrained* by markets (e.g., during acute economic crises). Control and constraint; empowerment and dependence; all these different aspects of the state–market relationship will be further analysed in due course. In the present context it is sufficient to emphasize that the view of 'state transformation' is a much more analytically useful starting point than the one-sided view of states either 'winning' or 'losing'.

The idea of 'state transformation' is not new, of course. It has been adopted by a large number of scholars from various disciplines (i.e., sociology, political science, IPE and international relations, or IR) in their various attempts to study the development and change of the state (e.g., Brenner *et al.* 2003; Cerny 1990; Clark 1999; Giddens 1992; Held *et al.* 1999; Held and McGrew 2002; Jessop 2002; Rosecrance 1999; Sassen 1997; Scholte 2000; Weiss 1998). Being an open analytical position, it is non-controversial and rather innocent; it does not tell us anything about what kind of transformation the state may be undergoing or what the consequences are for the state's role and significance in the international system.

The importance of history

History is important for one simple reason: we must have some notion of what existed before in order properly to assess the extent to which change has taken place. Transformation is always from one particular state of the state to another, and we cannot make sense of what has happened unless we know that earlier state of the state. This also means that there are at minimum two, and not one, possible sources of disagreement. Analysts can quarrel about the present shape and importance of the state but they can certainly also disagree about history (i.e., the state of the state in earlier days).

Many retreat scholars frequently overestimate the power and influence of the state in previous times. They are perhaps led to that view by IR researchers who tend to associate the sovereign state with a very high degree of autonomy: that is, with state elites that are unconstrained and which have full control over domestic and foreign affairs. State-centric scholars tend to take an opposite view, emphasizing how the state was always dependent on all kinds of people in civil society, such as merchants, money-lenders and food-producers, not to mention the availability of men (and women) for the armed forces. Stephen Krasner has shown how the actual content of sovereignty, 'the scope of authority that states can exercise, has always been contested' (Krasner 1993b: 235; 1999).

Krasner undoubtedly makes a valid point; but contested or not, the discussion cannot end here. We need some common perception of history – that is, of the historical development of sovereign statehood – in order to make sense of the changes that are taking place today. That historical baseline cannot be established through a one-sided focus on challenges to the power and influence of the state; it must be based on a positive vision of how the state has developed and changed over time. To set forth such a view with sufficient nuance and detail is of course a Herculean task, but fortunately that is not necessary for our present purposes. The aim in what follows is merely to give a rough indication of the development of the state in order to have a fairly accurate background picture against which more recent changes can be discussed. This will be accomplished by briefly addressing the main stages of historical state development and by outlining the major features of the modern state immediately after the Second World War.

Homo sapiens evolved from *homo erectus* about half a million years ago. For almost all of the time between then and now, humans have been hunters and gatherers living in small groups of somewhere between five and 80 people. Permanent settlement began only some 13,000 years ago. The groups began to grow in size and typically became tribes, which are villages or clusters of villages with hundreds of people, but they continue *not* to exhibit any of the major features (such as police forces, bureaucracy, tax collection) which we normally associate with states. Everybody still knew everybody else and outsiders would always be in mortal danger. The characteristics of statehood slowly began to emerge in the context of chiefdoms which appeared for the first time some 7,500 years ago. Chiefdoms comprise thousands of people; with their rise, 'people had to learn, for the first time in history, how to encounter strangers regularly without attempting to kill them' (Diamond 1998: 273).

States, defined descriptively by Diamond (1998) as permanent settlements of more than 50,000 people, arose less than 6,000 years ago in Mesopotamia; 2,300 years ago in Mesoamerica; 2,000 years ago in China, Southeast Asia and the Andes; and 1,000 years ago in West Africa. States introduce hierarchical leadership, and also develop writing, set up centralized control, economic specialization, bureaucratic administration, formalized rules of law, public works and taxation. But the process is slow – extremely so – and a full-blown modern state did not emerge until the twentieth century. Only then can we find states with developed and coherent national economies; with polities based on law, order and centralized rule; and with defined nations, groups of people who are citizens and who lend legitimacy to the state while they also define a cultural and emotional community. And only after the Second World War did the sovereign state become the universal format of political organization, replacing empire, the dominant form of organization for most of the recent centuries of human history.

So, even if early forms of statehood developed several thousand years ago, the most adequate view of history up to the mid-twentieth century is one of state formation rather than of a mature system of fully-fledged states. The present debate about the fate of the state does not address premodern forms of statehood. It unfolds against the background of the modern, Westphalian, states. More specifically, it unfolds against the background of the advanced, modern states as they had developed in Western Europe and North America by the mid-twentieth century. In that sense the debate is Eurocentric, of course; it does not tell us much about statehood in the areas that were colonies or – as in the case of China – subjected to other forms of European domination. But that is a subject for later; our present focus must be on Western Europe and the emergence of the modern state there.

Why did modern states emerge first in Europe? Several different causes have to be combined (cf. Sørensen 2001: ch. 6; see also the debate at H-world 1998; Gill 2003). The imperial structures of the Holy Roman Empire were weak; they gave way to competition among kings for territory and resources. At a later stage, this was combined with competition for power and position between religious and secular elites. New forms of production and technology emerged in the development of capitalism; states helped promote capitalism and were themselves much strengthened in the process, as a consequence of the new sources of revenue and resources.

It is important to emphasize that the consolidation of modern states in Europe from the early sixteenth until the mid-twentieth century took place against the background of a long period of fragmentation. In the Middle Ages, power was disjointed and personalized, without the formal political and administrative organization of the Roman Empire. Public power was privatized and centred on individuals who took control in military, judicial and economic matters. Larger kingdoms were subdivided into counties or fiefs where a similar structure of power was replicated on a smaller scale. The nobles pledged loyalty to the king; lesser knights to dukes and counts, and so on; at the bottom, peasants cultivated a plot of land owned by the lord of the manor. They completely depended on him for the land to yield their livelihood, for his interpretation of the law, and for military protection. In return, they paid rent in the form of labour, produce or money.

The power of kings increased between the sixteenth and the eighteenth centuries; that process laid the foundation for the modern state. Kings grew stronger because of changes in military technology and organization. Large armies became a necessary basis for power. That kind of force requires substantial resources; kings began taxation of the estates and of the bourgeoisie. Tax collection called for something to be delivered in return; kings and their fledgling bureaucracies created a monetary and legal order with a reliable system of credit, a guarantee of the value of money, and a legal framework for commodity exchange. Capitalist expansion was greatly facilitated and the bourgeoisie came to accept the burdens of taxation. The early form of the modern state began to take shape: a centralized system of rule, headed by the monarch, based on a set of administrative, policing and military organizations, sanctioned by a legal order (cf. Giddens 1992: 121; Mann 1993: 55; Skocpol 1979: 29).

It is common to focus on the Peace of Westphalia at the end of the Thirty Years' War in 1648 as the birthplace of the modern, sovereign state. That peace accord undermined the power of the church and strengthened secular power. The choice between Catholicism and Protestantism became the privilege of local rulers embodied in the principle of *cuius regio eius religio*. A corresponding secular principle gave the King authority over his own realm: *rex in regno suo est Imperator regni sui*. Dispersed medieval authority was replaced by centralized modern authority, the King and his government. In 1648, we could, according to Sir Ernest Barker, 'hear the cracking of the Middle Ages'.

However, the modern state as most of us would recognize it was by no means in place by 1648. There were over 200 European entities – state wannabes – involved in the Westphalian negotiations. Over the next 250 years, the number of European states would be reduced to a much smaller number. A process of state consolidation took place; stronger entities swallowed or coopted weaker ones. In many cases heads of state were jealous of their independence; amalgamation proceeded by coercion and competition. So, state consolidation in Europe took place in a context of fierce competition and violent conflict; states made war and war made and unmade states (Tilly 1992). It is important to note that the context for state development and transformation today is a fundamentally and completely different one: even the weakest states today need not fear extinction by conquest because the present norms of the international society do not accept that. This is certainly the most dramatic change when comparing state-making then and now and it greatly affects processes of state development today, especially in the weak states in the South, but also in the North.

To return to the consolidation of state power in European history, two major external aspects of that process have already been indicated. First, competition and conquest were a major factor; second, sovereign states also helped each other increase their power in relation to all other actors by creating a special international society of states. Hedley Bull defined international society as a group of states which 'have established by dialogue and consent common rules and institutions for the conduct of their relations, and recognize their common interest in maintaining these arrangements' (Bull 1995: 13). The year 1648 was, of course, a landmark in the creation of this international society; states confirmed their independence of religious authorities and their right to sole control of their internal affairs. States, so to speak, sent a message to all possible rival centres of authority and power – religious as well as secular – that they were in charge and they set the rules of the game for everyone else.

Domestically, the consolidation of state power involved the submission of rivals. For a long period, prospective heads of state thus fought battles on two fronts, against both external and internal rivals. The domestic conflict was concluded when the state ruled a territory within which it could claim 'the monopoly of the legitimate use of physical violence in the enforcement of its order' (Weber, quoted from Mann 1993: 55).

The build-up of state power changed the relationship between the state and the people. Before the modern state, persons at the bottom of society were subjected to several different authorities; as peasants, they were under the control of local feudal rulers; as Christians they were also subject to religious authority (i.e., priest, bishop, pope). With the concentration of power and authority at one point – the King and his government – peasants and Christians became the direct subjects of the King. The result was a large group of individuals within a defined territory, subject to one supreme authority: this group became 'the people'. 'The people' is a special kind of community with two main characteristics; on the one hand, they are subjects and citizens of a particular state, and on the other hand, they have a shared idea about themselves as a cultural and historical entity: they are an imagined community (Anderson 1991), or even a nation. 'The people', therefore, is a historical novelty which emerged only in the context of the modern state.

The transformation from subjects, who primarily have obligations, to citizens who also have rights happened only gradually. The centralization of power and the abandoning of private armies created a basis for a direct relationship between the King and his subjects. Domestic law and order erected a barrier separating the population and the sovereign from the outside. A notion of common purpose could now emerge: the good of the state and the good of the people depended on mutual support and shared obligation towards defending and supporting the state. Obligations (taxation, military service) became combined with rights: initially political rights and civil liberties, with economic and social rights emerging in a later phase in the context of the welfare state.

The people's rights and obligations in relation to the state can be considered the material basis of the nation because they define a foundation for community. The most important non-material aspects of community are a common language and a common cultural and historical identity based on literature, myths, symbols, music and art. That kind of national identity was to a significant extent shaped from above, by the state, through the system of mass education. Compulsory education began in earnest by the mid-nineteenth century. So, a national identity outside elite circles, in the general population, became firmly established in several states in Europe only rather late.

A modern state is a nation-state in the sense that the population shares the characteristics of citizenship (common rights and obligations towards the state) and nationhood (the cultural-historical ideas of an imagined community). A nation-state in this sense is not necessarily based on a homogeneous ethno-national group of people. Very few modern states are nation-states in this more narrow sense.

The modern state is based on a national economy. That economy emerged in the context of economic activity which was both globalized and localized. On the one hand, long-distance trade became increasingly important in the sixteenth century with improvements in shipbuilding and navigation. European states began to project economic interests and political power on a world scale. The profits supported national economic development at home. On the other hand, the economic space defining most people's lives continued for a considerable time to be highly localized. Economic, and indeed also social and political, life took place in and around market towns with an agricultural hinterland of some 20 miles. These 'microeconomies' remained in place well into the nineteenth century. In France in 1835, for example, 'only about 13 per cent of production was consumed more than 20 miles from its production site' (Schwartz 2000: 14). The creation of a national economic space required modern infrastructure – especially railroads – that emerged only in the context of the Industrial Revolution. For example, a trip between Paris and Lyons took about one week in 1800; by 1848, it was down to 55 hours (Zürn 1998: 41–63).

So, the national economy was literally built from the bottom up. The state helped create a national space for economic development by removing local barriers to exchange and supporting both industry and infrastructure. The modern national economy is characterized by the combined presence within its territory of the major economic sectors: that is, means of production and distribution as well as means of consumption. What particularly defines it as a national economy is the fact that the most important inter- and intrasectoral links are domestic (cf. Amin 1976; Senghaas 1985); in this sense the national economy is self-sustaining. There is external trade, of course, but the economic structure is introvert rather than extrovert.

The relationship between state and market has changed over time. Mercantilism put the state first; it was a theory about the need for a strong national economy as a necessary basis for a strong state. But classical liberalism also made a strong case for the creation of sound national economies; liberals argued that a certain minimum size of nations was needed for economic viability and they urged the state to support economic development (Hobsbawm 1993: 25–35). Classical liberals wanted the state to set up the minimal underpinnings necessary for the proper functioning of the market. More recent liberals have been highly influenced by Keynesian ideas about the need for more state interference and direction of the economy.

Over time then, there has been a tendency for an increasing state presence in the economy. A need to mitigate social tensions via redistribution and stronger state direction in times of war have been major factors in this development (Zürn 1998). French central state expenditures including social security, for example, tripled (in constant prices) between 1909 and 1920, and doubled again between 1938 and 1950 (Porter 1994). A similar pattern can be found in most of the advanced industrialized countries of the West.

It is now possible to summarize the typical features of the modern, Westphalian state as it had developed mainly in Western Europe and North America around 1950. There is certainly substantial empirical variation on specific dimensions within this group of countries. At the same time, states in the Eastern bloc as well as in the South were very different. Still, these typical modern features provide a helpful baseline against which more recent transformations of the state can be discussed. As already emphasized, we need an idea of the previous shape of the state in order to assess what has changed. The modern, Westphalian ideal type provides such an image.

Following Robert Cox, states are conceptualized as historical structures made up of material capabilities, ideas and institutions. The 'institutions' level focuses on the government; the 'ideas' level concentrates on nationhood (i.e., the community of people in the state); and the 'material capabilities' level focuses on the economy. Against this background the modern state is defined as in Box 1.1.

Box 1.1	*The modern state*
Government	A centralized system of democratic rule, based on a set of administrative, policing and military organizations, sanctioned by a legal order, claiming a monopoly of the legitimate use of force, all within a defined territory.
Nationhood	A people within a territory making up a community of citizens (with political, social and economic rights) and a community of sentiment based on linguistic, cultural and historical bonds. Nationhood involves a high level of cohesion, binding nation and state together.
Economy	A segregated national economy, self-sustained in the sense that it comprises the main sectors needed for its repro-duction. The major part of economic activity takes place at home.

Note that this ideal type by no means represents a picture of the state that has been valid for a long historical period. There was no modern state in the seventeenth, eighteenth or nineteenth centuries. There were political, economic and social developments, and also other changes that would eventually lead to the modern state. Transformation is there-fore the rule and not the exception. States have always undergone devel-opment and change; the present period of transformation only adds a new chapter to that story.

The importance of concepts and theories

Concepts and theories are important because they constitute an essen-tial part of the lenses through which we look at our subject. It is clear that the two concepts of 'state' and 'power' respectively are of primary importance for the present undertaking. A closer look at them is there-fore warranted. It will appear that conceptual differences – and some-times misunderstandings – are at least partly responsible for the disagreements about what is happening to the state. Having sorted that out, it is possible to give a clearer formulation of the argument in this book and the way in which it plays out in the following chapters.

There are three main ways of looking at states and power; the first is state-centric, and is connected to political science and to the realist tra-dition in IR; the second springs from the liberal tradition in political thought; the third – which I call the critical view – is linked to theories inspired by IPE and historical sociology. The state-centric view of the state is often connected to the realist approach while retreat scholars frequently draw on the liberal tradition. 'Transformation' scholars, finally, typically subscribe to the critical view but there are exceptions, and by no means all scholars are easily classified in this way.

In order to pursue this issue further, we need to take a closer look at the three main approaches. But before introducing them, readers should be warned that what follows is not a comprehensive introduction to theories of the state. Such wide-ranging treatments can be found elsewhere (e.g., Giddens 1992; Hall and Ikenberry 1989; Jessop 1990, 2002; Mann 1993: 44–92; Wendt 1999). For present purposes, focus is on those conceptualizations of the state deemed most relevant for the debate about state transformation.

State-centric analysis as represented by realism (Morgenthau 1966; Waltz 1979; for an overview, see Jackson and Sørensen 2003) simply assumes that the international system is a system of sovereign states. States control the means of violence; they set the rules of the game for all other actors, including corporations, individuals and organizations. States jealously guard their freedom and autonomy; for that reason there is no world government and there never will be. The international system is anarchic in the sense that power and authority is decentralized: it resides in the single state. Anarchy means insecurity; states cannot be sure of each other's intentions. In order to defend themselves states need power, especially military power. But when they build such power, they also threaten other states in the process. This situation represents the security dilemma: one state's increased security is another state's increased insecurity.

State-centric analysis focuses on the system of sovereign states and the game of power politics that states play. It is against the background of this view that we must understand the way in which scholars in this tradition conceptualize state and power. The state is a sovereign entity with a defined territory, a population and a government. The government acts on behalf of the population; no sharp distinction is made between the state as a government and the state as a territorial unit with population and resources. The state-centric, realist view is a systemic one; it looks at sovereign states from the outside, from the perspective of the international system. Seen from this perspective, states are *unitary* and *coherent* actors, rather like billiard balls rolling on the table that is the international system. They are unitary in the sense that state leaders speak and act on behalf of their respective states. They are coherent in the sense that the power of the government and the power of the state as a territorial unit with population and resources are seen as one and the same. State leaders/governments are always under pressure from the system because anarchy means insecurity and insecurity can lead to violent conflict with fatal consequences for the state. That external pressure is, of course, hardest on the smaller and weaker states; they are forced to adjust, to negotiate, as well as they can, a safe place in the balance of power. Bigger and stronger states have more degrees of freedom because the systemic pressure on them is less strong. The extent to which they are constrained depends on the balance of power. The USA and the Soviet Union held each other in check during the Cold War; they constrained each other. Today, the USA is much less constrained because the Soviet Union has disappeared and no other state can match its power (Krasner 1992).

For realists, power is the ability of one actor to make another actor behave in a certain way. But this use of power and the ability to control outcomes – that is, to make things happen the way you want them to – is difficult to measure. A may want B to behave in a certain way, but factors other than A's power over B may play a role in B's falling into line. In order to avoid these difficulties, realists focus on power as a resource. The assumption is that a strong arsenal in terms of power resources means a strong possibility for the actor to exercise actual power over other actors. Because of anarchy and the constant risk of violent conflict, military power (and especially nuclear weapons) is considered the most important power resource. But other resources, such as the size of the population and the economy, control over raw materials, and level of science and technology are relevant as well. Finally, power is fungible. Military power, for example, is not merely relevant for violent conflict; it can also be used as a power resource in other areas, such as the pursuit of economic interests.

Summing this up, states are unitary and coherent actors. Strong states (i.e., great powers) have a robust portfolio of power resources. Most important in this respect is a high level of military power relative to other states. Governments are constrained by the international system, but such constraints may not be strong enough to affect the great powers. Governments are highly autonomous in relation to their own societies; that is, they are able to act freely on their behalf.

Against this background, it is easy to understand why state-centric realists are sceptical faced with the idea about states in retreat. When the basic assumption is that states are special actors setting the rules of the game for everyone else, and when the power of states resides especially in arsenals of military force controlled by sovereign states that are unitary and coherent actors, then any claim about states being in retreat because of the increasing power of private corporations, or because of the advance of market forces in general, must be met with the highest scepticism. The short answer given by realists is: markets and corporations develop because states want them to and, when the crunch comes, when violent conflict looms again (and at some point, it always will), states, especially the strongest ones, remain in firm control.

Liberals have a rather different view of states and power. The liberal starting point is the individual citizen and the liberal model of the state is a 'Citizen-Responsive State Model' (Greenberg 1990: 11–41). States are not primarily concentrations or instruments of power; they are caretakers of the rule of law and the rights of citizens to life, liberty and property. From the beginning, therefore, individuals and groups in civil society are the major focus for liberals. They argue that transnational relations – that is, relations across borders between individuals and groups ('non-state actors') – have become of increasing importance in recent decades. That is one major reason for the 'erosion ... of state and governmental power' (Rosenau 1993: 274).

Furthermore, liberals reject the idea that states are unitary and coherent actors. States are complex entities, just like the societies they represent, and relations between states take place on many levels and through multiple channels. There is a multifaceted network of trans-governmental relations (Keohane and Nye 1977: 24). Finally, modernization and democratization have reduced the probability of interstate war; for that reason, the 'high politics' of military security no longer dominates the international agenda; the 'low politics' of economic and social affairs is increasingly important.

In sum, the state was never a strong, unitary, coherent and autonomous actor for liberals; it was always a guardian of individuals and groups in civil society and therefore strongly influenced by these 'non-state actors'. In recent decades, transnational and transgovernmental relations have increased significantly and this has accentuated the erosion and dispersion of state power.

The liberal view of power employs the same starting point as the realist view: power is the ability of A to make B behave in a certain way. Like realists, liberals also focus on power as a resource. But from there on, liberals develop their own view. In terms of power resources, they emphasize the importance of non-material, intangible sources of power, such as national cohesion; a universalistic culture; and influence in international institutions. National cohesion is the ability of society and state to stand together; a universalistic culture is a culture with universal appeal, such as the American lifestyle which is attractive to people in many countries. Liberal, American values also permeate international institutions. That gives the USA a substantial amount of 'soft power' or 'cooptive power': that is, the ability 'to structure a situation so that other nations develop preferences or define their interests in ways consistent with one's own nation' (Nye 1990: 91).

Furthermore, liberals see power as much less fungible. Power in one area whether, for example, shipping, computer technology, agriculture or military force, cannot necessarily or easily be put to use in other areas. As a result they see the power structure as inevitably a great deal more complex: small states, such as Denmark or Norway, may be powerful in shipping or oil; conversely the military might of large states is generally of little use in non-military affairs. In sum, power is distributed among many actors across a vast range of issue areas; and states are increasingly under pressure from the transnational relations conducted by individuals and groups. That is the basis for the 'retreat of the state' view supported by many liberals.

The third main way of looking at states and power is different from both the realist and the liberal view. The critical view emerges from various sources, particularly in sociology and IPE. It recognizes the existence of a system of sovereign states based on territory, population and government. But the critical view emphasizes the coexistence of sovereign states with a global economic system based on capitalism. Proponents of the critical view are mostly interested in the relationship between politics and economics, and especially in the ability of states to exploit the possibilities for economic and social development in a capitalist world system (e.g., Jessop 2002). Capable states in this respect are 'developmental states' (Evans 1995: 12) in the sense that being powerful is about being capable of promoting development.

Such states need administrative capacity in the form of effective institutions, but that is not enough. The argument is that state capacity (or power) with respect to economic development depends both on the *autonomy* of the government/state apparatus from society and on the *embeddedness* of states in their societies. Autonomy is important because without it the state would be a mere handmaiden of social forces in society. Embeddedness is important because states need the ability to 'work through' society: 'a state that was only autonomous would lack both sources of intelligence and the ability to rely on decentralized private implementation' (ibid.). The combination of autonomy and embeddedness is similar to what Michael Mann calls 'infrastructural power': that is, 'the institutional capacity of a central state ... to penetrate its territories and logistically implement decisions. This is collective power, "power through" society, coordinating social life through state infrastructures' (Mann 1993: 59).

The idea of embedded autonomy may be relevant for external coalitions of states as well: Linda Weiss uses the concept of 'catalytic' states for a kind of embedded autonomy that is externally oriented. 'Catalytic' states are states that seek to 'create more real control over their economies (and indeed over security)' by 'assuming a dominant role in coalitions of states, transnational institutions and private-sector groups' (Weiss 1998: 209). So, where the realist view emphasizes state autonomy and the liberal view underlines the primary role of civil society, the critical position argues that state power is based on a combination of autonomy and connection to (embeddedness in) civil society.

The other major focus for the critical view is the relationship between states and markets. The critical view follows Karl Polanyi (1957) in conceiving of that relationship as a dialectical one. That is to say, states create and regulate markets; but markets, once created, are also sources of power that may constrain states. Realists contend that states are in control of markets; many liberals see markets as a formidable force challenging and constraining states. The critical view perceives the state–market connection as an evolving relationship of interdependence in which each side needs (and benefits from) the other. At the same time, states and markets are sources of political and economic power and different kinds of balances are possible where either states or markets have the upper hand.

In sum, I have looked at the concepts of state and power through three different theoretical lenses: a state-centric realist, a liberal, and a critical one. The point of the exercise is to make clear that theories and concepts turn us in different directions and sometimes even lead us more or less by definition to take a particular view of a subject, irrespective of what might be happening in the real world. The realist state-centric view is predestined to argue that states remain firmly in the driver's seat facing no serious challenges from other actors. That is because realists assume that states are special players setting the rules for others. The states are exceptional because they control the means of violence and it is an insecure world out there with violent conflict always a possibility. The realist concept of power with its strong emphasis on the importance of military power is compelled to award a special role to states.

The liberal view is predestined to argue that individuals and groups from civil society are in the driver's seat. The state is nothing more than the custodian of civil society anyway and an increasing density of transnational relations contributes to the erosion of state power. At the same time, specific power resources are not highly fungible and that creates a complex distribution of power among various actors.

Finally, the critical view is focused on the relationship between politics and economics. The concepts of embedded autonomy and of state–market interplay point to an evolving relationship between states and civil societies on the one hand and between states and markets on the other. That leads towards a 'transformation' view where states are neither 'winning' nor 'losing' but where the relative power position of states (and other actors) may change over time and across issues.

The three theoretical approaches to the state are summarized in Box 1.2.

None of these three different views is inherently right or wrong. They are different grips on a complex reality; each of them is the starting point for an analysis that throws light on some aspects of that reality

Box 1.2 Three views of the state

	State-centric, realist	Liberalist	Critical
Approach	Focus on states as sovereign entities with defined territory, government and population.	Focus on states as a group of people. Government provides rule of law and rights of citizens.	Focus on capable governments interacting with a capitalist world system.
Major actors?	States/governments set rules for other actors.	Individuals and groups in civil society run states and set the rules.	States set rules in cooperation with actors from civil society.
Power?	Strong states have many power resources. Power concentrated in states/governments.	Non-material, intangible sources of power important. Power diffused among many actors.	Capable states have autonomy, administrative capacity, and are embedded in civil society (infrastructural power).
States in retreat?	No	Yes	Transformation rather than retreat

while leaving other aspects in the dark. Each may be useful for certain analytical purposes and less useful for others. In one sense, they are like different games; the realist focuses on states and the risk of violent conflict; the liberal focuses on the development of civil society; and the critical theorist studies the interplay between politics and economics. To the extent that they are different games, we cannot find a winner. Just as the golf player will remain unconvinced that tennis is a better game, the realist, the liberal and the critical theorist will continue their respective game no matter what the others say. In sum, just as we respect that people want to play different games, we must respect the individual merits of each theoretical perspective on its own terms.

At the same time, however, the three perspectives are not entirely different games. Overlaps exist, and all three views have something to say about states and power and how the power of states develops over time. It is this area of overlap that is the focus of the present book. The aim is to find out how states are changing and what the consequences are for the power of states relative to other actors. As we have seen earlier in this chapter, this calls for an open theoretical view. That is to say, we cannot begin by assuming that the state remains in the driver's seat or by assuming that individuals and groups in civil society are in control; neither can we begin by presupposing that states are always getting ready for violent conflict or by taking for granted that the world is now peaceful and violent conflict between states is impossible. We must begin with the open analytical position that states are being transformed. That can happen in ways which both increase and reduce their power and influence in the international system; starting from there, we can evaluate the relative merits of theoretical views.

At the same time, we must be careful not to confuse the different ways in which the analytical perspectives conceptualize their ideas about states and power, and we must also be ready to accept that each of the various theoretical perspectives can provide helpful insights even if we may disagree with some of the theoretical assumptions on which this or that perspective is based.

That is the starting point. The goal is to find out exactly how states are being transformed and what the consequences are. When that is accomplished, we can return to the different theoretical positions and re-evaluate them against our findings.

Conclusion

The world is changing and a fresh debate about the fate of the state has begun. The state remains the universally dominant form of political organization; but it appears to be challenged from many different quarters, including global market forces, international institutions and popular movements. Is there a 'retreat of the state' or is the 'state-centric' view the more convincing one? Scholars disagree, but instead of getting locked into the 'state losing' or 'state winning' contest, there is a more attractive position: namely, the idea of 'state transformation' which is open to changes in both directions.

The modern state developed over several centuries; transformation was always the order of the day. States, like other human organizations, have never stood still; they have always developed and changed. In order properly to assess the extent of more recent state transformation, we need a baseline. That baseline is the modern state with its major features – in ideal typical terms – as they had developed by the mid-twentieth century. Those features are summarized in Box 1.1.

Concepts and theories shape the way in which we look at our subjects. The three major ways of looking at states and power – the realist, the liberal and the critical view – make profoundly different assumptions about what states are and how states can have power, and therefore they arrive at very different assessments of what has happened. Based on the theoretically open view of 'state transformation' and employing the baseline of the modern state at the mid-twentieth century, we can set out to examine what has happened to the state. Afterwards, it is possible to evaluate the different theoretical perspectives.

Chapter 2

Economic Globalization and State Transformation

The elusive concept of globalization
From national to globalized economies?
States and markets interacting in new ways
Economic globalization and the welfare state
Conclusion

What happens to the state as a consequence of globalization? The previous chapter recorded how retreat scholars were convinced that globalization was putting states under pressure; some even thought that states were being removed altogether from the centre stage of human development. State-centric scholars were confident that states maintained their position; some argued that globalization was controlled by states and served to strengthen them rather than the opposite. I have claimed that we should focus on state transformation instead of states 'winning' or 'losing'. The appropriate question is this: are states transformed as a result of globalization and, if so, in what way? To answer that question, we first need to find out what globalization is. The reflections on that in the following section will identify different major aspects of globalization. The chapter will then seek to clarify how economic globalization transforms the economies of modern states. It will also consider the effects on social welfare.

The elusive concept of globalization

Globalization means, in the broadest sense, the expansion and intensification of economic, political, social and cultural relations across borders (this is the definition offered in Holm and Sørensen 1995: 1). Globalization is uneven in terms of cross-national intensity, geographical scope, and national and local depth. The process of globalization is pushed by several factors, including economic, technological, political and social ones. Globalization is both a cause and a consequence. It increasingly shapes the context for interstate relations as well as for the everyday lives of ordinary citizens. But states and other actors are not merely passive objects exposed to the swell of globalization; states are active players and their policies are probably the single most important determinant of the scope and direction of globalization, although some states have more capacity to act than others. In sum, there is an interplay between the processes of globalization and the policies undertaken by states.

Globalization has been described as a 'polyvalent, promiscuous, controversial word that often obscures more than it reveals' (Jessop 2002: 113). This is most certainly true; but nonetheless, the concept has, in a surprisingly short period of time, become a key entity in social science. Rival notions such as internationalization, interdependence or transnationalization have been left in its wake.

There are certain advantages of this dominance by a new concept: it facilitates the tying together of debates across a range of different disciplines and issue-areas and thus creates good possibilities for cross-fertilization. Globalization is important in many disciplines because of the time–space compression which it portends. The fact that individuals, groups, companies, organizations and indeed states are much more affected by far-away events than they used to be is of importance in many aspects of human life. Sociologists, economists, political economists, international relations specialists, political scientists, students of law, historians and various branches of the humanities all have debates on globalization which link up with each other and sometimes provide fresh insights compared with more compartmentalized research undertakings.

There are also drawbacks, however. A major downside is that the concept is simply too big to theorize. 'Social relations' is basically everything, and one cannot have a theory about everything. 'Social relations across borders' comprise, for example, Internet communication, refugees, direct investment, interstate relations, NGOs, immigration, tourism, television, terrorism, transnational enterprises and trade. It is hardly possible to have one meaningful theory covering all that and much more. Theories are distinguished by focusing on certain aspects of social reality and leaving others in the dark; staying with the totality of 'social relations' leads to a one-to-one picture of social reality, an impossible candidate for theorizing. Bob Jessop emphasizes that 'far from globalization being a unitary causal mechanism, it should be understood as the complex emergent product of many different forces operating on many scales' (ibid.: 114). In other words, to understand what is going on behind the all-encompassing processes of globalization, the concept needs to be unpacked and looked at in its component parts; only then can we meaningfully discern what 'globalization' really involves.

We clearly cannot cover all, or even all the most important, aspects of globalization in this chapter or even in this book. We want specifically to look at the relationship between major aspects of globalization and the process of state transformation, given the debate between retreat and state-centric scholars. For present purposes, the flood of literature on globalization can be classified according to two major sets of distinctions. The first is between, on the one hand, globalization as a primarily *economic* process involving, for example, production, distribution, management and finance (e.g., Boyer and Drache 1996; Cox 1987; Hirst and Thompson 2000; Hoogvelt 2001; Jessop 2002) and, on the other, globalization as a broader *sociological* process involving all aspects of social activity including, for example, culture, communication, belief systems, attitudes, everyday life, and so on (e.g., Albrow 1996; Beck 1992; Giddens 1990).

The second major distinction is between 'Globalization Believers' and 'Globalization Sceptics'. According to the former, globalization is changing, or has already changed, both the economic and the social world in fundamental ways. We are entering a qualitatively new reality where national economies are subsumed by a globalized economic system, and where individuals and groups face radically different conditions of existence in a world where sovereign states have lost most of the power they used to have. Clearly, most of the retreat scholars named in the previous chapter belong in this category.

According to 'Globalization Sceptics', nothing much is new. The processes behind the broad 'globalization' label have been at work for many decades. There was a high level of economic interdependence between countries before the First World War; and, in broader terms, the increasing interconnectedness between societies at social, cultural and political levels began a very long time ago. In short, globalization is nothing new; it has been around for some considerable time. Most of the state-centric scholars identified in the previous chapter are in this category. The two sets of distinctions can be summarized as shown in Box 2.1.

The distinction between a narrow and a broad concept of globalization is analytical, meaning that the choice between them depends on what one wants to analyse. As already indicated, given the focus of the book this chapter will concentrate on economic globalization.

The 'Believers' versus 'Sceptics' debate has become extraordinarily confused because the available information is ambiguous; it can be subjected to different interpretations. For example, when world exports grow as a percentage of world output, 'Sceptics' will see this as an instance of 'more of the same': economic interdependence between national economies is intensifying as we have seen in earlier periods, especially at the beginning of the twentieth century. 'Believers', by contrast, will interpret this as an indication of a new, globalized economic system in the making. When states and markets interact, 'Sceptics' will

Box 2.1. *Dimensions of globalization*		
Aspect of globalization	Consequences of globalization	
	'Globalization Sceptics'	'Globalization Believers'
Narrow: Economics	Economic interdependence: nothing new	Globalized economic system: qualitative shift
Broad: Comprehensive social change	Interconnectedness increases: nothing new	Globalized societies redefine conditions of life for individuals and groups

tend to see states as having the upper hand, with the capacity to control and regulate markets to the extent that they see fit. 'Believers' will tend to see markets as having the upper hand, with states having to adapt their policies to the demands of the global market forces.

In short, it is not at all easy to settle the debate between 'Sceptics' and 'Believers' because the available evidence can be interpreted to point in different directions. In a manner of speaking, we are looking at a glass of water which is half full and half empty. 'Sceptics' will focus on the empty part of the glass and strongly emphasize that it is indeed half empty, meaning nothing much is new. 'Believers' will focus on the filled part of the glass and maintain that a great deal is new. Undeniably, both views have a point.

Fortunately, however, this debate is merely another version of the zero-sum logic invoked by retreat and state-centric scholars. We do not have to choose between 'nothing is new' and 'all is new'. The broader process of transformation can contain both 'more of the same' and qualitatively new elements. The 'transformation' view, however, still leaves us with the complex task of finding out how much of globalization is 'more of the same' and how much is really new. The baseline is the economy of the modern state. In what ways has it changed due to economic globalization?

From national to globalized economies?

Economic globalization is surely taking place; in several ways, the national economies of the world hang closer together than ever before. In a sense, a global economy is in the making (Dicken 1998; Scholte

1997), but vast national and regional differences remain. The national economy has not been obliterated. If we focus on the idea of transformation and lay aside for a moment the most extreme statements of 'Sceptics' and 'Believers', it would appear that most observers will agree that economic globalization takes place in the following ways:

- internationalization of national economic spaces through growing penetration (inward flows) and extraversion (outward flows)
- formation of regional economic blocs embracing several national economies – including, most notably, the formation of various formally organized blocs in the triadic regions of North America, Europe and East Asia – and the development of formal links between these blocs, notably through the Asia-Pacific Economic Cooperation forum (APEC), the New Transatlantic Agenda and the Asia-Europe meetings
- growth of more 'local internationalization' or 'virtual regions' through the development of economic ties between contiguous or non-contiguous local and regional authorities in different national economies, ties that often bypass the level of the national state but may also be sponsored by it
- extension and deepening of multinationalization as multinational companies, transnational banks and international producer services firms move from limited economic activities abroad to more comprehensive and worldwide strategies, sometimes extending to 'global localization' whereby firms pursue a global strategy based on exploiting and/or adjusting to local differences
- widening and deepening of international regimes covering economic and economically relevant issues
- emergence of globalization proper through the introduction and acceptance of global norms and standards, the adoption of global benchmarking, the development of globally integrated markets together with globally oriented strategies, and 'deracinated' firms with no evident national operational base. (Points quoted from Jessop 2002: 115–16)

The economy of the modern state was national in the sense that all stages of manufacture typically took place within the country, in enterprises and industries that were also national. The economic crisis of the 1930s that led to protectionism in many countries, and the Second World War in the first half of the 1940s, both strengthened this tendency for national firms operating within national economies. The ideology of the period further emphasized the national economy. A frequently quoted passage from the renowned liberal economist J.M. Keynes makes the point: 'let goods be homespun whenever it is reasonably and conveniently possible; and, above all, let finance be primarily national' (Keynes 1933: 237).

International trade at the time reflected the predominance of national economies (see Table 2.1). Trade involved the exchange of raw materials and agricultural products for finished goods and it involved procurement of the necessary inputs for the national systems of manufacture. To the extent that economic exchange or integration between countries existed, it was '*shallow integration* manifested largely through arm's length *trade* in goods and services between independent firms and through international movements of portfolio capital' (United Nations Conference on Trade and Development 1993: 113).

With the postwar Bretton Woods system, a political framework was created that liberalized economic relations, especially between Western Europe, North America and Japan. Trade and foreign direct investment now grew at faster rates than production. At the same time, new technological possibilities in transport, communication and production gradually emerged; they much improved the possibilities for setting up manufacturing systems on a regional or even global scale.

New ties developed between the advanced economies; this process of *deep integration*:

> meant that larger parts of economic activity became organized primarily by transnational corporations (TNCs). 'Deep' integration extends to the level of *production* of goods and services and, in addition, increases visible and invisible trade. Linkages between national economies are therefore increasingly influenced by the cross-border value adding activities within…TNCs and within networks established by TNCs. (United Nations Conference on Trade and Development 1993: 113)

Table 2.1   *Foreign trade (exports and imports) as a percentage of GDP*

	USA	Germany	France	UK	Japan
1950	9	19	28	47	18
1960	9	35	27	44	21
1970	11	40	31	45	20
1980	21	53	44	52	28
1992	22	60	45	49	18

Source: Adopted from Beisheim *et al.* (1999: 273). Based on data from Penn World Tables: http://datacentre.epas.utoronto.ca:5680/pwt/pwt.html.

A 'production chain' describes the different stages in the production of goods and services, from procurement of materials over manufacture, to sale, distribution and service (Dicken 1998: 6). Production chains are increasingly transnationally organized on a regional or even global level. Instead of the national corporation, the typical firm is the transnational corporation (a firm operating in more than one country). Today, it is possible to carve up the various segments of a production chain and situate each component in locations where the conditions are optimal in terms of labour cost, availability of inputs, technological environment, proximity of markets, and so on. Some industries are, of course, frontrunners in the process: the car industry, textiles and clothing, the electronics industry and the chemical and pharmaceutical industries are examples. It is quite sometime ago that a Swedish Volvo was made in Sweden; today, the car combines inputs from many countries and the final product is marketed worldwide. These are the so-called producer-driven production chains that dominate capital- and technology-intensive industries. Another type of production chain is buyer-driven; large retailers – such as Nike – set up a global production and marketing network (Gereffi 1994).

At the same time, a company such as Volvo is now part of a larger network of car manufacturers, overall controlled by Ford, an erstwhile purely American producer. That illustrates a further general tendency across industries: mergers, acquisitions and strategic alliances. The initial investments required in order to market a new model or product are very substantial indeed. Another famous car producer, Jaguar, sold out to Ford because it was unable to bear the cost of developing a new generation of engines and models. The general tendency is thus industrial concentration, the dominance of fewer and larger companies (or, rather, networks of firms). However, this global concentration is combined with increasing competition in local markets, because the dominant players all want to be present in attractive markets worldwide (see Table 2.2).

As a result of these developments, international production, meaning production by transnational enterprises outside their home countries, now exceeds world trade and has done so since the 1980s. A further major change has taken place in the structure of international trade. In earlier days, trade was typically between different sectors or industries (i.e., exchange of finished goods for raw materials or foodstuffs for other consumer goods). Today, trade is typically intra-industry (i.e., import of one car part or model and export of other parts and models). Only one-quarter of international trade is of the traditional kind today. Moreover, trade increasingly takes place within the context of the same company or network of companies. Such intrafirm trade now accounts for roughly one-third of world trade; in the case of the USA, the share is more than 40 per cent (Ruggie 1997: 2). Paradoxically then, the

Table 2.2   *Selected top 100 TNCs, ranked by transnationality index,* 1995

Corporation	Economy	Industry	Transnationality index
Nestlé SA	Switzerland	Food	94.0
Electrolux AB	Sweden	Electronics	88.3
Shell, Royal Dutch	UK/ Netherlands	Oil, gas, coal and related services	73.0
Bayer AG	Germany	Chemicals	69.3
Sony Corporation	Japan	Electronics	59.1
IBM	USA	Computers	54.9
Honda Motor Co., Ltd.	Japan	Automotive	52.6
Transnationalization index, top 100 world TNCs			51.0
Daewoo Corporation	Korea (Rep.)	Diversified	47.7
GTE Corporation	USA	Telecommunications	14.9

* The 'transnationality index' is calculated from the average ratios of foreign assets to total assets, foreign sales to total sales, and foreign employment to total employment.
Source: Based on United Nations (1997).

creation of global markets has led to a sharp relative decline of free trade (i.e., arm's length exchange between independent parties) because the global division of labour is being internalized at the level of the firm.

Another indicator pointing to the increased importance of cross-border economic activity is the growth of the general level of trade. World exports represented about 7 per cent of world output in 1950; today, the figure is approximately 17 per cent (Krugman 1995). Export growth is a global phenomenon, but the developed countries in the Organization for Economic Cooperation and Development (OECD) have always taken the lion's share; they accounted for 64 per cent of world exports in 1950 and 70 per cent in 1996. These trade figures refer to merchandise trade and do not include services, but there is a similar level of OECD dominance in services as well.

It was mentioned earlier that liberalization – that is, the removal of impediments to cross-border economic transactions – was a very significant factor behind the development of economic globalization. This is true also for the emergence of a globally integrated financial market. Deregulation has paved the way for increasing integration between national financial systems. It is most visible in the area of foreign exchange markets, where the volume of transactions exceeds world trade by a ratio higher than 60:1 (*The Economist*, 1995). But there are many other kinds of financial flows, including bank-lending, bonds, derivatives, options, swaps, and so on. Integration is taking place here as well; the World Trade Organization (WTO) concluded a Financial Services Agreement in December 1997 which was designed to open national banking and insurance industries to foreign competition. A new negotiation round on the liberalization of financial services was launched by the WTO in February 2000.

So, the national economy of the modern state has been transformed. Transnational corporations organize production chains on a regional and global basis. That development has been supported by political measures liberalizing economic exchange between countries. Technological progress has facilitated globalized production and marketing in the sense described above. The structure of trade has changed from interindustry exchange on an arm's length basis to primarily intraindustry exchange, much of which is intrafirm trade. Trade has grown much faster than production, and other areas of economic activity (including financial services) are also undergoing a process of globalization.

However, a unified, homogeneous, and totally integrated global economy has certainly not been created. It is rather a process of uneven development where some national economies – particularly those in the triad of Western Europe, North America and East Asia – participate much more actively than others while the least developed Third World economies tend to become marginalized. And even among the advanced economies in the triad, significant national differences remain in place because states respond to the challenges of economic globalization in different ways. They conduct different industrial, macroeconomic and welfare policies and that leads to national economies with different characteristics (Boyer and Drache 1996; G. Garrett 1998).

Economic globalization takes place in the ways indicated in the points above. As a result, the national economy of the modern state is being transformed. What are the results of this transformation? I have rejected the zero-sum choice between a radical 'Believer' and a radical 'Sceptic' position, but it still remains for the reader to decide where to put the accent when the evidence is pulled together. Transformation, yes, certainly; but how much is really new, compared to earlier phases of global capitalist development? My own ideas about how the modern state has been transformed are presented in Chapter 9.

States and markets interacting in new ways

This section will further inspect the relationship between states and markets under the conditions of economic globalization. The issue is important because it is a major element in the debate between state-centric and retreat scholars. The former believe that states continue to be in control of markets, while the latter argue that markets are now much stronger and states correspondingly weaker. The reader will know by now that the present analysis stresses the idea of 'transformation' rather than the idea of states or markets 'winning' or 'losing', so how has the relationship between states and markets been transformed?

Advanced capitalist countries have always agreed that states and markets are both necessary for the achievement of growth and welfare; but different models and ideologies about the appropriate combination of 'state' and 'market' have dominated in different periods. The Second World War meant a much higher level of state direction of, and involvement in, the economy than was seen earlier. The high level of state interference was continued – especially in Europe – in the context of Keynesian economic policies during the three decades after the war. Keynes had suggested that with the appropriate policy instruments, states could sustain growth and welfare at high levels. This model, the 'Keynesian Welfare National State' (Jessop 2002: 55–95), contained a particular set-up of the state–market relationship. That set-up was:

- *statist* insofar as state institutions ... were the chief complement to market forces ... To the extent that markets failed to deliver the expected values of economic growth, balanced regional development inside national borders, full employment, low inflation, a sustainable trade balance, and a socially just distribution of wealth and income, the state was called on to compensate for these failures and to generalize prosperity to all its citizens.
- *national* insofar as the national territorial state assumed the primary responsibility for developing and guiding Keynesian welfare policies on different levels ... In particular, economic and social policies at the urban and regional level were orchestrated in top-down fashion by the national state and primarily concerned with equalizing economic and social conditions within each of these national economies. (Jessop 2002: 60, 61)

This state–market set-up underwent a crisis from the late 1960s to the 1970s. The primary crisis indicators were stagnation and inflation. The crisis paved the way for a new state–market set-up emphasizing neoliberal ideas. The dominant thinking about the state–market relationship in this new set-up has been termed the 'Washington consensus' (Williamson 1990). It contains the major elements shown in Box 2.2.

It is the rise of this neoliberal state–market arrangement in the context of economic globalization which has persuaded retreat scholars that the state is being squeezed by the market. Susan Strange was quoted

> **Box 2.2   The 'Washington consensus'**
>
> - Fiscal discipline
> - A redirection of public expenditure priorities towards fields offering high economic returns
> - Emphasis on education and infrastructure
> - Tax reform (to lower marginal rates and broaden the tax base)
> - Interest rate liberalization
> - A competitive exchange rate
> - Liberalization of foreign direct investment inflows
> - Privatization
> - Deregulation (in the sense of abolishing barriers to entry and exit)
> - Secure property rights

to that effect in Chapter 1: 'where states were once masters of markets, now it is the markets which, on many crucial issues, are the masters over the governments of states' (Strange 1996: 4). But it can be argued that the new emphasis on 'market-oriented' economic activity does not mean a *reduced* role for the state; rather, it means a *different* role compared to the earlier state–market set-up. That is to say, the introduction of 'more market' in the context of the neoliberal Washington consensus means not less, but 'more state' as well. The reason is that the pursuit of intense economic globalization requires an elaborate and complex regulatory framework which calls for comprehensive state activity. Let us briefly look at some of the major features of the state–market relationship under the new conditions.

First, the activity of states has moved away from stressing functions of economic management towards stressing procedural–regulatory functions. For example, the activity of 'regulation for deregulation' meant that the number of regulatory measures taken in the Thatcherite neoliberal UK of the 1980s grew much faster than in the socialist France of François Mitterrand. As emphasized in a recent analysis, 'in contrast to neoliberal assumptions that more market means less state, market economization produces an enormous demand for legal regulation of money relations which increases state intervention at least with respect to regulations' (Altvater and Mahnkopf 1997: 456). Similarly, the creation of a single market in the context of the European Union has involved a huge number of regulatory directives aimed at enabling the free movement of goods, services, capital and people.

Second, political authority is no longer primarily represented by an all-powerful central state. It is being disaggregated into distinct parts, each of which interacts with a diverse compilation of private companies, groups and organizations as well as with their counterparts in other countries. One group of scholars label this a specific type of multilevel governance which they call 'type II governance' (Hooghe and Marks 2001). In this system, citizens are served 'not by "the" government, but by a variety of different public service industries … We can then think of the public sector as being composed of many public service industries including the police industry, the fire protection industry, the welfare industry, the transportation industry, and so on' (Ostrom and Ostrom 1999: 88–9).

These various 'micro' units of the states help organize the activities of global markets in conjunction with a variety of private groups. One scholar has studied a particular global economic network: the production and marketing of the Barbie doll (Snyder 1999). Although originally American, the doll is a truly global product, marketed from California, produced in China, with components from Japan, Saudi Arabia, Taiwan, the USA, Europe and Hong Kong. Snyder argues that such a global economic network is organized and structured by 'global legal pluralism'. By that, he means 'a variety of institutions, norms, and dispute resolution processes located, and produced, at different structured sites around the world' (ibid.: 15).

Breaking up this example of a global economic network into its component parts helps demonstrate how various types of regulation emerging from many different quarters are involved in determining the shape of the network. They include US intellectual property law, competition law and antitrust law; international customs rules; Chinese central and local legislation; the organization of power in the global toy commodity chain, including the role of dominant buyers; NGOs, such as the Toy Coalition; American buyers and national and international trade associations; the European Union (EU) toy directory and EU import quotas; EU trade legislation; and WTO rules on trade and intellectual property.

It is clear that there is a multitude of different 'sites' of global legal pluralism involved in structuring the Barbie doll economic network. 'Some sites are market-based, being generated by economic actors as part of economic processes. Some are polity-based, in that they form a part of established political structures. Others are convention-based, deriving from agreements between governments' (ibid.: 28). The example demonstrates how various parts of 'the state', together with different players in the market and also with NGOs and international organizations, are involved in setting up the organization of a global economic network. In this way, a large number of different public institutions are getting involved in the marketplace in new ways, unlike the standard picture of a centralized state governing the market.

A further example of this development of new 'sites' is 'public policy networks'. Such networks also involve government agencies, organizations from civil society, international organizations and private sector groups, but, in contrast to the Barbie doll case, public policy networks are concerned with providing solutions where market forces or existing public arrangements are insufficient. One example is the Global Reporting Initiative (GRI) which involves governments, private firms, NGOs and professional associations. It helps to develop harmonized standards for calculating the environmental impact of private corporations. 'Although many firms are voluntarily producing and releasing such assessments, each employs its own indicators and measurements, making it virtually impossible for investors, environmentalists, or consumers to compare reports and make informed decisions' (Reinicke 2000: 50). Public policy networks thus engage both private and public units in order to complement existing market-based or government-based arrangements considered insufficient. In short, the state–market arrangement is growing increasingly complex, involving a multitude of different actors connected to various 'sites'; it is no longer a situation of centralized state institutions regulating a well-defined national realm.

The above examples have all concerned cases where the state is getting involved with or participating in the market in new ways. But the reverse process is taking place as well: market-based solutions are increasingly finding their way into areas previously dominated by states. The privatization of a range of state services corresponds to placing under 'market conditions' a number of activities which were earlier exempt from the market. The period immediately after the Second World War saw the nationalization of industries; private firms were put under public control. Privatization is a movement in the opposite direction. State bureaucracies are increasingly busy conducting 'marketization' of activities. The notion of 'reinventing government':

> means the replacement of bureaucracies which directly produce public services by ones which closely monitor and supervise contracted-out and privatized services according to complex financial criteria and performance indicators ... Furthermore, the substance of regulation itself has shifted from structural regulation (that is, *ex ante* attempts to design market structures and to control market outcomes) to regulation which penalizes anti-competitive or fraudulent behaviour through *ex post* litigation, such as 'prudential regulation' in the financial markets. (Cerny 2000: 129)

So, states and markets are brought closer together. The state is becoming a more polymorphous entity, diffused into complex networks involving a range of other actors. On the one hand, there is a movement away from the 'central role of the official state apparatus in securing state-sponsored economic and social projects and political hegemony towards an emphasis on partnerships between governmental, paragovernmental and non-governmental organizations in which the state apparatus is often only first among equals' (Jessop 1997: 574). On the other hand, the formulation of state regulation now, to a much larger extent than before, takes place in transgovernmental networks which also involve a diverse group of other actors.

How can we summarize the various changes in the state–market arrangement? These changes are still under way, so no definite conclusion can be drawn, but there are some clear trends. One insightful analysis conceptualizes the changes as a move away from the Keynesian Welfare National State, towards a different model, the Schumpeterian Competition State. A 'competition state' is:

> a state that aims to secure economic growth within its borders and/or to secure competitive advantages for capitals based in its borders, even where they operate abroad, by promoting the economic and extra-economic conditions that are currently deemed vital for success in competition with economic actors and spaces located in other states … [A]n important aspect of the activities of competition states concerns their attempts either alone or in conjunction with other forces (including other states) to project power beyond their political frontiers to shape cross-border or external economic spaces relevant to capital accumulation and social reproduction … the competition state's strategies … are always mediated through the operation of the world market as a whole. (Jessop 2002: 96)

So, instead of the earlier focus on correction of market failures within national borders, states are pursuing strategies to secure competitive success in a world market context. There are major variations between the advanced states, of course; not everybody is doing exactly the same things. But the general trend that can be discerned is one of moving towards a competition state.

It remains to sort out what this means for the role of the state as seen from the debate between state-centric and retreat scholars. To repeat, retreat scholars tend to see a reduced role for the state in these developments, and an erosion of public authority ('state power') to the advantage of private authority ('market power'). It is true that political authority is increasingly disaggregated and less focused on economic management. It is also true that the much increased opening up to the world market has made it more difficult for states to control completely what goes on within their own borders. States are now more exposed to the economic forces of the world market. Certainly, economic globalization has much decreased the possibilities for national economic management.

There are at least three reasons for not seeing the changed state–market relations as a case of the state 'losing', however. First, states have much increased their activity in terms of regulatory and supervising functions. In other words, traditional forms of state regulation may have decreased but new forms develop to take their place. Direct management of the economy has decreased; instead, regulation of private actors has increased. This calls for more negotiation between public agencies and private actors; negotiation potentially increases the influence of private actors. States are certainly not left powerless, but they operate under new, and sometimes more difficult, conditions (cf. Vogel 1996).

Second, the more closely intertwined state–market relations in the context of the competition state play out within a macro framework very much constructed by states. A recent analysis identifies five levels in this framework.

1   Governance through agreement between the major political entities, particularly the G3 (Europe, Japan and North America), to stabilize exchange rates, to coordinate fiscal and monetary policies and to cooperate in limiting speculative short-term financial transactions.
2   Governance through a substantial number of states creating international regulatory agencies for some specific dimension of economic activity, such as the WTO to police the General Agreement on Tariffs and Trade (GATT) settlement.
3   The governance of large economic areas by trade and investment blocs such as the EU or NAFTA ... The blocs are big enough markets in themselves to stand against global pressures if they so choose.
4   National-level policies that balance cooperation and competition between firms and the major social interests.
5   Governance through regional level policies. (Hirst and Thompson 2000: 191–2)

That is to say, states attempt to compensate for their decreased national capacities for regulation by increasing their *inter*national capacities for regulation through cooperation with other states. In place of national regulation, regional and international cooperation has much increased, as will be further argued in the next chapter.

Finally, it is misleading to imply that 'market forces' actively seek the erosion of state power. Private actors in the marketplace need stable rules and predictable conditions of operation. The rule of law, the enforcement of property rights, secure circumstances of production, trade and exchange are all conditions that companies cannot create themselves; they need states to do that. In the absence of such stable rules and regulations, the market would be a 'mafia market' based on the random use of force, threats or bribes. Companies are strongly reluctant to operate under such conditions, as evidenced by the lack of investment in many less developed countries. And even in properly-functioning systems, state supervision is needed in order to avoid financial fraud and other illicit activity as confirmed by the recent debates about such problems in the USA. 'The market' will surely not always correct itself. In general terms, states must be considered as being 'necessary to advanced social life' (Mann 1997: 495). In sum, states have not 'lost' to markets; they have changed to interact with markets in new ways. There has been a change in relative emphasis, from one mode of market involvement to another.

State-centric scholars argue that states remain in control of markets, now as before. To some extent this is true, as the above considerations demonstrate; but the new state–market set-up is also a highly unstable one. Stability is needed in order to provide secure conditions for economic growth and welfare. Many observers question the stability of the current state–market arrangement. The financial expert, George Soros, put it the following way: 'I cannot see the global system surviving... Political instability and financial instability are going to feed off each other in a self-reinforcing fashion. In my opinion we have entered a period of global disintegration only we are not yet aware of it' (quoted in Soederberg 2001). Financial crises in Asia and Latin America are evidence of the vulnerability of the system. Financial and trade liberalization open economies up to more dramatic fluctuations than under the old Bretton Woods system. At the same time, the USA does not appear willing to pick up the mantle of responsibility for a more stable system and the European Union, willing or not, is not yet able to do so. The result is a volatile system which has too little to offer that half of the world's population which exists on two dollars or less per day. State-centric scholars are surely right that states can manage markets provided they make serious efforts to do so, but there is an element of serious instability in the current state–market matrix which powerful states appear unwilling to confront.

In conclusion, states as well as markets have been transformed under conditions of economic globalization. Instead of a *reduced* role for the state, the role of the state has *changed*. States operate under different circumstances now. In some ways that means new constraints on states, but states have also developed new means of regulating the market and thus the transformation that has taken place contains elements of both 'losing' and 'winning'. Again, it remains for the reader to decide where to put the accent when the evidence is pulled together.

Economic globalization and the welfare state

What are the consequences of economic globalization for the welfare state as we know it in Western Europe and North America? The question is complex because these countries are differently involved in economic globalization and they have different historical traditions shaping their involvement in welfare politics. And there is a further complication which may be the most serious one: economic globalization does not determine or even influence welfare policies and outcomes in a simple way. Remember that economic globalization itself is a complex product of different forces, including the policy measures taken by states. Some political forces may use references to 'globalization' as an excuse or alibi for changes made for other reasons. Welfare systems are the result of many different factors, including demographics, changing family structures, work patterns and lifestyles in the advanced capitalist states, and of course policy traditions, institutional structures and different configurations of political forces.

In spite of these serious complications, there is a comprehensive debate about economic globalization and the welfare state. Many retreat scholars argue that welfare systems are under severe pressure and that they are exposed to a 'race to the bottom' in welfare standards. Increased international competition, improved exit options for firms, and rapid reactions from global financial markets compel states to fiscal discipline, decreasing levels of social protection, and the lowering of corporate tax levels (e.g., Gray 1998; Hoogvelt 2001; Scholte 1997; Strange 1996;). Most state-centric scholars claim that this is pure myth because states remain fully capable of handling the welfare challenges of economic globalization (Esping-Andersen 1999; Swank 2001, 2002).

This debate is not new: it was also conducted by the great economists of the mid-twentieth century. John Maynard Keynes, Joseph Schumpeter, Gunnar Myrdal and several others agreed that the rise of the welfare state would impede economic integration and interdependence across borders. They were convinced that 'international economic disintegration will be the price paid for a stable and democratic national polity' (Rieger and Leibfried 1998: 364). Their argument is based on the idea that economic openness will be a threat to welfare policies; for that reason such openness will not be pursued.

The eminent economists turned out to be wrong. The Bretton Woods system became the basis for the model called 'embedded liberalism'

(Ruggie 1982). It went a long way towards liberalizing economic relations between the industrialized countries, but instead of curtailed welfare this was combined with an increasing level of state intervention in the economy and rising tax levels. Furthermore, in Western Europe especially, there were also several measures of economic redistribution to the less privileged, including social safety nets for exposed groups (including the old, the young, and those in poor health). How was that possible? It was possible for two main reasons, one economic and one political. The economic reason is that liberalization involving increased economic openness led to rapid economic growth over a sustained period. In other words, a larger pie was created, some of which was available for welfare purposes. The political reason is that powerful political coalitions were established among the groups potentially negatively affected by liberalization. These social democratic-cum-liberal coalitions were behind the measures of welfare expansion. Instead of a negative relationship between economic openness and welfare state intervention, a positive relationship emerged; 'more open economies have bigger government' (Rodrik 1998: 997; see also G. Garrett 2001).

Some scholars even go a step further and argue that welfare policies were a precondition for economic liberalization, not merely a reaction to negative effects of it. Their argument is that economic liberalization would not have taken place at all if compensating welfare mechanisms had not been in place (Rieger and Leibfried 1998). The issue cannot be pursued here, but it emphasizes that the relationship between economic liberalization and welfare policies is not merely one-way; the two interact and affect each other in a complex manner.

The model of embedded liberalism had its heyday in the late 1950s and the 1960s. By the 1970s, the model faced a crisis. Western Europe and Japan had been rapidly rebuilt after the war; instead of candidates for economic aid, they were now serious competitive challengers to the USA. The US response – named the 'Nixon Shokku' by the Japanese – included protectionist measures (import duties) and the abandoning of the dollar's convertibility to gold. But that did not lead to a comprehensive pursuit of protectionism by the countries in the triad (Western Europe, Japan and North America). Instead, domestic shifts in the dominant political coalitions led to the neoliberalism of the 1980s where the political and economic agenda was set by such leaders as Ronald Reagan in the USA and Margaret Thatcher in Britain.

The neoliberalism of the 1980s sparked a further round of more intense liberalization. The result was the process of economic globalization described above. Former national economies are now globalized in the sense of being deeply involved in cross-border production chains and increasingly markets, financial services and other major areas of economic activity are functioning in a global or regional environment. The question in the present context is whether these developments put welfare policies under unbearable pressure (see Box 2.3). Some scholars certainly find that to be the case:

> In the absence of an alternative, the major default option for government is the 'denationalized' economic policy posture of competing with other, similarly situated, capitalist countries in providing a friendly policy environment for transnational capital irrespective of ownership or origins. A British scholar (Phil Cerny) calls this model 'the residual state'. (Quoted from Ruggie 1997: 6)

Box 2.3   *Globalization and the welfare state*

To imagine that the social market economies of the past can renew themselves intact under the forces of downwards harmonisation is the most dangerous of the many illusions associated with the global market. Instead social market systems are being compelled progressively to dismantle themselves, so that they can compete on more equal terms with economies in which environmental, social and labour costs are lowest. (Gray 1998: 92)

Few governments would now hope to be able to manage the business cycle. Stability has been removed; the degree to which governments believe they can affect welfare through state intervention is strictly limited; and modernization is no longer a function of state control. The tools which the nation-state can use to achieve its ends in this diminished realm are also reduced. The result has been a dispersal of the power which the state accumulated in the post-war years; to the market and to different forms of international economic co-operation. The price of an open global economy run by weak states has been very heavy for those at the bottom of the social scale. Taking account of inflation, in real terms US median family income declined in the 1970s, plummeted in the 1980s and did not return to 1973 levels until 1990. The wages of average workers are below 1979 levels; family incomes were often only sustained by both partners going to work. The trend towards a greater gap between rich and poor prevailed throughout the industrialized world. (Horsman and Marshall 1994: 98)

The capacity of nations to control their own affairs has been checked by finance and eroded by free-roving commerce, but politicians continue to pretend they are in charge. The nation-state faces a crisis of relevance. What remains of its purpose and power if authority over domestic social standards is yielded to disinterested market forces? If governments are reduced to bidding for the favours of multinational enterprises, what basis will citizens have for determining their own destinies? (Greider 1997: 334)

An important reason for these concerns is that more intense economic globalization, especially in the areas of finance and production, poses more severe challenges to welfare policies than does international trade. The integration of financial markets requires increased financial discipline from governments in order to reassure markets about financial stability; the underlying threat is that capital will go elsewhere (Ruggie 1997; Scharpf 1991). The integration of production provides much improved exit options for firms. If they find tax burdens or other liabilities too demanding, they can set up shop somewhere else (Rodrik 1997; Steinmo 1993). In sum, the current intense economic globalization poses a much more severe threat to the welfare state than earlier measures liberalizing arm's length trade.

Retreat and state-centric scholars cannot agree about the consquences of economic globalization for the welfare state. There are many reasons for this and, as we have seen, the issue is complex because many different factors help determine welfare policies. Since the seminal work of Peter Katzenstein (1985), a large literature has emerged on the subject. In the present context, a highly simplified model can help clarify some of the major issues at stake in the debate. The model is presented in Box 2.4.

Table 2.3   *Structure and change in the welfare state, 1960–95**

Social policy dimension	Level 1960–4	Level 1980–4	Level 1990–3/5
Total social welfare	11.6	21.6	24.4
Income maintenance:			
• Cash transfers	8.7	16.9	18.4
• Social wage	25.0	40.0	44.0
Public health spending	2.8	5.8	6.3

* Based on data from 15 countries: Australia, Austria, Belgium, Canada, Denmark, Finland, France, Germany, Italy, Japan, the Netherlands, Norway, Sweden, the UK and the USA.

Variable definitions:

Total social welfare: total government expenditure for social welfare programmes (OECD definition) as a percentage of gross domestic product, or GDP (to 1993).

Cash income maintenance: cash payments for old-age and disability assistance, sickness and health benefits, unemployment compensation, family allowances, and social assistance as a percentage of GDP (to 1994).

Social wage: percentage of average production worker's gross income replaced by unemployment compensation, unemployment assistance, and various entitled social welfare benefits during first year of unemployment (to 1995).

Public health spending: government spending on health programmes as a percentage of GDP (to 1993).

Source: adopted from Swank (2002: 69).

Box 2.4 *Economic globalization and welfare: a simplified model*		
Politics: Response by state	Economics: Response by firms	
	Remain in country	*Resort to exit or non-investment*
Market-conforming liberalization	1 Welfare endangered	2 End of welfare state
Regulation to protect welfare	3 Strengthen welfare state	4 Welfare endangered

The simple model presents the consequences of economic globalization for welfare as the product of reactions by firms/capital on the one hand and policies by states on the other hand. Cell 1 is the result of the interplay between capital pushing for liberalization and politicians conforming to that pressure. According to John Ruggie, among others, this is what has happened in many OECD countries in the 1980s and 1990s. There is a shift towards 'neo-*laissez-faire*' (Ruggie 1997: 6) which helps increase inequality in society and frequently involves cutbacks in welfare expenditures.

Cell 2 is the worst-case scenario for welfare: the state liberalizes but still fails to attract investment and capital resorts to exit. There are no strong examples of this in the OECD area, but several developing countries in Africa, Asia and Latin America have had such experiences. They compete amongst each other in terms of presenting the most favourable climate for capital, but still fail to attract significant investment. Cell 3 is what happens in many OECD countries according to state-centric scholars. The state continues to protect welfare but firms remain in place because there are other incentives (e.g., attractive markets, a qualified labour force, political stability, and so on) that induce them to carry on business. There is thus no 'cruel choice' between welfare and economic openness (e.g., G. Garrett 1998). In cell 4, finally, state policies to protect welfare lead to a lack of incentives for capital to invest in the country and may also involve exit by existing undertakings. According to one commentator, such processes have been at work in Germany (Stelzer 1999: 29).

The simple model makes it easier to understand why the debate about the welfare consequences of economic globalization remains difficult to resolve. Theoretically, very different outcomes are possible and scholars cannot agree about the empirical evidence. On the one hand, for example, greater openness of economies is associated with lower rates of capital taxation (Rodrik 1997); on the other hand, corporate tax burdens in the OECD have on average *increased* over the 1970–97 period (Weiss 2003). At the same time, Swank (2002) shows an increasing total welfare effort in all of the three types of welfare state identified by Esping-Andersen (1990), (see Table 2.3).

The appropriate approach to economic globalization and welfare is that the changes wrought by globalization, in combination with a host of other factors, set a new context for welfare policies. The new context is in some ways more constraining than before, but it does not necessarily put an end to the welfare state, or even seriously threaten it.

What are the major elements of transformation taking place? First, countries are pursuing similar economic strategies of development and growth; that is, all are liberal democratic regimes basing themselves on a market economy oriented towards openness and international cooperation. The common pursuit of that model has integrated and synchronized the advanced economies so that crises or disturbances are quickly related to all parts of the system. Technological levels, the level of information among firms, interest rates and economic policy instruments are to some extent converging across countries.

Still, it is only a cluster of countries that have pursued strictly neoliberal policies; they include the USA, the UK, New Zealand and, in some measure, Australia and Canada. The overall trend in advanced capitalist countries, however, is that welfare policies are upheld, albeit with a new emphasis which includes the following:

- the use of social policy to enhance the flexibility of labour markets and to create flexible, enterprising workers suited to a globalizing, knowledge-based economy
- the redesign and reorganization of social policy to put downward pressure on the social wage, which is now regarded more as a cost of international production than as a source of domestic demand. (Quoted from Jessop 2002: 168)

In sum, welfare policies are upheld and expanded even in the face of economic globalization. At the same time, economic globalization presents new challenges to welfare policies. This may or may not lead to welfare curtailment. The welfare regime is upheld, but it has been transformed in ways that may endanger at least some aspects of welfare provision. Once again, it remains for the reader to decide where to put the accent.

Conclusion

Globalization means the expansion and intensification of economic, political, social and cultural relations across borders. This concept is too big to theorize. Instead, the chapter focuses on major aspects of economic globalization.

The modern economies of Western Europe and North America have been transformed as a result of economic globalization. Regional and global production chains organized by transnational corporations and a globally integrated financial market are major elements in this transformation, but it is not at all certain that such changes spell an entirely new phase of capitalist development as some globalization 'Believers' will say.

The state–market relationship in the modern state was statist and national. The state–market arrangement under the conditions of economic globalization is focused on competitiveness in the world market. Instead of a *reduced* role for the state, the role of the state has *changed*.

The changes wrought by economic globalization in combination with a host of other factors set a new context for welfare policies. Welfare policies are upheld and expanded even in the face of globalization, but the process of economic globalization also presents new challenges to welfare policies.

The transformation that is taking place contains elements of the state both 'losing' and 'winning'. As I have already made clear, the reader must decide where to put the accent once the evidence is pulled together. My own summation of the transformation of modern states follows in Chapter 9.

Chapter 3

Economic Globalization and the Third World

States and markets in the least developed Third World countries
Conclusion

The debate between state-centric and retreat scholars is focused on the advanced states in Western Europe, North America and Japan. Both sides in the debate have a certain contrast picture, a certain historical view of the state in mind when they discuss the development and change that has taken place with respect to the state. In other words, both sides use 'the modern state' as the baseline for their considerations, as explained in Chapter 1. But many states in the world today do not belong to this group, and of special interest here are the states in the Third World.

Even if Third World states are very different from the type of state dominating the debate between retreat and state-centric scholars, a further discussion of them will help shed new light on this dispute as well. It will reveal forms of state with weaknesses more severe than even the most radical retreat scholars had ever contemplated and it will demonstrate to state-centric scholars that effective and capable statehood can in no way be taken for granted.

What happens to Third World economies as a result of globalization? Many liberal scholars argue that economic globalization is a blessing that will vastly strengthen Third World economies (e.g., Bhagwati 2000). More critically oriented scholars assert that the Third World is being marginalized in the process of globalization and does not benefit from it at all (e.g., Hoogvelt 2001). This chapter will clarify the arguments in favour of each view and will demonstrate why the debate is not easily settled. In relation to that debate, it will be examined how economic globalization transforms (or does not transform) the Third World economies.

Critics emphasize the uneven nature of economic globalization and they are quite right to do so. The label 'economic globalization' is entirely misleading because most of the transactions across borders are not of a truly global reach: that is, they are neither intercontinental, nor interregional. As already indicated, it is the advanced capitalist

46

countries in the triad of Western Europe, North America and Japan that are mostly involved in economic globalization. Many Third World countries, especially the least developed countries (many of them in sub-Saharan Africa), are minimally involved.

This state of affairs is reflected in a core element of economic globalization, the flows and stock of foreign direct investment (FDI). Developing countries held 30 per cent of the world FDI stock in 1997; industrial countries took the rest. The lion's share of those 30 per cent went to a select few developing countries: China (6 per cent); Brazil (4 per cent); Mexico (3 per cent); Indonesia (2 per cent); and Malaysia, Argentina and Saudi Arabia (1 per cent each: figures from World Bank 2000: 38, 73).

Behind these figures on the distribution of total *stocks* of FDI are several important changes in *flows* of direct investment. Southeast Asia (China, Malaysia, Singapore, Indonesia and Thailand) emerged as the most important recipients of FDI in the 1990s whereas investment in Brazil and Mexico declined sharply compared to the late 1970s. This change is related to a shift in the source of FDI; the US share has declined whereas the West European and East Asian shares have increased. Three-quarters of the direct investment flowing into China over the last 15 years arrived from other Asian countries (Dunning 2000: 47).

So economic globalization is uneven partly for the simple reason that international investment capital is particularly interested in some locations and not at all interested in other locations. The decisions about location of investment are related to two major factors: one is the source of investment – that is, where it comes from – and the other is the set of motivations for making the investment. As to the source, there has been an increase in the FDI share of Japan and of Asian developing countries. The bulk of that investment goes to other Asian countries, in particular to China. China's rising popularity as an investment location is thus connected to the increasing economic muscle of Chinese business communities elsewhere in East Asia; they direct their investment to China (Dunning 2000: 37).

As to the set of motivations, firms invest abroad to make money of course; but firms were always in business to make money so the more recent patterns of foreign investment require some further explanation. A basic element behind FDI is that firms have developed competencies that can be exploited through foreign investment. These 'monopolistic advantages' (Hymer 1976) can be related to various aspects of production, distribution and marketing. They may have to do with technological know-how as well as expertise in production, design and marketing, or they may have to do with capabilities in other areas, such as administration, finance or sales. We noted the general development of regional and global production chains earlier in this book. Behind these chains are thus specific firms with a variety of skills that can help them to profit from participation in international activity.

The advantages related to firms help explain why they invest abroad, but they do not explain why investments arrive in a specific country. In order to understand that, we need to focus on the incentives that various investment locations have to offer. Investments have traditionally come to the Third World for three major reasons, the first being natural resources. These were the early investments in iron, gold, copper, oil and so on. The second reason is attractive local markets: for example, access to lucrative domestic markets with high barriers of protection was a major factor in US foreign investment in Latin America between the 1950s and the 1980s. Finally, there is the incentive of access to valuable conditions of operation. They may have to do with the availability of cheap labour or labour with special skills. A strategic location and special transport/communication facilities (such as in Singapore) are other relevant elements.

In recent years, these traditional reasons for FDI have been supplemented with an additional set of factors having to do with the intensification of economic globalization. As indicated earlier, enterprises now set up strategic alliances and networks, and they want to be present in countries and regions that offer a wider range of facilities – that is:

> an adequate supply of cost-effective semi-skilled or skilled labour, a good physical infrastructure, government policies which are market-friendly, and minimal distance related transaction costs ... In the 1990s, FDI is determined less by the country-specific costs of factor endowments or size of local markets, and more by those variables which facilitate firm and/or plant economies of scale and scope; and the effective exploitation of regional and/or global markets. (Dunning 2000: 29)

In order to appreciate the effects of foreign investment on Third World economies we need one further element, and that is the ability of the host country to profit from FDI in its own process of economic development. This is a very large topic because many different factors are relevant in this regard. To simplify, we may focus on what are arguably the two most important aspects: the economic and the political capacities of the host country. If economic and political capacities are very low, foreign investors will simply control their respective sectors, pay low wages and repatriate profits to the home country. If economic and political capacities are high, local firms can benefit from foreign investment in terms of technological transfers, market access, product upgrading and competence development. As for the political aspect, a capable state can help create the optimum framework for foreign investment. This will often require sophisticated regulations concerning technology, profit transfers and relations to local firms. In short, the better equipped a host country is in terms of economic and political capacities, the greater the likelihood of getting a process of economic development under way with the help of foreign investment. And the reverse is also true: very poorly equipped host countries cannot expect significant contributions from foreign investors to their economic development (cf. Sørensen 1983).

Foreign investment is a core element in economic globalization. We now have the necessary building blocks to evaluate the consequences of foreign investment for Third World countries. The first important dimension concerns the readiness of international firms to invest in the host country; the second important dimension concerns the economic and political capacities of host countries. These two dimensions are combined in Box 3.1.

Several Southeast Asian countries have been able to attract substantial foreign investment. At the same time, these countries have high capacities for extracting developmental benefits from such investment. Taiwan is a good example. Industrial development in Taiwan has proceeded in three stages: import substitution in the 1950s, export of manufactured consumer non-durables (toys, shoes and so on) in the 1960s, and a process of industrial upgrading with emphasis on producer goods and some consumer durables (electronic equipment and computers) beginning in the mid-1970s (Sørensen 1991: 128–31). That is to say, when foreign investment started coming in on a larger scale, Taiwan had already built an industrial base of its own: local industrial capacity which could benefit from foreign investors existed. Furthermore, the state oversaw the process of FDI and directed it to export industries, urging foreign investors to cooperate with local firms. A famous

Box 3.1 *Foreign investment in the Third World: development or not?*		
Host states: Economic/political capacity	**Firms: Will they invest?**	
	Yes	*No*
High	Southeast Asia	(India?)
Low	(Latin America?)	Sub-Saharan Africa

example is the investment by the Singer Sewing Machine Company. Singer was urged by the state to 'locally procure 83 percent of required parts one year after operation and ... assist Taiwan's producers in meeting specifications. Singer ended up transferring technology, upgrading the entire industry, and boosting exports' (Gold 1986: 85). In spite of state demands, the general conditions of operation in Taiwan remained favourable enough to attract investors. In the Taiwanese case, economic globalization in the form of FDI helped produce economic development.

Compare this situation to the weak states in sub-Saharan Africa. These countries have never been able to create coherent national economies. In economic terms, they are incoherent amalgamations of traditional agriculture, an informal petty urban sector and some fragments of modern industry, mostly controlled by external interests. Exports consist of one or a few primary products and the economies are highly dependent on imports of manufactured and technology-intensive products. Political institutions are inefficient and corrupt, frequently run by self-serving elites offering what state services there are to the highest bidder. FDI is not very interested in coming into these countries in the first place because of the lack of stability and attractive conditions of operation; less than 2 per cent of total FDI (World Bank 2000: 38) goes to sub-Saharan Africa. And when investment does come in, it has monopolistic control over pockets of the economy with little or no links to local undertakings. Foreign investment under these conditions does not help to produce economic development; rather, it perpetuates underdevelopment. And sure enough, the 'investors' coming in are often arms dealers, gold and diamond traders, drug smugglers and so on.

Thus, it is easy to understand why scholars cannot agree on the impact of economic globalization on Third World countries. In some cases economic globalization does help perpetuate marginalization and underdevelopment; in other cases it does promote economic development. It all depends on the willingness of investors to come in and the capacity of host countries to benefit from the presence of FDI. The extreme examples in this regard are sub-Saharan Africa on the one hand and several countries in Southeast Asia on the other. In-between cases include India, which has the capacity to benefit from FDI but which has long made investors hesitate to come in because of exceptional regulations, and also several Latin American countries where investment has arrived but host states have not had sufficient economic and political capacity to benefit from it. This, of course, raises the complex question of why conditions in the various parts of the Third World are so different in the first place. A full answer to that question involves explaining the different historical trajectories of development, a task I cannot take up here (but for Southeast Asia and India, see Sørensen 1991; for sub-Saharan Africa, see Jackson and Rosberg 1982; for Latin America, see Cardoso and Faletto 1979).

We noted earlier in this chapter how the modern economies in North America and Western Europe were transformed from national towards globalized economies as a result of globalization. In what ways are Third World economies transformed? This is a more intricate question because variation is much greater in the starting points for Third World economies and so are the trajectories as a result of globalization. Many of these countries have never been able to construct modern, national economies in the first place. At the lowest levels of economic and political capacity – such as in many countries in sub-Saharan Africa – economic globalization further perpetuates underdevelopment and marginalization. In the most successful cases, including several countries in Southeast Asia, economic globalization helps further strengthen national economic capacities. At the same time, in these cases globalization also amplifies a transformation from purely national economies towards more globalized economies. In other regions, such as Latin America and South Asia, the picture is even more mixed.

States and markets in the least developed Third World countries

The previous chapter dealt with the relationship between states and markets and how it has been transformed under conditions of economic globalization. But that earlier discussion focused on the advanced states; it is important to be aware that the state–market arrangement has different characteristics in Third World countries, and in particular in the least developed ones.

There is a close relationship between states and markets in successful processes of economic development. States set up the rules that enable the market to function properly. Market dynamics affect states because the economic resources available to states and the concrete scope for state intervention are influenced by the way markets function. One influential analysis (North 1990) has formulated four institutional conditions that states need to provide in order to secure an appropriate framework for economic growth and development: (a) secure property rights; (b) an efficient and unbiased juridical system; (c) a clear and transparent regulatory framework; and (d) an institutional framework promoting impersonal forms of exchange and interaction, including rules of contract and regulations of entry/exit for private firms.

In more concrete terms, think of a real estate transaction: the buying and selling of a house and how each of North's conditions would relate to this: for (a), as a buyer, you need to be certain that you actually get to own the house when you have paid a large sum of money for it. For (b), if the relationship with the seller turns sour, you need to be sure about fair treatment in court. As regards (c), regulations shaping the deal, such as concrete terms, credit, insurance, technical specifications on the house, building regulations and so on, need to be clear in order for the transaction to run smoothly. Finally, in relation to (d), you would prefer a selection of real estate agents operating in a proper manner, and not on the basis of personal whims and favours.

These necessary institutional conditions for a market economy are frequently far from sufficiently developed in the least developed Third World countries. One of the most serious problems is the lack of secure property rights. People very often cannot document ownership to the house they live in or the land that they cultivate. The reason is that the road to legal ownership has been bureaucratized in the extreme and there are vested bureaucratic and other interests in keeping things that way. In the Philippines, it requires 168 steps involving 53 public and private agencies to formalize ownership of a squatter's house built on state-owned land; the process takes from 13 to 25 years. In Peru, a team of researchers set up a one-man clothing workshop in the suburbs of Lima and tried to register it so that the property rights and the legal framework for the business were in good order. It took 289 days to get through the process, involving a cost of $1,231, a sum which represents more than 30 times the monthly minimum wage in Peru (*The Economist* 2001: 22; de Soto 2001).

The lack of well-defined property rights and clear regulation of transactions stifle economic growth. This can be illustrated by a story from Malawi. The Tarera family raises goats and sells the meat; business is good, they want to expand. They need the local equivalent of $250. They have built a house worth more than that, so it should be a simple thing to borrow the money with the house as security. But they cannot prove that they own the house. It is built on 'customary' land, bought informally through the local chief who took a fat cut for his services. No bank will accept the contract signed by the chief as collateral because the contract is not enforceable in a court of law. The house is 'dead' capital.

The lack of institutional conditions for a market economy perpetuates poverty (World Bank 2002). Malawi's dictator for more than 30 years (1964–94), Hastings Banda, encouraged formal ownership. 'But his habit of grabbing large tracts of land for his cronies undermined the rule of law. Banks were forced to lend for political rather than commercial reasons, which prevented the evolution of property-backed lending' (*The Economist* 2001: 22). So, the rule of law is a luxury that most people in weak, postcolonial states enjoy, at best, sporadically. Most of the time 'they have suffered the whims of strongmen, who have undermined judicial independence, detained opponents, countenanced (or practised) rent-seeking and corruption, and ... empowered public tribunals to confiscate private property and jail businessmen for "economic crimes"' (Sandbrook 2000: 120, writing about Ghana).

To the extent that weak states have actually set up and enforced rules governing the market, these regulations have frequently been counter-productive in terms of growth and welfare. Instead, they have benefited leaders and their select groups of clients. Robert Bates (1981) argued that the ways in which African governments regulate markets are harmful to the interests of most farmers. The purchase of farm produce through state controlled marketing boards means that farmers get artificially low prices for their products. In this way, political leaders subsidize their urban supporters who get access to food at low prices. At the same time, the protection of domestic industry from competition means that farmers pay exorbitant prices for manufactured goods.

While these pricing policies hurt farmers badly, some of them have been offered development projects and other forms of aid as a compensation. In terms of general economic development, this is not an effective system: higher prices increasing the farmer's incentive to raise output would be much better. However, in terms of a powerful ruler's patron–client system, it is highly attractive. Selected groups of friends and supporters can be rewarded and the possibilities for skimming off rents in the process are good.

Such policies have alienated farmers; they have no incentives to increase output beyond what they need for survival. Instead of helping to promote the development of a market economy, they retreat into what one scholar has termed 'the economy of affection' (Hydén 1983). This is a peculiar peasant mode of production where the participants are linked together on the basis of ethnicity, kinship or religion. Their obligations to each other have nothing to do with standard market relationships between buyers and sellers, or producers and consumers; instead, they are based on tradition and social status. 'The economy of affection' is linked in complex ways to the patronage system of political rule, not least because most rural families have links to relatives in the city and in the state apparatus, so the two systems reinforce each other. This intricate system of giving and returning favours has been comprehensively unable to promote a process of sound economic growth.

At the same time, weak states faced severe external economic constraints, as indicated earlier in this chapter. Decline in the prices of primary produce and expensive import of oil increased external debt dramatically. It was against this background that the international financial institutions (the International Monetary Fund, or IMF, and the

World Bank) began advocating a policy of structural adjustment in the Third World. The new policies, formulated during the 1980s, were indebted to the ideas of the 'Washington consensus' presented above (p. 33). It was strongly felt that 'government failures' were a much more serious problem than 'market failures'. Consequently, the policy of structural adjustment aimed at 'regulation for de-regulation': that is, to liberalize economic exchange. Regulations should help set economic exchange free by removing the heavy, and distorting, hand of direct state intervention. In concrete terms that meant:

- lifting trade restrictions and currency regulations
- fiscal discipline, public sector cutbacks, tax reform
- liberalizing trade in agricultural product and better inputs for farmers
- removal of industrial protectionism, privatization of state enterprises, facilitation of the establishment of private enterprises. (Taylor 1997: 148–9)

The Structural Adjustment Programmes (SAPs) were evaluated by the World Bank in 1994. On the one hand, the Bank gave 'a qualified yes' to the question of whether adjustment was paying off in sub-Saharan Africa (World Bank 1994: 131). On the other hand, an editorial in *Codesria Bulletin* a few years earlier was in no doubt that the SAP 'completely undermines Africa's sovereignty, [and] creates and/or further strengthens authoritarian regimes who will have to implement an inherently anti-democratic set of socio-economic reforms entailed in the programmes' (quoted from Barya, 1992). A similar debate has taken place concerning the use of SAPs in Latin America.

There appears to be little doubt that structural adjustment has had some positive effects in a number of countries, especially in improving the conditions for agricultural production. But it is equally true that there have also been harmful consequences. Most of the time, the possible beneficial effects have tended to be cancelled out by the short- and medium-term negative effects of rapidly increasing prices, more unemployment, cutbacks in public services and so on.

The international financial institutions (IFIs) and the African states share responsibility for the problems connected with SAPs. The IFIs pursued a 'one-size-fits-all' approach that was far too ambitious in its assumptions about the swift adaptability of weak states to liberalizing measures. Lack of capital, of local entrepreneurs and of any effective market economy framework made it extremely difficult to succeed in the short and medium term. At the same time, governments had their own ways of adapting to the new pressures for reform. For them, the game quickly became one of extracting as many fresh resources as possible in new aid and loans, while offering as little as possible in terms of actually implemented policy reforms. This was:

> a perfectly understandable attitude for African rulers, who were anxious to get their hands on the money, but whose long-established practices and possibly political survival were threatened by the conditions which accompanied it; African governments, indeed, rapidly became as adept at evading the demands of international financial institutions as their people were at evading those of their own governments. (Clapham 1996: 177)

Evading reform altogether was certainly no durable solution to anything. That strategy was tried by Kenneth Kaunda in Zambia in 1987. The economy of a corrupt, self-seeking system of rule merely accelerated its progress of economic decline, further pushed by the lack of economic inflows from external actors (Callaghy 1991: 49). By the early 1990s, the IFIs were well aware of the problems. Reforms had to go beyond policy changes and try to create a new context for a functioning market economy. Following the end of the Cold War, the institutions increasingly began to push for democratization and 'good governance', meaning states that are more effective, more responsive and less corrupt.

This is actually a fresh turn in Western thinking; many observers used to see strong, developmentalist states as more likely to be non-democratic, using the experience of the authoritarian, developmentalist states in East Asia (South Korea and Taiwan) as empirical support. An early analysis of Japan by Chalmers Johnson argued that 'soft authoritarianism' could provide political stability and order. Here, the idea is quite the opposite: political pluralism is dangerous because it can challenge the goals of the developmental elite. The Japanese experience demonstrated the successful combination of 'an extremely strong and comparatively unsupervised state administration, single-party rule for more than three decades, and a set of economic priorities that seems unattainable under true political pluralism during such a long period' (Johnson 1987: 137).

However, it was never quite clear that authoritarianism was a necessary element in a developmentalist state (Baeg-Im 1987; Hamilton 1987). And comparative analysis could quickly reveal that the special conditions surrounding a 'soft authoritarian' developmentalist state in East Asia were not present elsewhere, least of all in the weak, postcolonial states. The East Asian experience cannot be generalized; the variants of 'soft' and 'hard' authoritarianism found in Africa, Latin America and South Asia have all failed to generate a state geared towards economic development (Sørensen 1993).

So, democratization and good governance are the new demands on Third World states. The hope is to boost the states' institutional, technical, administrative and political capacity, this last including legitimate authority and responsive and representative government (Grindle 1996; World Bank 1997). The underlying idea is that democracy will help discipline the state, making it more responsive to society, and less inefficient, corrupt and incompetent. A more effective state, in turn, can take the lead in promoting processes of economic development which will help change society and thereby help 'produce' social groups more conducive to further rapid socio-economic development.

This may sound very good in theory, but practice has been somewhat less successful. Early elections in less developed Third World states have not produced the expected results; rather, they have superimposed a thin layer of democratic coating upon a system of corrupt patron–client rule without major change in the basic features of the old structure. According to one astute observer:

> elections appear to be the wrong place whence to start a process of democratization ... In recent years, African elections have typically been organized in a hurry, in some cases before parties had time to consolidate or armed movements had agreed to disarm. As a result, losers have found it easy to reject election results, and voters had little choice but to vote on the basis of ethnic or religious identity ... Elections held under wrong conditions can be a real setback for democratization. (Ottaway 1995: 245; for a similar view see Elklit 1994)

Another major drawback of the early democratization processes in the least developed Third World states is that there has been little change for the better in the economic policies of the new regimes. A recent analysis found that:

> elections may actually increase the use of patronage ... Traditional patron–client relations have often been critical in winning recent elections, indicating that the nature of African politics has not changed despite the new liberalization. Ghana, Nigeria, and Kenya have all reported massive overspending as governments sought to reward traditional supporters, notably members of particular ethnic groups and civil servants, to smooth the transitions process or to gain votes ... The particular circumstances of political liberalization in Africa cause leaders' horizons to be relatively short and therefore to induce particular strategies such as clientelism which may be unnecessary where democratic structures are more institutionalized. (Bienen and Herbst 1996: 38–9)

In sum, democratization appears to be a sound long-term answer to the question of how to promote effective statehood and economic development in weak states. State elites that are not accountable to 'their' societies in some meaningful way may conduct development 'experiments' or act in self-seeking ways that have disastrous consequences for the people, as demonstrated by autocratic rulers in sub-Saharan Africa and elsewhere. But democracy takes a considerable amount of time to develop, especially where the societal conditions are adverse, as is mostly the case in weak states. Therefore, early results from scattered electoral processes should not be expected. Democracy cannot be installed overnight. There might even be a need for developing new models of democracy which are different from the standard models of the West and better suited to weak state conditions, but this is by no means an easy task.

In conclusion, there is a peculiar relationship between states and markets in the least developed Third World countries. These states are so feeble that they are unable to set up and enforce the rules and regulations necessary for the market to function. As a result, there is a lack of well-defined property rights, of an efficient and unbiased juridical system, of a clear and transparent regulatory framework and of an institutional framework promoting impersonal forms of exchange. Instead, norms of exchange have developed which benefit self-seeking rulers and their favoured group of clients. The attempts by external actors to liberalize the system, and to make it more democratic and responsive, have come up against serious problems indeed. There are probably no 'quick fixes', no miracle cures, that will turn around the weak states and swiftly put them on the road to economic development and democracy.

The situation in the least developed Third World states clearly demonstrates why it is misleading to adopt a zero-sum view of the relationship between states and markets. Markets positively *need* a properly-functioning regulatory framework in order to operate efficiently. In that sense, there is no 'free market' outside the reach of the state. There are markets regulated in different ways, but regulation is always needed. In its absence, a 'free market economy' cannot function.

Many Third World states are, unfortunately, an example of exactly that. The lack of economic progress in sub-Saharan Africa illustrates the situation. Real growth rates have stagnated or dropped since the mid-1960s; the states are plagued by debt, disinvestment and decreasing export earnings. According to the World Bank's most recent estimate, the gross national income of 674 million Africans amounted to $317 billion in 2001; the corresponding figure for 5 million Danes was $166 billion. The more realistic figures of purchasing power parities (PPPs) which better reflect differences in real purchasing power are: $1,094 billion for Africa, and $150 billion for Denmark. Life expectancy at birth in sub-Saharan Africa stood at 47 years in 2000 (all figures from World Bank 2003; PPP measures are in terms of domestic purchasing powers of currencies, thereby avoiding the distortions of official exchange rates). There are a few countries with better track records, such as Botswana and Mauritius (Carroll and Carroll 1997), but such 'success stories' are few and far between.

Conclusion

The conclusion in terms of the state–market relationship is clear: when the state retreats in a really dramatic way, the market retreats as well. Effective markets depend on strong and effective states; the zero-sum view is wrong. This is the lesson for retreat scholars. State-centric scholars need to take note of the fact that there are a large number of sovereign states in the world today which are significantly weaker than the state-centric view assumes. State-centric scholars tend to portray the state as the modern state ideal type presented in Chapter 1. But far from all states are modern: there are a significant number of ineffective, less developed states in the present international system. State-centric scholars will have to take note of that fact, or their analysis will remain seriously incomplete.

Chapter 4

Political Changes: From National Government to Multilevel Governance?

Towards a global polity?
The development of regional cooperation
Multilevel governance: consequences for the state
Challenges to democracy in the new context
The least developed states in the Third World
Conclusion

In this chapter our attention shifts to the ways in which the political level of the state has been transformed compared to our starting point, the modern state of the early 1950s. There are two major aspects to this: first, we need to know about the changes in the institutional organization and the exercise of politics as they have developed in context of economic globalization and a host of other relevant factors. Second, there is the issue of democracy: what are the challenges to democracy in the new political situation? Is democracy possible at all when politics takes place in a new multilevel context, very different from the well-defined territorial container of the modern state? Traditionally, this entire debate has focused on the modern states in Western Europe, North America and Japan. For our purposes, it is necessary also to ask about changes in the political level pertaining to the weak states in the Third World.

The political changes in question have been interpreted quite differently by retreat and state-centric scholars. State-centric scholars portray international cooperation as dominated by states, taking place in international institutions that leave states free to pursue their own interests. Retreat scholars depict international cooperation as more demanding, frequently constraining the freedom of manoeuvre of states. Furthermore, so they claim, new sources of governance not controlled by states have emerged in the context of globalization.

Towards a global polity?

Many commentators diagnose changes at the political level as a consequence of new developments elsewhere, not least because of economic globalization. With globalization, the socio-economic space that states

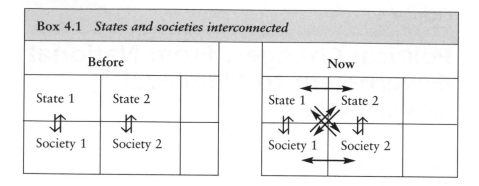

Box 4.1   *States and societies interconnected*

have to deal with is extended across the territorial border. Put differently, states are now increasingly influenced by events and decisions made beyond their territorial reach, and vice versa: activities undertaken by states increasingly have consequences not merely within their own juris-diction, but elsewhere as well. More and more, then, a lack of congruence develops between the formal reach of political decisions on the one hand, and the integrated socio-economic space which is influenced by the state and affected by its decisions on the other hand (cf. Zürn 1999; and also see Box 4.1). The result is an increasing demand for political cooperation across borders; only in that way, so the argument runs, will states be able to reclaim the regulative powers lost due to globalization.

Liberal observers emphasize three major developments pointing to more cross-border cooperation (Keohane and Nye 1977, 2001; see also Tables 4.1 and 4.2). First, the growth of *interstate* relations, especially through cooperation in IGOs. The number of such organizations rose from 123 in 1951 to 260 by the mid-1990s (Held *et al.* 1999: 54; Zacher 1992: 65). At the same time, many international organizations within the UN system, the Bretton Woods system (i.e., the IMF and the World Bank), and even the OECD have expanded their roles so that they are of increasing importance for the member states. The IMF and the World Bank monitor economic performance in all parts of the world and are central players in situations of economic crisis; UN institutions have

Table 4.1   *Bilateral agreements*

Number of new agreements	USA	Germany	France	UK	Japan
1950–4	666	90	101	243	56
1960–4	696	90	213	270	35
1975–9	1,250	537	264	242	140

Source: Adopted from Beisheim *et al.* (1999: 333), and based on data in UN, *Treaty Series*, http://www.un.org/Depts/Treaty/collection/series/search.htm.

significantly developed international law in such areas as human rights and minority rights. The OECD has also increased its policy surveillance of member states. Membership of the World Trade Organization is considered a very high priority for states that want integration in the global economic system (Held *et al.* 1999: 65–85; Scholte 2000: 148–51).

The second important development is the expansion of *transgovernmental* relations. They indicate that states are connected with each other at many different levels; external relations are no longer the sole responsibility of the ministry of foreign affairs and the head of state. Ministries and other units of government (such as regulatory agencies, courts and executives) are connected with their counterparts in other countries in a dense web of policy networks. According to one observer, 'transgovernmentalism is rapidly becoming the most widespread and effective mode of international governance' (Slaughter 1997: 185). Transgovernmental activity is especially developed among national regulators, the officials responsible for corporate supervision, environmental standards, antitrust policies and so on. A recent German report looked at German ministries as actors in global governance and found a rapidly increasing level of transgovernmental activity in individual ministries. At the same time, ministries were progressively more involved in issues that contained an international dimension (Eberlei and Weller 2001).

The third important development is the expansion of *transnational* relations; that is, cross-border relations between individuals, groups and organizations from civil society (non-state actors). The number of international non-governmental organizations (INGOs) increased from 832 in 1951 to 5,472 by the mid-1990s (see Tables 4.3 and 4.4). There is great diversity among INGOs; on the one hand, many of them are critical of governments and international organizations. Whether it concerns issues of trade policy, the environment, disarmament, or human rights, they 'keep saying things governments do not want to hear' (Ingram 1995: 5). On the other hand, INGOs increasingly work alongside governments and international organizations in a number of areas, including, for example, development aid, environmental protection and health care.

Table 4.2 *Multilateral agreements*

Number of new agreements	USA	Germany	France	UK
1950–4	94	87	182	144
1960–4	118	177	158	170
1970–4	151	177	258	197

Source: Adopted from Beisheim *et al.* (1999: 335), and based on data in UN, *Treaty Series*, various years.

Table 4.3   *Number of IGOs and INGOs*

	IGOs	INGOs
1909	37	176
1951	123	832
1996	260	5,472

Source: Data compiled from Held *et al.* (1999: 53) and Zacher (1992: 65).

According to one observer, governance is increasingly managed by global public policy networks: that is, 'loose alliances of government agencies, international organizations, corporations, and elements of civil society such as nongovernmental organizations, professional associations, or religious groups that join together to achieve what none can accomplish on its own' (Reinicke 2000: 44). A study by the World Bank has identified 50 such networks in a variety of areas, such as crime, fisheries, public health, agricultural research, environment and water resources.

The argument is that a significant change is taking place. In earlier days, national *governments* ruled within well-defined territorial borders. Today, politics is increasingly taking the shape of international or global *governance*, a term that refers to activities everywhere – local, national, regional, global – involving regulation and control. Governance is thus an international, transgovernmental and transnational activity that includes not only governments or units of government and traditional international organizations, but also non-governmental organizations and other non-state actors. Put differently, we may distinguish between three aspects of governance; the first is *governance by government* which is the traditional picture of hierarchical national regulation and control. The second is *governance with government*; governments are still involved, but they negotiate with a host of other actors and act more like a *primus inter pares*. Such processes may take place both in the international and in the domestic realm. International accords – such as the agreement to protect the ozone layer – provide an example of this. Finally, there is *governance without government* where actors set up patterns of regulation without government interference. For example, this has been done by sports associations, defining rules of their games and anti-doping regimes (the argument in this paragraph draws on Zürn 1998: 169–71).

The argument by radical 'retreat scholars' is that when globalization in the broad sense gradually expands and intensifies, governance *by* government will tend to be replaced by governance *with and without* government. Ulrich Beck, for example, defines globalization as the

Table 4.4   *Selected countries in world politics*

	USA	Germany*	France	UK	Japan
IGO memberships					
1950	59	25	67	62	14
1996	64	83	87	71	63
INGO participation					
1960	612	841	886	742	412
1996	2,418	3,204	3,255	3,031	1,970

* Federal Republic of Germany data prior to 1996.
Source: Adopted from Held *et al.* (1999: 83–4); data compiled from Held *et al.* (1999: 53) and Zacher (1992: 65).

processes 'through which sovereign national states are criss-crossed and undermined by transnational actors with varying prospects of power, orientations, identities and networks' (Beck 2000: 101).

Another approach to these complex developments has been termed 'the global polity'. The idea is that a global polity is emerging. The 'global polity' is simply defined as 'that totality of political structures, agents and processes, with transnational properties, that in the current historical context have developed a high level of *thick* interconnectedness and an element of *thin community* that transcends the territorial state' (Ougaard and Higgott 2002: 12). The notion of 'thin community' implies 'a robust community although still vague and general and with only few concrete manifestations' (ibid.: 13). The issue of community will be dealt with in detail in the next chapter.

The global policy networks briefly mentioned earlier are, according to several scholars, a core element in the global polity:

> networks allow resources to be mobilized towards common policy objectives in domains outside the hierarchical control of governments ... This tendency towards alliances, coalitions or partnerships is particularly noticeable in the global polity where governance structures are more diffuse and lack the central coordination hierarchies characteristic of national polities ... There are several competing and overlapping network concepts. They include: quasi-official *policy communities*, broadly participatory *transnational advocacy networks*, scientific *epistemic communities* or *discourse coalitions* defined by language, symbols and ideas. (Stone 2002: 131–2)

In sum, a global polity contains two important changes compared to an earlier phase of national government. First, governments are increasingly enmeshed in a complex network of international organizations to which they make a variety of commitments, some of which are of a more binding nature than previously. Second, many non-state actors influence the processes of governance; regulation and control is no longer a sole preserve of states.

Is a global polity really in the making and, if so, does it imply a much less pronounced role for the state when it comes to governance? Retreat scholars are certain that the answer is affirmative, but state-centric scholars reject the idea that states are losing control. States are themselves the primary architects of globalization: they have created the liberal framework of international exchange which made economic globalization possible in the first place. We return to that debate below, but first a few words about regional cooperation.

The development of regional cooperation

Cooperation across borders is frequently not global in scope; it is regional. Variations in the intensity of regional cooperation testify to the different conditions prevailing in different regions. Björn Hettne has usefully distinguished between five levels of regional complexity or 'regionness' as follows:

1   Region as a *geographical and ecological unit*, delimited by natural geographical barriers: 'Europe from the Atlantic to the Urals', 'Africa South of Sahara', or 'the Indian subcontinent'.
2   Region as a *social system*, which implies translocal relations of a social, political, cultural and economic nature between human groups.
3   Region as *organized cooperation* in any of the cultural, economic, political or military fields.
4   Region as *regional civil society* which takes shape when the organizational framework promotes social communication and convergence of values throughout the region.
5   Region as *acting subject* with a distinct identity, actor capability, legitimacy, and structure of decision-making. The organizational expression of this level of complexity naturally also tends to become more complex, as the current transformation of the European Community into a European Union shows. (Hettne 1997: 226–8)

There is a progression in the five levels, from lower to higher stages of integration and cooperation; but it is not a 'stage theory' where all regions must progress from level one to reach level five.

Regional cooperation has developed the most in Western Europe. Conditions for it were especially favourable following the end of the

Second World War. The former foes wanted to avoid new confrontations in the future; West Germany was politically reconstructed by the Allies and a political elite very strongly committed to European cooperation emerged in that country. The USA also pushed for closer links between West European states. And there was a common enemy, the Soviet Union and the Eastern Bloc.

The European Union has developed into the most ambitious and far-reaching example of regional cooperation. The EU contains a significant element of supranational governance, meaning that EU institutions in some areas have the powers to write the rules for member states. The European Court of Justice, the European Commission and the Council of Ministers can make decisions going against single members. Rulings by the European Court take priority over rulings by national courts. Successive treaties have stipulated ever closer cooperation in more and more areas; the single market and the common currency are merely the most visible elements of an integration process that already touches upon all significant policy areas. Member states have bargained with their sovereignty so as to achieve influence over the domestic affairs of other member countries. In return, they allow these other states to influence the regulation of their own domestic affairs (Keohane 1995; Sørensen 1999; for more on sovereignty see Chapter 6).

The EU, then, is the clearest example of what could be called multi-level governance: that is, a situation where political power is diffused and decentralized. Instead of purely or mainly national political regulation, a complex network of supranational, national and subnational regulation has developed (see Table 4.5). At the same time, integration at the political level has stimulated integration between societies (and vice versa). So multilevel governance in the EU is matched by a high level of interconnectedness between member societies in general (i.e., in economic, cultural and other areas).

It should be noted that multilevel governance is a complex phenomenon covering different types of political regulation; the common denominator is that in addition to national government, a number of other actors are closely involved in the process of regulation. One form

Table 4.5 *Number of European Community administrative and legal acts, selected years*

1961	36
1971	376
1981	684
1990	618

of multilevel governance was instituted in the EU in 1988, when the Union's cohesion policy was reformed. Cohesion policy aims at reducing regional disparities by supporting regional projects through so-called 'structural funds'. The reform stipulated that policy networks involving representatives from the regions, from member states and from the EU Commission collaborate in the policy-making process. 'Thus, in addition to affecting the content of cohesion policy, the reform had the significant effect of changing boundary rules, by widening the circle of policy-participants, and decision-rules, by introducing horizontal co-decision. Hierarchy was repudiated and networking promoted' (Kjær 2004, forthcoming; see also Hooghe 1996: 12).

Different variants of multilevel governance are at work in other EU policy areas. In implementing the single market, the harmonization of product standards takes place in a way which circumvents complicated intergovernmental bargaining; the task is undertaken by the Commission which has set up committees involving national producers and other groups. This 'comitology' arrangement has been acclaimed for greatly facilitating the reaching of unanimity (Scharpf 1997: 528). In industrial relations, corporatist arrangements involving a tripartite representation of employers, employees and member states are emerging at the European level. Even in policy areas that substantially remain the preserve of the EU's national governments, new forms of cooperation are emerging. Although not formally binding, common guidelines and performance indicators for economic policy are set forth and debated in the Economic and Finance Committee; as regards foreign and security policy, a similar process of coordination and consultation is taking place. Some scholars argue that these measures are important instruments in creating a common view of the world among national policy-makers (Jørgensen 1997).

There are several other examples of regional cooperation in the world. One set of arrangements is focused on economic cooperation, such as the North American Free Trade Agreement (NAFTA) and the Mercosur (Mercado Commún del Sur) free trade agreement between several South American countries (Brazil, Argentina, Uruguay, Paraguay). APEC is a framework for economic cooperation between 14 countries on the Asian side of the Pacific, and ECOWAS (Economic Community of West African States) as well as SADC (Southern African Development Community) are similar examples from Africa. Other groups, such as the OAU (Organization of African Unity), the OAS (Organization of American States) and ASEAN (Association of Southeast Asian Nations), are more focused on broader political cooperation.

The European Union is in a class by itself in terms of the intensity and extensity of regional cooperation among member states. The other regional initiatives are of a more traditional kind, limited to more narrowly defined economic or policy areas, and without impinging on the sovereignty of their members, defined as their autonomous right to regulate domestic affairs. Therefore, regional cooperation is clearly becoming of increasing importance in general, but it varies greatly in terms of concrete content and level of ambition.

A similar conclusion is warranted in the case of global governance. International cooperation, together with transgovernmental and transnational undertakings, serves to increase the importance of global governance. In some areas of global rule-making supranational elements exist; that is to say, some global institutions can make rules that constrain states in that they stipulate the behaviour of states and have some room for sanctions if states do not comply. Such elements can be found in the WTO (concerning dispute settlement), the International Criminal Court (jurisdiction over persons for the most serious crimes of international concern), and in the covenants against race discrimination and torture (cf. Zürn 1999). But a very substantial part of global governance continues to be of a more conventional kind where states do work together and consult each other, but retain their autonomous right to implement and supervise regulations at home.

There appears to be a general trend, then, away from governance in the context of national government and towards multilevel governance in several interlocked arenas overlapping each other. Some of that governance reflects a more intense conventional cooperation between independent states; some of it reflects a more profound transformation towards supranational governance in a context of highly interconnected societies. The extent to which one or the other form of multilevel governance has developed in the real world varies greatly between countries and groups of countries.

Multilevel governance: consequences for the state

We must consider whether the changes that have taken place are in accordance with the diagnosis made by retreat scholars as regards states being less powerful and influential than before. In order to approach this issue, a distinction between major aspects of multilevel governance is helpful (see Box 4.2).

The major axis in Box 4.2 is from top left to bottom right; multilevel governance begins with interstate cooperation in traditional international organizations frequently setting up regimes: that is, rules which govern state action in particular areas such as shipping, investment, environmental regulation, trade or human rights. The most developed

Box 4.2 *Major aspects of multilevel governance*		
Society level	**State-as-government level**	
	'Shallow integration': *sovereignty intact*	*'Deep integration':* *sovereignty affected*
Societies segregated	1 Traditional international organizations (e.g., UN system)	2 Supranational elements of WTO, International Criminal Court
Societies interconnected	3 USA/Canada States of former Soviet Union	4 The European Union

form of multilevel governance is where societies are interconnected in the sense that there is a high density of transnational relations. At the same time, governments cooperate closely, having created significant elements of supranational governance.

As indicated, the best example of the advanced cooperation in cell 4 is the EU. We do not know, of course, whether the current EU is an example of the 'final stage' of such close cooperation because it keeps developing new features. At present, however, there is little likelihood that it will become a federation, a 'United States of Europe'. We cannot know for sure to what extent supranational governance will emerge in other parts of the international system. Economic globalization, or any other single factor, does not alone determine future developments.

There are four major controversies between state-centric and retreat scholars tied in with the issue of multilevel governance. The first is about history; state-centric scholars claim that the change towards multilevel governance is exaggerated because the starting point is wrong: the 'before' model of 'pure' national governance is a fiction. To repeat from Chapter 1: there has not been 'any golden age of state control. States ... have never been able to free themselves from concerns about external and internal challenges' (Thomson and Krasner 1989: 198).

According to this view, there has not been a big change at all. But following the argument presented above, there has been important change because the starting point was a situation of much less multilevel governance for the modern state around 1950. Clearly, the model of the modern state employed here as a description of 'before' is an ideal type; it does not include every empirical detail. Therefore, the view presented above is a comparison of ideal types which may tend to exaggerate the differences between then and now.

The second controversy concerns the type of cooperation that is taking place between states. On the one hand, state-centric scholars tend to emphasize the traditional interstate relationship of cell 1 in Box 4.2. The claim is that because cooperation is shallow, states remain in the driver's seat: they dominate international organizations anyway and no such organization can turn against the interests of the most powerful states. Retreat scholars, on the other hand, tend to emphasize the more demanding cooperation that contains supranational elements and thus affects the sovereignty of states. They also claim that even traditional international organizations can set up regimes with rules that constrain states. In other words, even strong states cannot push international organizations around as they wish.

The third controversy concerns the concrete consequences for states of being involved in international cooperation through the various types of international institutions. State-centric scholars argue that such cooperation serves to strengthen states. By cooperating they achieve powers of regulation they would not otherwise have had. International agreements – for example, on environmental regulation, currency stability or crime prevention – allow states to set up rules together that benefit them all. States cannot make such regional or global rules on their own, but cooperation gives them new capabilities of regulation.

Retreat scholars argue that cooperation constrains and therefore potentially weakens states. International institutions become more powerful, especially in the case of deep integration, such as in the EU. Here, the Council or the European Court can stipulate rules going against the wishes of single states. But even in the case of shallow integration, international bureaucracies in the United Nations (UN), the IMF and the World Bank are much more influential than earlier because of more intense cooperation. Retreat scholars see this as power devolving away from the sovereign state; there is a diffusion of power and for that reason, states are less influential than they used to be.

This debate is especially virulent in the case of the EU (for an overview, see Marks, Hooghe and Blank 1996). The state-centric scholars see states (i.e., national governments) 'as ultimate decision-makers, devolving limited authority to supranational institutions to achieve specific policy goals. Decision-making in the EU is determined by bargaining among state executives. To the extent that supranational institutions arise, they serve the ultimate goals of state executives' (ibid.: 344). The alternative view is that 'European integration has weakened the state' for several reasons: first, 'decision-making competencies are shared by actors at different levels rather than monopolized by state executives. That is to say, supranational institutions – above all, the European Commission, the European Court, and the European Parliament – have independent influence in policy-making that cannot be derived from their role as state executives.' Second, 'collective decision-making among states involves a significant loss of control for individual state executives'; third, 'political arenas are interconnected rather than nested ... states do not monopolize the links between domestic and European actors, but are one among a variety of actors contesting decisions that are made at a variety of levels' (ibid.: 346).

It should take only a moment's reflection to appreciate that both state-centric scholars and retreat scholars make valid points. International cooperation offers both new opportunities for regulation as well as new constraints on states. In that sense, states are becoming both more and less powerful and influential simultaneously. The net result can hardly be calculated beforehand; it will vary substantially across states and across issue-areas. What we can say on the general level is that states have changed; a calculation of their power and influence now requires a fresh analysis because the context has been transformed from one of primarily national government towards one of significant multilevel governance.

The final controversy is about the relationship and relative power of states (as governments) and non-state actors (individuals, groups and organizations from civil society). The retreat view is that non-state actors are significantly increasing their influence on political processes and decisions. Whereas political decisions were earlier taken primarily by state officials, they are presently being diffused into networks of actors involving states negotiating with NGOs and other civil society associations, as exemplified by the public policy networks mentioned above. Susan Strange is very clear on this point: 'Depending on the issue, it may be that banks or the oil companies, or the drug barons of Colombia, or large multinational enterprises are just as important as states in determining the who-gets-what questions that have always lain at the centre of the study of politics' (Strange 1996: 68).

State-centric scholars maintain that states remain special players. States are the core units of the international system; they set the rules other actors play by, and these 'other actors' – including most NGOs – would amount to very little if they did not enjoy the support of states. It is often states that provide most of their funding; it is states that invite them in, in the UN system, the World Bank and elsewhere, in order to consult them. And NGOs, like most other civil associations, do indeed spend most of their time attempting to influence states and their policies. All this confirms the special role of states.

Furthermore, the distinctive role of states is emphasized every time a crisis appears. If the economic system is in trouble, as in the so-called 'Asian crisis' of finance in the late 1990s, states are called upon to re-create order. When terrorism strikes, as in the outrageous attacks on the World Trade Center and the Pentagon in 2001, states are called upon to provide security, order and justice.

Again, it should be clear that both views are correct; they merely portray different aspects of a complex reality. Political decisions *are* increasingly made in the context of networks involving many different types of actors. A recent analysis refers to this as 'networking minimalism' (Nye and Donahue 2000). But at the same time, states *do remain* special players, with exceptional powers and prerogatives. They set the ground rules for others and they retain primary responsibility for security, order and justice.

In sum, retreat and state-centric scholars both make valid points, but they tend to focus narrowly on certain selected aspects of what is going on. When those aspects are generalized so as to represent the whole picture, the result becomes distorted, biased and misleading. States are undergoing a process of *transformation* that probably makes them stronger in some respects and weaker in other respects. It is that complex transformation which merits our analytical interest. To decide whether the transformation amounts to a 'net gain' or a 'net loss' for states is a very complicated task because many different elements of change are in play. Nonetheless, the debate provokes us to think about it and clarify the arguments.

Challenges to democracy in the new context

The growing importance of the various forms of multilevel governance presents new challenges to democracy. Democracy means rule by the people; the large debate about what that actually stands for cannot be addressed here (see Sørensen 1998). In the present context, democracy is defined as political or liberal democracy, which Robert A. Dahl calls polyarchy. A political system is democratic if it involves three major elements: *competition* among individuals and groups for all important positions of governing power; *political participation* in the selection of leaders and policies; and *civil and political liberties* (e.g., freedom of expression and of the press) sufficient to ensure the integrity of political competition and participation.

So far, democracy has only developed within the context of independent states. Many theorists of democracy have argued that the sovereign nation-state is a necessary precondition for democracy.

The independent nation-state makes up the framework for a community of people that build democracy, and without such a well-defined community democracy is not possible in the first place. Dankwart Rustow has set forth a much-used model describing the main phases in a transition to democracy (Rustow 1970); that model contains one background condition, national unity, which must be in place before it is possible to conceive of a transition towards democracy. According to Rustow, national unity simply indicates that 'the vast majority of citizens in a democracy-to-be ... have no doubt or mental reservations as to which political community they belong to' (ibid.: 350). National unity was an issue in India and Pakistan; it also emerged when Yugoslavia and the Soviet Union disintegrated. Democracy, in other words, must be based on a well-defined community; in the absence of such a community, we do not know who 'we, the people' really are. As one observer stated, 'the people cannot decide until somebody decides who are the people' (Jennings, quoted from Rustow 1970: 351).

Against this background, there are obvious problems with democracy outside the framework of an established, independent nation-state, precisely because there is no obvious *demos*; that is to say, there is no well-defined political or moral community outside that context. And with no such *demos*, democracy cannot be realized. That is the reasoning behind the following statement: 'the only forum within which genuine democracy occurs is within national boundaries' (Kymlicka 1999: 124).

There are additional problems associated with democracy outside the nation-state context. Multilevel governance is not based on a distinct constitutional framework; therefore, core decision-makers are not subject to sufficient democratic accountability and control. Decisions are made behind closed doors, frequently by high-ranking bureaucrats without a clear democratic mandate. Robert A. Dahl has summarized the requirements that international organizations would have to meet in order to qualify as democratic:

> Political leaders would have to create political institutions that would provide citizens with opportunities for political participation, influence, and control roughly equivalent in effectiveness to those already existing in democratic countries. To take advantage of these opportunities, citizens would need to be about as concerned and informed about the policy decisions of international organizations as they are about government decisions in their own countries. In order for citizens to be informed, political and communication elites would need to engage in public debate and discussion of the alternatives in ways that would engage the attention and emotions of the public. To ensure public debate, it would be necessary to create an international

equivalent to national political competition by parties and individuals seeking office. Elected representatives ... would need to exercise control over important international bureaucracies about as well as legislatures and executives now do in democratic countries. (Dahl 1999: 31)

All this creates what appear to be formidable obstacles to democracy in a new context of multilevel governance. And what is more, there is hardly any turning back: as argued earlier, a major part of the world *has* changed away from a system of modern states with sharply segregated political, economic and social structures. Economic and other forms of globalization *have* taken place; governance *is* moving away from its clear context of national government towards a multilevel framework. So, the challenge to democracy will not go away; instead, it will become more and more urgent.

Fortunately, the sceptical view emphasizing democracy's problems in a context of multilevel governance is not the whole story. First, not all aspects of such governance are negative when seen from a democratic point of view. Second, different groups of scholars make the claim that the new challenges to democracy can be successfully confronted.

The democratically positive aspect of multilevel governance concerns the fact that regional and global processes of development are brought under political control; seen from the individual state this means an increasing scope of democracy. That *national* political procedures within a single country are highly democratic is not so reassuring when – because of intense interconnectedness – economic, social and other significant developments in that country are determined or highly influenced by external forces over which the national polity has little or no control. Increasing the country's influence over such vital external forces is a democratic gain, not a loss. Fritz Scharpf (1997) refers to that gain as an increase in *output legitimacy*: that is, because of involvement in multilevel governance, the political system is better capable of regulating the forces that shape people's lives, and that in turn creates political legitimacy because the political system is more effective than before.

Let us turn to the proposition that the challenges to democracy can be successfully confronted. There are different lines of argument to choose from, some of them more optimistic and ambitious than others. Joseph Nye (2001) represents a liberal view. He notes that many international organizations are not very strong; their budgets and staffs (even including the much-maligned WTO) are rather moderate. Therefore, most of such traditional multilevel governance is not very threatening to democracy in the first place because the important decisions continue to be taken within national democratic frameworks.

Furthermore, international institutions, such as, for example, the UN system, are highly dominated by national governments. Because national governments hold (or ought to hold) clear democratic mandates, international organizations dominated by such governments are at least provided with indirect democratic legitimacy. That situation is not very different from that of many domestic institutions in liberal democracies (such as the US Supreme Court or the Federal Reserve Board) whose democratic basis is indirect as well.

Joseph Nye suggests that the democratic legitimacy of multilevel governance can be safeguarded if international institutions are designed in such a way that they 'preserve as much space as possible for domestic political processes to operate' (Nye 2001: 3). This can then be combined with measures that increase the transparency of international organizations. Better access for NGOs to these organizations, and improved procedures such as disclosure of records and justifications of decisions, are suggested as moves to improve democracy. These deliberations are based on the premise that the challenge to democracy from multilevel governance is not that serious in the first place. It is also assumed that nearly all of such governance can be kept within cell 1 of Box 4.2. It has already been indicated that both premises can be questioned, the latter because globalization and other developments will continue to increase the demand for more far-reaching international cooperation, and the former because international institutions appear to move in the direction of more and not less autonomous influence *vis-à-vis* their member states. What then?

The answer, of course, depends on a closer analysis of the problem, including the underlying theory of democracy (cf. McGrew 2000). There appear to be three different, major types of response. The first is based on radical democratic pluralism; the second is committed to cosmopolitan democracy; and the third believes that democracy's future outside the context of the independent state is regional rather than global.

Radical democratic pluralism wants to create democracy 'from below'. The claim is that existing structures of governance benefit the rich and powerful. Real democracy, by contrast, requires the empowerment of the people. Critical social movements struggling for gender equality, peace and a healthier environment are the central forces of a global democratic order. Democracy is not located in nation-states. It is:

> located in a multiplicity of self-governing and self-organizing collectivities constituted on diverse spatial scales – from the local to the global ... This is a vision of direct democracy which considers substantive transnational democracy issues from the existence of a

plurality of diverse, overlapping and spatially differentiated self-governing 'communities of fate' and multiple sites of power without the need for 'sovereign' or centralized structures of authority of any kind. (McGrew 2000: 26)

Radical democratic pluralism is thus based upon a tradition of direct, participatory democracy. The problem with this approach to democracy is that it rejects the existing foundation of a democratic order – the rule of law and the system of sovereign states – without providing a clear idea about what should replace it. Some form of democratic multilevel governance is clearly seen as both feasible and attractive, but the institutional and legal framework for the envisioned 'empowerment of the people' is not specified at all.

The *cosmopolitan* view is much more positive towards the democratic elements in the existing world order. It builds on consolidated liberal democracy as it has developed within the states of the triad in particular and is emerging elsewhere also. The idea is both to deepen democracy within states and to extend it to the transnational realm in a mutually reinforcing process (Held 1995). Cosmopolitan democracy is based on an ensemble of organizations at different levels, but they are all bound by a common framework of cosmopolitan democratic law with a charter of rights and obligations. The creation of a global Parliament is envisioned, together with an international criminal court. The monopoly of violence, currently resting with the sovereign states, would gradually be transferred to regional and global institutions; the ultimate aim is demilitarization of all states.

These are all long-term goals; in the short term, the cosmopolitan approach foresees a reform of the UN Security Council involving better representation of developing countries and enhanced decision-making capacities. The creation of a UN second chamber is the first step towards a global Parliament. The international court and a new, international human rights court are awarded compulsory jurisdiction. An international military force would be created, and regional political cooperation would be improved (ibid.: 279).

Even when focus is on the short-term goals, it is clear that the vision for cosmopolitan democracy is enormously ambitious. Many powerful countries would most certainly be highly sceptical about the creation of a framework in which they would be subject to new obligations without receiving any clear, tangible benefits in return. Behind such obstacles is a major problem mentioned above: the lack of a sufficiently developed political and moral community that binds peoples from different states together. Cosmopolitans claim that such a community is currently being created in the context of democracy's progress, both in single states and at the transnational level (ibid.: 237). The sceptical view, however, holds that democratization of the world is a very long-term process; therefore the conditions for cosmopolitan democracy cannot be expected to emerge for some considerable time.

The project for cosmopolitan democracy is a sympathetic one and it is also very detailed in its concrete plans for institutional and legal changes; but, at the present juncture, it must be considered at least mildly utopian. That leads us to more modest considerations about democracy in a context of multilevel governance. These deliberations do not contain a global vision for democracy; they find that transnational democracy has much better possibilities in a *regional context* of consolidated democratic states. Michael Zürn has argued that if we take a closer look, some major aspects of a political and moral community have actually developed among triad countries and especially in Western Europe (Zürn 2000: 196). First, there is a common recognition of civil liberty *rights*, including the rights of political participation. Second, there is a high level of *trust* that accepted obligations are met with compliance. Third, a *public spirit* has emerged in the sense that at least a 'weak form of collective identity' exists (ibid.: 198), and that civic identity is 'a consensus around a set of norms and principles, most importantly political democracy, constitutional government, individual rights, private property-based economic systems, and toleration of diversity in non-civic areas of ethnicity and religion' (Deudney and Ikenberry 1999: 193).

These are important aspects of a *demos*; what is lacking is, on the one hand, an even stronger sense of solidarity with an acceptance of economic and other redistribution within the community and, on the other hand, a common public discourse in the sense of a developed transnational sphere of public debate and the formation of public political opinion. Jürgen Habermas has emphasized that the future of Europe needs to be discussed 'throughout Europe in interlinked public spheres; that is, the same issues must be discussed at the same time, so as to foster the emergence of a European civil society with its interest groups, non-governmental organizations, civic initiatives, and so forth' (Habermas 1999: 58).

This will take time, of course; it will require school systems that provide a 'common grounding in foreign languages' (ibid.) and the construction of a European party system. Given the current partial development of a *demos*, can democracy be improved, for example in the context of West European multilevel governance in the EU? Philippe Schmitter argues that the EU is the only region where cooperation is so intense that an emerging 'Euro-polity' can be identified. But the Euro-polity suffers from a democratic deficit. In order to confront that problem, member states will have to 'experiment with new forms of citizenship, representation and decisionmaking' (Schmitter 1999: 941). Several different reform proposals are set forth, among them (summarized from Schmitter 1999):

- direct elections to the European Parliament are made 'special' through electronic or postal voting, distinguishing them from national elections
- 'advisory' referenda on European issues
- 'universal citizenship': that is, granting of voting rights at the moment of birth but assigning them to parents until maturity
- enhancing the role of Euro-parties in candidate nomination and list formation, through financial and other support
- enhancing the role of European level associations and movements by letting voters distribute vouchers to those entities that they believe can best defend their interests and passion, and providing such associations with economic support
- protection of small countries and European minorities. Continued overrepresentation and overweighting of votes for small countries in the European Parliament and in the Council of Ministers.

There is no need to discuss these proposals in detail here. They serve to support the idea that democracy has a solid future even outside the confines of the independent state, in a new context of regional multilevel governance that goes beyond traditional interstate cooperation without amalgamating into a new federal state.

In sum, democracy was always situated within the context of the independent state. Multilevel governance with intense transnational linkages between states therefore presents new challenges to democracy. There are obvious problems with democracy outside the national context and some observers are highly sceptical about the possibilities for democracy in combination with multilevel governance. More optimistic observers suggest rather different remedies. One approach is to preserve maximum space for domestic, national political processes, but this will not be enough in cases of more demanding supranational cooperation. Radical pluralists look to the creation of democracy from below, but more or less completely reject the existing basis for a democratic order without devising any alternative framework. Cosmopolitan democrats want to create democracy on a global scale; that is an extremely ambitious and therefore mildly utopian undertaking. Finally, several scholars find that democratic multilevel governance has the best prospects in a regional context. They especially focus on the EU and propose democracy-enhancing reforms of the Euro-polity (see the summary in Table 4.6).

Table 4.6 *Multilevel governance and democracy*

	Democracy possible with multilevel governance?	Content of democracy?	Big changes needed?
Sceptics *(Dahl)*	No. National democracy cannot be re-created outside the nation-state.	Political participation and control by the people.	Yes. But hardly possible to really democratize international institutions.
Moderate liberals *(Nye)*	Yes. Preserve space for domestic political processes to operate.	Political participation and control by the people.	No. But transparency of international organizations must increase.
Radical pluralism	Yes. If the people were empowered.	Rule from below, of and by the people.	Yes. In order to create real rule by the people.
Cosmopolitan democracy	Yes. By building on existing democracies.	Political participation and control by the people.	Some. Strengthen national democracies and extend it to the international realm.
Regional approach	Yes. But only within regions.	Political participation and control by the people.	Some. Create a regional *demos* and democratize the regional polity.

The discipline of political science has worked on the assumption that democracy always develops within the framework of sovereign states. Therefore, the study of democracy and democratization has, overwhelmingly, focused on the prospects for democracy in single states (see, e.g., Diamond, Linz and Lipset 1988, 1989). The national focus is clearly no longer sufficient. It is necessary to devote much more attention to the challenges to democracy in the context of multilevel governance because that will increasingly be the new framework for democracy. It must also be expected that the liberal proposal of preserving maximum space for national democracy will not be sufficient. Therefore, political science needs to confront the challenges to democracy and democratization in the new context much more aggressively, and political scientists will need help from political philosophers to speculate about the appropriate democratic institutions and processes in a multilevel context that is neither purely conventional interstate cooperation, nor a new supranational, federal entity.

The least developed states in the Third World

The debate above about retreat or state-centric theories is entirely focused on the advanced states, primarily in Western Europe and North America. Third World states hardly ever enter into the picture. As already indicated in the previous chapter, Third World countries are an extremely diverse group. Some of the most advanced states are based on fairly well developed national economies and they participate in the process of globalization; others are abysmally backward and utterly marginalized, lacking in the economic and political capacity to participate effectively in international exchange. Since it is the weakest states in the Third World that are most dramatically different from the advanced states discussed above, my remarks in this section will focus on them. I shall argue that the weak Third World states are involved in a very special kind of 'multilevel governance' with its own peculiar characteristics. Those characteristics are a combination of the following features:

1   At the national level, institutional and administrative structures are weak and ineffective. They are controlled by state elites who do not primarily seek to provide public or collective goods. The state apparatus is rather a source of income for those clever enough to control it. The spoils of office are shared by a group of followers making up a network of patron–client relationships.

2   At the global level, international institutions and stronger states increasingly attempt to constrain, influence and direct policy measures in weak states. Their ticket to influence is the high level of external dependence, economically and otherwise, of weak states. Being desperately dependent, weak states have to comply with recommendations and dictates by the international institutions and the countries that finance loans and supply aid. But state elites continue to struggle for maximum autonomy and preservation of their privileged positions.

3   At the local level, some groups attempt to get access to state resources and international aid. They do this by securing a place on the lower rungs of the state elite's patron–client network, but the great majority of the population attempts to cut itself loose from any

state influence whatsoever. People know very well that the state is a source of pillage, threat and exploitation. It is by no means a provider of welfare, security and order. Instead, ethnic communities attempt to build their own 'self-help systems' in order to compensate for the absence of state services.

In sum, the vast majority of the people in weak states are left in a situation where effective governance is lacking. It has come to that through a long and unfortunate chain of events where external dominance and exploitation has been replaced by internal dominance and exploitation. Entrenched political and social structures create a context where well-meaning measures by aid donors and other progressive forces have little effect. The story typically begins with colonization of the areas that became the Third World. There is of course great variation between regions: Latin America had already been colonized by the Spaniards and the Portuguese in the sixteenth and seventeenth centuries. At the other extreme, the 'scramble for Africa' led by Britain, France, Germany and several other European powers took place in the late nineteenth century. Most of the weak states are located in sub-Saharan Africa so, for simplification, let me focus on that region.

Colonizers were not particularly interested in economic and political development of the areas they took into possession; they were more interested in maximizing profits, so the focus was on the extraction and export of natural resources combined with an effort to minimize the cost of controlling the colonies. In the worst cases, such as King Leopold's rule in the Congo, this produced nothing in terms of development, only misery and exploitation. In the better cases, some infrastructure, together with some political as well as social and economic institutions, was left for the domestic regimes that took over upon independence.

No coherent national communities existed, however. Africa had always been a patchwork of overlapping ethnic groups and the colonizers had built on that fact in their strategy of divide and rule. It was extremely difficult to create nations, upon independence, out of the very diverse ethnic groups with different languages, beliefs and ways of living. The new state elites quickly abandoned any such nation-building project; instead a system of 'personal rule' (Jackson and Rosberg 1982) emerged. The key positions in the state apparatus are manned with loyal followers of the leader; loyalty is strengthened through the sharing of the rewards of office. This is the network of patron–client relationships referred to above. It comprehensively characterizes the political rule in the weak states of sub-Saharan Africa. Attempts at democratization and other measures (cf. Sørensen 1998) have had little effect in terms of changing the system.

The old colonial motherlands have helped to create this system and they employed it for their own purposes to some extent during the Cold

War. But as aid donors, they have also become increasingly disgusted with it and have initiated a variety of measures aimed at reforming the system. So, the weak states are increasingly subjected to demands for good governance: that is, the creation of more democratic, effective and responsive political systems and administrations. They have also been directed to liberalize their economies and to increase their involvement in international economic exchange, but these measures have not had significant success. Incumbent state elites remain a part of the problem rather than a part of the solution.

For people at the bottom, this means trying to survive as best they can without any assistance from the political system. People do organize in different ways in order to carry on, but this hardly amounts to any comprehensive process of state-building from below. These activities have little effect in terms of building national communities, and neither do they lead to social infrastructures that can offer the citizen the benefits of health care, education, protection or the rule of law on a sustained basis.

In sum, it may require too much stretching of the imagination to call the system characterizing weak states a peculiar form of 'multilevel governance'. In basic respects, effective and responsive government and governance is lacking because the state apparatuses are so weak and because they are captured by self-interested elites. The increasing external demands in terms of political and economic conditionalities (Sørensen 1993) insisting on good governance and economic improvement do not amount to an alternative system of rule. Therefore, people at the bottom are most often left to their own devices; the formal systems of rule have much too little to offer.

Conclusion

The growth of interstate, transgovernmental and transnational relations amounts to a change in governance from what existed in the modern state. The transformation leads away from governance in the context of national government towards multilevel governance at overlapping national, local and international levels.

Retreat and state-centric scholars offer very dissimilar analyses of the new situation, but at the end of the day they both make valid points. Their common bias is to focus too intensely on different, selected aspects of the changes that are taking place. Once we realize that states are undergoing a transformation that makes them stronger in some respects and weaker in other respects, we can formulate a broader, and much more relevant, analytical agenda.

The new context of governance creates new challenges to democracy because, historically, democracy has always developed within a well-defined context of independent nation-states. Some scholars of democracy are highly sceptical when evaluating the prospects for democracy outside the nation-state; others are much more optimistic, but the remedies they suggest vary greatly because they subscribe to different theories of democracy and substantially different analyses of the nature of the problem. Political scientists and political philosophers will need to focus with much greater force on the analysis of democracy and democratization in the new context.

The least developed states in the Third World have their own peculiar structure, created through colonization, external dominance and domestic supremacy by self-serving elites. National institutions are weak and ineffective. International institutions and aid donors have taken disciplinary measures in order to improve the situation, but that is not easily done and ordinary people at the local level are most often required to manage on their own.

Chapter 5

Nationhood and Identity: Community beyond the State?

Community of citizens and community of sentiment in the
   modern state
Challenges to the community of citizens
Challenges to the community of sentiment
The debate about retreat and state-centric views revisited
Citizenship and collective identity in the least developed states
Conclusion

This chapter brings us to the third major component of the modern state as identified in Chapter 1: nationhood. Nationhood in the context of the modern state was defined as a people within a territory making up a community based on citizenship (including political, social, and economic rights and obligations), and on a 'community of sentiment' (meaning a common language and a common cultural and historical identity based on literature, myths, symbols, music and art; see Box 5.1). A unique feature of the modern state is the welding together of the state and the nation: the state is an expression of the nation, representing it and catering for its basic social values: security, freedom, order, justice and welfare. At the same time, citizenship is connected with a specific form of collective identity as the community of citizens also shares linguistic, cultural and historical bonds that distinguish it from other

Box 5.1 *The nation in the modern state: two types of community*	
Community of citizens	*Community of sentiment*
Relation between citizens and the state: Political, legal and social-economic rights (and obligations).	Relation between citizens as a group: Common language, common cultural and historical identity, based on myths, symbols, music, art, and so on.

groups (though, as mentioned earlier, a nation in this sense is not necessarily based on a homogeneous ethno-national group of people).

This chapter begins with a brief survey of the 'community of citizens' and the 'community of sentiment' in the context of the modern state. That provides the necessary background for the claims made by retreat and state-centric scholars about changes in this area. The claims are set forth and systematically evaluated. A further section touches upon the special conditions concerning nationhood in weak states.

Community of citizens and community of sentiment in the modern state

The connection between the two aspects of community is a complex one and there are several different theoretical approaches to it. In the present context, it is sufficient to note that a close relationship exists between the 'sentiment' and the 'citizen' community; one supports the development of the other so that changes on one dimension affect the other. Both emerged in the context of the consolidation of the sovereign state and they are also connected to the development of capitalism. Further aspects of the relationship will be touched upon below. I try to draw together only the major aspects of the development of national community; there is, of course, much more variation in the historical world.

The early development of national community began when medieval kings centralized power and abandoned private armies; that created a direct relationship between the king and his subjects. Order, protection and the rule of law were valued by the people; in return, they paid taxes and offered military service. For a very long time, however, citizens were not all equal; citizenship rights were highly unequally distributed. Only a tiny elite – first the aristocracy, then the bourgeoisie and later on the intellectuals – were citizens in a meaningful sense. Citizenship rights for the larger population were earned the hard way, in struggle against privilege and hierarchy, rather than granted from above by benevolent rulers. Therefore, a larger community of citizens including the broad masses of people appeared in Europe only during the nineteenth and early twentieth centuries.

A classical account (Marshall 1950) points to a successive introduction of citizenship rights in three overlapping areas: legal, political and social rights. Legal rights are basically equality before the law, and the right to own property and to conclude contracts. Political rights concern the right to political participation in free and fair elections as well as civil and political liberties (i.e., freedom of the press, and freedom to form and join organizations). Finally, social or welfare rights involve the provision of social welfare for those in need: unemployment benefits, health care, social pensions and so on.

Social rights were the last generation of rights to be developed. In most Western countries they emerged during the first half of the twentieth century. This demonstrates how the introduction of rights is a process that involves contest over inclusion and exclusion. Citizenship rights, or at least parts of them, are always up for debate; groups in society always quarrel over whether this or that right should be extended to this or that group. So, when citizenship in the modern state is defined as including a certain set of rights, this is a static summary of what has been achieved over a long period of time. Rights are always under development because of the constant debate about them.

This more dynamic picture of a contested entity always being debated also applies to the other major aspect of nationhood, the 'community of sentiment'. National community in this sense was shaped by a number of different factors. One succinct account (Royal Institute of International Affairs 1968: 221–5) identifies seven major factors in this process. Although the analysis focuses on England and France, it has general relevance in demonstrating how nationality was created both from 'above' and from 'below'. The factors are outlined below:

1 A common language: 'The need to express orders and inquiries in a form which would be intelligible to all broke down the monopoly of Latin as the language of every one who mattered and brought about the gradual acceptance of the native tongue as the regular medium of intercourse.'

2 A single set of laws for all: 'Along with the law, and partially incorporated in it, went a vast body of conventions of social behaviour. The extension of the law created another common link between members of the State, which also served to distinguish them from other states.'

3 New middle classes: 'The rise of the new merchant class, as well as of the bureaucracy who were the king's agents, meant a vast increase in the number of those who owned property and who had what is commonly called "a stake in the country".'

4 The growth of education and culture. Compulsory education was a vital element in the incorporation of common people in the nation. Intellectuals and artists helped develop a common cultural and historical identity based on literatures, myths, symbols, music and art.

5 War. Interstate wars 'not only compelled co-operation between the members of one State, but also intensified the differences which distinguished them from the members of the other'.

6 The move from religious to secular authority. 'The political implications of the reformation were as important as the religious ones, and

it is no accident that Luther should be regarded as a pioneer of German national feeling.'

7   Democratization 'not only enabled those citizens who had become politically conscious to feel that they had a share and personal responsibility in the State, but also stimulated the growth of political consciousness. Thus were laid the foundations of [the] association between nationalism and democracy.'

It ought to be clear from this brief overview how the 'sentiment' and the 'citizenship' components of nationhood are woven together. The emotional attachment to the nation was highly stimulated by the reward of citizenship rights. The achievement of rights stimulated the feeling of affection for the nation. Both strengthened the division between insiders and outsiders, between 'us' and 'them'. The collective identity of national belonging was greatly amplified in times of war. National patriotism introduced an emotional element of commitment and sacrifice.

Nationhood in the modern states of the mid-twentieth century was particularly strong. The populations had experienced the Second World War and many people had memories of the First World War. Furthermore, there was a new Cold War rivalry between East and West, so both the emotional and the material bonds between the nation and the state were at a high point. Let us now turn to the challenges to the 'community of citizens' and the 'community of sentiment' in the context of the current transformation of the state.

Challenges to the community of citizens

Let us look at the 'community of citizens' first. One major development in this area is that civil and other rights are no longer being granted solely by the sovereign state. At the global level, a set of universal human rights has been defined; in some regional contexts, close cooperation has led to common rights for citizens of different countries.

The most important regional example is the European Union. A Union citizenship was fully established with the Maastricht Treaty of 1992 even though some of the rights pertaining to that status existed before the treaty. Citizens of the EU have the following rights in the member states (Soysal 1994: 148): (a) free movement, gainful employment and residence within the boundaries of the community; (b) discrimination based on nationality among workers of the member states with regard to employment, social security, trade union rights, living and working conditions and education and vocational training is disallowed according to Community law; (c) states are obliged to facilitate teaching of the language and culture of the countries of origin within the framework of normal education; (d) full political rights in the long run are recommended for Community citizens living in other member states. At present, they have the right to vote and stand as candidates in local and European elections.

This may not look dramatic, but EU rights indicate a break-up of the close link between statehood and citizenship; they illustrate that the intimate connection between a sovereign, territorial state, a 'community of citizens' and a 'community of sentiment' is not logically given. It is a historical construct, completed with the development of the modern nation-state. The question is, then, what will be the fate of the state once this unity is abandoned, recalling the close link between 'citizenship' and 'sentiment'? We will return to that question in due course.

The link between 'community of sentiment' and 'community of citizens' is also being weakened in another way in Western Europe. Yosemin Soysal has studied the guestworkers coming into the EU from non-member states. Many of the guestworkers residing in Germany, for example, do not have German citizenship, and neither are they members of a German 'community of sentiment', but they still make claims on the German political and social system. They 'participate in the educational system, welfare schemes, and labor markets. They join trade unions, take part in politics through collective bargaining and associational activity, and sometimes vote in local elections. They exercise rights and duties with respect to the host polity and the state' (ibid.: 2). At the same time, a formal, legal framework stipulates the incorporation of these workers into the national systems and provides them with a series of rights concerning social security, working conditions, wages and so on.

Soysal argues that this indicates a transformation of citizenship 'from a more particularistic one based on nationhood to a more universalistic one based on personhood' (1994: 137). These developments are not exclusive to Western Europe: 'As the transnational norms and discourse of human rights permeate the boundaries of nation-states, the post-national model is activated and approximated world-wide' (ibid.: 156). This leads to the view that national citizenship is in the process of being replaced by 'postnational membership' based on universal human rights rather than on the national rights flowing from shared national citizenship and a national community of sentiment. 'The postwar period has witnessed a vast proliferation in the scope and categories of universalistic rights. Human rights have expanded beyond a conventional list of civil rights to include such social and economic rights as employment, education, health care, nourishment, and housing' (ibid.: 157). Again, this may not sound dramatic, also because 'the nation-state is still the repository of educational, welfare, and public health functions and the regulator of social distribution' (ibid.: 157). But according to Soysal, it demonstrates an emerging incongruence between identity and rights in the postwar era: 'Rights increasingly assume universality, legal uniformity, and abstractness, and are defined at the global level. Identities, in contrast, still express particularity, and are conceived as being territorially bounded' (ibid.: 159). In other words, it indicates a break-up between citizenship rights on the one hand and the cultural-historic community on the other, the two elements that were woven closely together in the modern nation-state.

I have looked at one set of factors nibbling at the strong and coherent community of citizens that characterized the modern state. They concerned the growth of citizenship rights which were not granted by the sovereign state and rights forwarded to non-nationals in a new context of 'post-national membership'. Let me turn to a second factor that may weaken the community of national citizens. It has to do with the ability of governments to deliver the goods, the social values contained in citizenship. The account above identified citizenship rights in three areas: legal, political and social rights. Several scholars (Habermas 1975; Hobsbawm 1996; Horsman and Marshall 1994) claim that it is becoming increasingly difficult for the state to actually protect and honour rights, and for that reason the legitimacy of the state is weakened.

The claim is that it is difficult for the state to provide rights because its ability to do so is increasingly put into question. The scholars especially emphasize the new context of a globalized or transnational economy 'whose transactions are largely uncontrolled or even uncontrollable by states' (Hobsbawm 1996: 272). The new context tends to reduce the authority of states, and loss of authority leads to loss of democratic accountability:

> Accountability means calling politicians to order. When decisions are made by officials, often at international rather than national level, or by transnational corporations, or by politicians in other countries, the myth of accountability is difficult to sustain. This is particularly the case when the decisions that count are made in the corporate sphere, resulting in environmental disaster, lost jobs, or financial risk. (Horsman and Marshall 1994: 221)

It is not merely accountability that suffers. For large groups of citizens, the new economic context puts social rights into potential jeopardy: the state cannot or will not deliver (ibid.: 216–34). When the state does not deliver, loss of legitimacy and support can easily follow.

It was noted above how the reward of citizenship rights stimulated people's emotional attachment to, and support for, the state. That link between citizen and state is now potentially severely weakened. This debate about the state's ability to deliver on citizenship rights is, of course, connected to the discussions in Chapter 2 on economic globalization and the welfare state, and the discussions in Chapter 4 on multilevel governance and democracy. The results obtained there will be taken into account later when the general debate about state and citizenship is evaluated. For now, we continue the identification of challenges to the community of citizens.

The third and final challenge concerns what one scholar calls the practice of 'citizenship without moorings' (Rosenau 1997: 282). The argument comes in different variants; it is perhaps most developed in a series of analyses by James Rosenau (1993, 1997). His reasoning is as follows: people, especially in the OECD world but increasingly elsewhere also, are becoming more and more analytically competent because of improved education systems and much better access to information. People can use that competence to make their voice heard in politics, not merely at the national level, but at regional and global levels as well. At the same time, global issues – including environment problems, economic crisis and terrorism – are progressively more important for the daily lives of billions of individuals.

The various aspects of globalization, including much improved possibilities for interaction and communication between people on a world scale, provide the means for people to address such global issues in a transnational dialogue between concerned individuals (rather than between defined groups of national citizens). The ability visibly to affect the global agenda and to help change the course of events puts traditional, national political leadership as well as citizen loyalty and support much more into question than it ever was before. Citizens 'are thus more ready to rethink the collectivities with which they identify and to redefine the balance between their own and society's interests' (Rosenau 1997: 286). One interesting aspect of these developments is that an increasing number of people today are entitled to dual citizenship, not least because children born to parents of different nationalities inherit both (Martin and Aleinikoff 2002). The variety of challenges to the 'community of citizens' is summarized in Box 5.2.

In sum, a number of different forces are at work to transform the coherent 'community of citizens' as it existed in the context of the modern state. None of the three factors discussed here indicates a complete break-up of the national community of citizens; the critical issue, then, concerns the precise extent to which that community is being

Box 5.2 *Challenges to the 'community of citizens'*	
Source of challenge	*Nature of challenge*
Citizenship rights granted by non-states: • Regional level: EU grants rights to its citizens. • Global level: Emergence of 'post-national membership' based on universal human rights.	Loosening or break-up of relationship between citizen and state
Decline in the state's ability to honour citizenship rights	Weakening of state legitimacy; loss of popular support
Citizenship 'without moorings'	Weaker link between citizens and the state

transformed or maybe even undermined by the new developments. Before taking on that question, it is relevant to look at changes related to the 'community of sentiment'.

Challenges to the community of sentiment

What about the emotional attachment to the nation? It is clear that the national 'community of sentiment' must also be exposed to changes in a new context characterized by the increased salience of globalization and the transnational relations that go with it. Perhaps the clearest sociological analysis of these changes and their importance for identity comes from Anthony Giddens. His central argument is that in the new context, self-identity 'becomes a reflexively organized endeavour' (Giddens 1991: 5). Individuals no longer 'rest content with an identity that is simply handed down, inherited, or built on a traditional status. A person's identity has in large part to be discovered, constructed, actively sustained' (Giddens 1994: 82).

In other words, the creation of identity becomes a project for the individual. Religious beliefs, for example, are not simply taken over from previous generations; they are reflected upon, evaluated, and then actively accepted or rejected. The end result of that process may be highly unorthodox, of course. People will declare that they sympathize with Christianity, Buddhism or Hinduism in a particular mixture, tailor-made for that individual. In a similar way, political convictions are no longer preordained from a certain social class affiliation or other tradition. They are created from the great selection of ideologies and values and the end result may not correspond to well-defined party affiliations. This is one reason why Western countries have experienced the emergence of many new types of political parties in recent decades. In every area of existence, including the most intimate ones associated with sexual and marital life, modes of behaviour and feeling have become 'mobile, unsettled and "open"' (Giddens 1991: 12). Nothing is given; identities must be actively created.

When identity is something that has to be actively created and sustained by individuals, the attachment to the national 'community of sentiment' can no longer be taken for granted. It was noted above how both the 'community of citizens' and the 'community of sentiment' were dynamic entities because the portfolio of rights – as well as items of national culture – was always being debated. But that is a view from 'above' reflecting how large groups of people always argue about what can and should characterize their national community. Giddens' view is from 'below', emphasizing how individuals freely choose their degree of affiliation and commitment to 'national community'. It highlights how identities are in flux, and, in this situation, attachment to the national 'community of sentiment' is changing from a given to one source of possible identification among a whole range of different possibilities.

What – if anything – is complementing or even replacing the attachment to the national 'community of sentiment'? There are several possibilities; on the one hand, collective identities may be losing importance altogether compared with personal identities. That means that any kind of collective 'community of sentiment', whether religious, ethnic, cultural or social, is of much reduced significance in the new context. On the other hand, these various modalities of collective identity certainly seem to continue to be important for many people. Against that background the task is to discover the reference points of collective identity that are currently gaining rather than losing importance.

One such reference point is collective identity 'above' the nation. A recent liberal analysis identifies a common civic identity for the Western political order (Deudney and Ikenberry 1999):

An essential component of the Western political order is a widespread civic identity that is distinct from national, ethnic, and religious identities. At the core of the Western civic identity is a consensus around a set of norms and principles, most importantly political democracy, constitutional government, individual rights, private property-based economic systems, and toleration of diversity in non-civic areas of ethnicity and religion. Throughout the West, the dominant form of political identity is based on a set of abstract and juridical rights and responsibilities which coexist with private and semi-public ethnic and religious associations. (Deudney and Ikenberry 1999: 193; see also Linklater 1998)

In other words, the argument is that a Western civic identity has developed which is distinct from national and other identities in that it embraces a certain set of common values. These values have less to do with people's national affiliations; they are values common to the entire community of Western populations. Such a Western civic identity need not replace the national 'communities of sentiment'; it may coexist with them. But Deudney and Ikenberry indicate that it is a non-national form of community that competes for attention with other collective identities. In that sense, the nation is a less dominant fixture of collective identity than it used to be; 'national identity has declined' (Deudney and Ikenberry 1999: 194).

Furthermore, it is quite possible that the Western civic identity is strong among some groups of the Western populations and much less strong among other groups. Could it be that the Western civic identity is an elite phenomenon? The analysis by Deudney and Ikenberry indicates as much in emphasizing:

the widespread circulation of elites and educational exchange. The advanced industrial countries contain many transnational networks based on professional and vocational specialization ... Also significant is the great increase in the volume of international education activities, most notably the increasingly transnational character of the study bodies in elite universities and particularly graduate professional schools. These developments have produced a business, political, cultural, and technical elite with similar educational backgrounds and extensive networks of personal friendships and contacts. (Deudney and Ikenberry 1999: 194)

Perhaps it is the case that developments analysed by Giddens, Rosenau, and Deudney and Ikenberry really pertain mainly to elites and not to the less educated and less well-to-do sections of Western populations? Recall that Rosenau speaks of analytically competent people who interact across borders and put pressure on national political leaderships. And Giddens speaks of self-identities created in sophisticated processes of reflexive endeavour. This could all be read as something undertaken by elites, but hardly by most common people. Perhaps, then, the general challenge to the national 'community of sentiment' is not serious at all; I return to this issue below.

Another analysis made some years ago (Sunkel and Fuenzalida 1979) clearly argues that a transnational community is emerging which is made up of the elites that control and benefit from the global economic system. They are the owners and managers of companies and the professional, technical and bureaucratic staff of public and private institutions. This transnational community has 'similar values, beliefs, ideas (and a *lingua franca* – English), as well as remarkably similar patterns of behaviour as regards career patterns, family structures, housing, dress, consumption patterns and cultural orientations in general. The transnational community, then, shares what could be considered a transnational culture' (ibid.: 73).

All this is not conclusive evidence, of course, but it does seem reasonable to assume that a transnational community with a Western civic identity is much more developed among elite sections of the population than it is among other groups. That leads us to think about what happens with the collective identities among those for whom economic globalization and the expansion of transnational networks is more of a threat than an opportunity. Manuel Castells argues that these exposed groups will tend to take on a *'resistance identity*: generated by those actors that are in positions/conditions devalued and/or stigmatized by the logic of domination, thus building trenches of resistance and survival on the basis of principles different from, or opposed to, those permeating the institutions of society' (Castells 1998: 8).

In other words, we may look at the emergence of transnational communities with a Western identity as an offensive, integrating response to globalization and other changes. But there is also a defensive, fragmentating response. One significant challenge to the national community of citizens comes from regional movements that vie for secession, or at least for a substantial increase of regional autonomy. Such movements are, of course, mostly active in states that were never consolidated as modern nation-states in the first place. That includes a large number of states in the Third World, but also the former Soviet Union, Yugoslavia and other states in what was Communist Eastern Europe (Gurr 1993).

In the present context, we are mostly interested in what were the modern states of the OECD world. Even here, a number of very active subnational, regional movements seek to achieve a special status for their communities. One analysis counts some 35 regional or ethnic groups seeking a higher level of autonomy or secession (Zürn 1998: 259). They include movements in Scotland, Wales, Northern Italy, Quebec, Spain (Catalonia and the Basque country) and the conflict in Belgium between Flemings and Walloons.

None of these movements has suddenly sprung from the earth; they are part of a longer history of intranational conflict and processes of national community-building that were unsuccessful. But several movements have become more active and visible in the context of the political and economic changes analysed in earlier chapters. With the growth of supranational cooperation, an institutional level 'above' the nation-state is emerging that can become a new partner for the regional movements. In other words, Scottish nationalists prefer dealing with Brussels rather than with London because the latter is seen as an old centre of repression and control. This regional sentiment was succinctly summarized by the Lombard leader, Paul Friggerio: 'We care about being Lombards first and Europeans second. Italy means nothing to us' (quoted in Rosenau 1997: 99).

At the same time, processes of uneven economic globalization impact on the regional movements. Not only countries, but also regions within countries, have different experiences with globalization for a host of reasons, the most important of which were discussed above, in Chapter 2. Successful regions, such as, for example, Northern Italy, may want to distance themselves from the other, less successful parts of the country. One way of doing that is through the achievement of more autonomy from the national centre and consequently fewer economic and political obligations towards all the other regions (Zürn 1998: 261).

This should not be taken to mean that there is any simple relationship between movements for regional autonomy and globalization. Several other factors are relevant for the analysis of such movements, not least the political and administrative structures of the countries to which they belong. It is noteworthy that Germany and the USA – states with decentralized, federal structures and thus with high levels of local self-government – have not seen strong movements for regional autonomy (ibid.: 260).

Nationalistic movements stressing a very exclusive definition of national identity can be seen as another defensive, fragmentating reaction. Le Pen's *Front National* in France, Jörg Haider's *FPÖ* in Austria, the German *Republikaner*, the *British Movement* in the UK, *Alleanza Nazionale* in Italy and the *Danish People's Party* in Denmark are all examples of movements or parties that turn against immigration and want to emphasize a much more narrow understanding of national identity. These organizations see transnational integration and increased interdependence as a two-pronged threat. First, it threatens the social and economic well-being of 'original' citizens because of the new claims made on the state by immigrants and other types of outsiders, including external institutions such as the EU. Second, it threatens a historically specific, narrow conception of national identity in which there is no room for newcomers. On that view, integration across borders and immigration is a threat to the community of citizens because its original core is diluted and ultimately undermined. Some of these movements are highly focused on the issue of immigration; but most of them are also highly sceptical about more intensive cooperation and exchange across borders.

Another set of movements is centred on the local community. Globalization tends to strengthen local identities because more intense relations with others reinforce the awareness of local identities. At the same time, local community movements act as a refuge from the wholly individualistic lifestyles and atomized self-identity projects that were discussed earlier. Many people will 'tend to cluster in community organizations that, over time, generate a feeling of belonging, and ultimately, in many cases, a communal, cultural identity' (Castells 1998: 60). Urban movements focus on three sets of goals, in different combinations: local living conditions and collective consumption; local cultural identity; and local political autonomy and participation. According to Castells, several other types of 'resistance identity' exist, including religious (fundamentalist) movements, and ethnic movements. But they tend to be most active in countries other than the industrially advanced, liberal democracies that interest us here.

In sum, this section has discussed challenges to the 'community of sentiment' that is the nation (see Box 5.3). In various ways, the attachment to the national community is put into question. One major tendency is that the creation of identity becomes a project of individual construction which gives increased salience to collective identity 'above' the nation.

Box 5.3 *Challenges to the 'community of sentiment'*	
Source of challenge	*Nature of challenge*
Self-identity becomes a project for the individual	Possibly less commitment to the national 'community of sentiment'
Emerging collective identity 'above' the nation: a Western civic identity	Possible decline of national identity
Sub-national, regional movements seeking greater autonomy	More narrow definition of national community
Exclusivist national movements	More narrow definition of national community
Local community movements	Local identities of increasing importance compared to national identities

The emergence of a common Western civic identity is an indicator of that. But several more defensive 'resistance identities' are also gaining importance, among them regional, nationalistic and local identities.

The debate about retreat and state-centric views revisited

What happens to the state when both the 'citizenship' and the 'sentiment' dimension of nationhood are being transformed? Retreat scholars argue that with the transformation of nationhood, loyalties are projected in new directions and additional sources of citizenship rights emerge; the state is weakened because the link between the state and its people is diluted. State-centric scholars argue that nationhood remains strong in both the 'community of citizens' and the 'community of sentiment' aspects. The bond between state and people is not weakened, and in that sense the state remains strong.

The arguments made by retreat scholars have been reviewed above. The community of citizens is under pressure in three ways: first, the emergence of citizenship rights granted from bodies other than the sovereign state; second, an allegedly reduced ability of states to deliver on social and welfare rights; and third, the practice of 'citizenship without moorings'. The community of sentiment is also being challenged in the ways summarized above.

The state-centric response to all this is an emphasis on the continued importance of nationhood, even in the face of these developments. Nationhood has not been replaced or even severely weakened, either in its 'citizenship', nor in its 'sentiment' aspect. National citizenship remains strong because people's rights continue, in overwhelming measure, to be granted by states and not by other instances. And to the extent that such supranational instances have emerged, as in the context of the EU, they can – and that is indeed the case – be identified with the state. That is because it is really through the efforts of the state and through the citizenship in the state that people have access to such rights in the first place. In other words, supranational citizenship rights have not served to create a more direct link – sidelining the state – between citizens and supranational institutions. In the context of the EU, 'citizenship of the Union has not superseded nationality of the Member States' (Closa, quoted in Welsh 1993: 17). Therefore, the existence of such rights has not led to the emergence of strong bonds of legitimacy between people and supranational institutions.

As for the alleged reduced ability of states to deliver on social and welfare rights, it was demonstrated in Chapter 2 that welfare provisions need not necessarily suffer because of economic globalization; and Chapter 4 argued that there were ways to preserve democratic account-ability even in the context of multilevel governance. In sum, the 'com-munity of citizens' might not be under severe pressure after all.

Neither is the 'community of sentiment' in severe danger, in the opin-ion of state-centric scholars. According to Anthony Smith, the national community contains special qualities based on 'primordial' elements of a common history and culture. National political authority draws basic legitimacy from the loyalty and trust of citizens; that special relationship cannot be replaced by other collective identities based on class, gender or religion because those identities do not contain similar virtues. Among Europeans, the national community of sentiment cannot easily be replaced by a supranational commitment to the EU. That is because European citizenship rights, or even a European Constitution, cannot be based on a shared historical experience, common values, symbols and myths; such elements are simply not sufficiently developed at a European level. It would be a 'memoryless scientific culture' (Smith 1992: 74) with little emotional appeal to people. In sum:

> as long as states protect and fashion national identities while draw-ing for their power and solidarity on the mobilized historic culture-community at their core, so long will national states remain the prime political actors in the modern world, and so long will the peoples of our planet place their loyalty and trust in the sovereign, territorially finite, national state. (Smith 1995: 115; see also Mann 1998)

State-centric scholars clearly have a point in emphasizing the contin-ued importance of nationhood. Both the national 'community of citi-zens' and the 'community of sentiment' continue to be of primary importance, even in the face of the new developments. What are we to make of the changes discussed above: are they significant or not?

First, we need to confront the question of whether identities are zero-sum or non-zero-sum. Is it the case that people can take on any number of new identities without discarding what they already have? Or are identities in conflict, so that, say, the taking on of a European identity in the context of the EU can only take place to the extent that the old, national identity is rejected? A moment's reflection ought to make clear that the answer to these questions depends on the level of analysis: that is to say, individuals can and do have multiple identities; furthermore, these identities will often be situational, depending on the concrete context (professional, private, religious and so on) in which individuals find themselves (cf. Smith 1995: 123). At the community level, by con-trast, the collective bond that exists between people is of a certain nature, a particular collective identity that either contains or does not contain specific elements (such as commitment to a Western civic identity).

That leads to the next question: to what extent have collective identities changed away from a traditional emphasis on nationhood in context of the sovereign state and towards more different and more complex identities? The nation is not under pressure in the sense that national communities are being replaced by other types of community; it is rather the case that *the content of nationhood itself* is being transformed to incorporate new aspects. In other words, national identities are themselves changed so that they increasingly contain supranational elements. This is what is happening in Europe in the context of EU cooperation. Take France, a country with a very clear and well-defined conception of nationhood. French national identity is changing to include European cooperation in the understanding of what it means to be French, so that a clear commitment to close European cooperation is now a part of a French 'national' identity (Waever 1998).

In Germany, such a commitment to Europe is even stronger as it became an explicit part of the constitution after their defeat in the Second World War. The preamble to the West German constitution, the so-called Basic Law, reads as follows: 'The German people, animated by the resolve to preserve their national and political unity and to serve the peace of the world as an equal partner in a united Europe ... have enacted ... this Basic Law' (quoted from Gruner 1992: 202).

The appropriate view, then, in my opinion, is one of nationhood undergoing a transformation so as to increasingly include supranational elements, both with respect to the 'community of sentiment' and the 'community of citizens'. That transformation does not necessarily weaken the state, contrary to what many retreat scholars have implied. That is because the transformation is not diluting – at least not at the present time – national identity affiliations. A national German or French identity now includes a supranational element of commitment to Europe, but that element is not in opposition to or in conflict with the national attachment. The concrete content of national identity has changed; it has not been superseded or replaced.

Citizenship and collective identity in the least developed states

Just as with the debate on political changes discussed in the previous chapter, the debate about transformation of nationhood and identity discussed in this chapter is exclusively focused on the advanced states in Western Europe and North America. The issue of nationhood and collective identity is somewhat more complex in the Third World because these countries are in a very different situation. If we use the modern nation-state ideal type as a baseline, Third World countries differ from it in a variety of ways. The weakest states in sub-Saharan Africa – those most different from the advanced states – are the focus of what follows.

Ethnic identities connected to tribal, religious and similar characteristics continue to dominate over the national identity in weak states. These ethnic identities are not primordial in the sense that they reflect ancient characteristics maintained over a long period of time. It is true that pre-colonial Africa was not neatly divided into territorially separate entities with clear-cut authority structures; it was rather a continent of overlapping entities where people had multiple group affiliations. But present-day ethnic groups were first created by colonial rulers employing ethnic labelling as a 'divide and rule' instrument, and then by postcolonial leaders appealing to ethnic identities as part of their own ambitions of power.

A national 'community of citizens' was created at independence, but only in a formal sense of providing people with identity cards and passports. This was combined with some scattered attempts to launch nation-building projects that would develop a common idea of the state. But the real substance of citizenship – legal, political and social rights – was not provided by the new states for a considerable period of time. Only recently have some elements of legal and political rights been promoted. When the state does not deliver, or only delivers so to a very limited extent, two consequences follow. First, people turn elsewhere for the satisfaction of material and non-material needs. In sub-Saharan Africa, they have primarily turned to the ethnic communities that are the focal points for a 'moral economy':

> The moral economy enables individuals in various contexts to rely on nonbureaucratic mutual aid networks and to reciprocate toward those who belong to a common society. Examples include those better off helping relatives and clan members find jobs or pay school fees, as well as regular contributions to weddings and funerals, even for persons with whom face-to-face contact has never been established but who are imagined to belong to one's community. The moral economy can be formalized in ethnic organizations (such as hometown funeral associations) that provide social insurance in the absence of state welfare programs. (Ndegwa 1997: 601)

The second consequence is that the bond of right and obligation between people and the state does not develop; as a result, bonds of loyalty leading to state legitimacy do not mature. When the ethnic communities become the primary focus for the satisfaction of people's needs, loyalties are projected in that direction and ethnic identities are reinforced. Ethnic rituals are important in that context:

> For instance, such initiation rites as circumcision continue to represent among most groups in Kenya the acquisition of full citizenship in the ethnic community. Among the Kikuyu, uninitiated men (rara) cannot inherit property or adjudicate in clan disputes, and parents of initiates ascend to an elder class which holds putative power in clans. Such rituals establish a hierarchy of power within the community that, when combined with other icons of power and status in the modern state, enables elites to mobilize within the ethnic community for interests in the secular state. At the same time, individuals can hold such persons accountable within the communal realm for actions in the state realm and especially for extracting resources from the state on their behalf. An example is traditional oaths, which affirm identity and obligation within the ethnic community but which often have a purpose in the state arena, such as securing electoral victory or political succession. These oaths are recurrent motifs in national politics in Kenya. (Ndegwa 1997: 602)

In sum, weak states are characterized by a situation where neither the 'community of citizens' nor the 'community of sentiment' has developed to become the primary bond for people. Nationhood has simply not taken on the significance that it has in the modern states. Instead, ethnic identities and affiliations remain of crucial importance.

One would hope that the democratic openings over the last decade could create a new momentum with a positive circle of increased state accountability and efficiency, combined with a population more and more inclined to take on the identity of a national community of citizens. But in many countries the opposite has happened: the early phases of democratization have emphasized ethnic cleavages in the populations. First, democratization increases the possibilities for different ethnic groups to present their views and formulate their demands; the result of that process has frequently been more rather than less conflict between various groups. Second, the spread of democracy has meant the quick holding of elections, often pushed by aid donors wanting to see a democratic transition. But elections organized in a hurry can be a destabilizing event in weak states. According to one scholar:

> elections appear the wrong place whence to start a process of democratization in a collapsing, conflict-ridden state. In recent years, African elections have typically been organized in a hurry, in some cases before parties had time to consolidate or armed movements had

agreed to disarm. As a result, losers have found it easy to reject election results, and voters had little choice but to vote on the basis of ethnic or religious identity. (Ottaway 1995: 235)

Third, state elites may actively enforce links with ethnic groups in their attempt to gain power. A recent analysis found that elections 'may actually increase the use of patronage ... Traditional patron–client relations have often been critical in winning recent elections, indicating that the nature of African politics has not changed despite the new liberalization. Ghana, Nigeria and Kenya have all reported massive overspending as governments sought to reward traditional supporters, notably members of particular ethnic groups and civil servants, to smooth the transition process or gain votes' (Bienen and Herbst 1996: 38).

In sum, weak states lack a strong national community both in the 'community of citizens' and in the 'community of sentiment' sense; instead, ethnic identity dominates. Recent democratizations have not improved on that because early processes of democratization tend to reinforce rather than weaken ethnic affiliation (see Box 5.4).

Conclusion

Nationhood in the modern state consists of an emotional attachment to the nation – 'community of sentiment' – and of citizenship rights and obligations, a 'community of citizens'. Nationhood in this sense forms a significant part of the modern nation-state, the ideal type identified in Chapter 1.

Box 5.4 *Citizenship and identity in the least developed states*	
Problems with community of citizens	*Problems with community of sentiment*
The state does not deliver on political, social and legal rights ⇒ lack of state legitimacy Ethnic communities step in ⇒ ethnic identities are reinforced	Ethnic (tribal, religious) communities are primary ⇒ they satisfy needs and provide bonding via rituals and myths Patron–client relations reinforce ethnic loyalties

The 'community of citizens' is challenged by rights not granted by the sovereign state; by a shrinking ability to deliver the social values of citizenship; and by the tendency for individuals to practise 'citizenship without moorings'.

The 'community of sentiment' is challenged in several ways. First, identities, including national identity, are not handed over or given any more; they have to be actively created and sustained. Second, there is an increased salience of identities 'above' and 'below' the nation. The former refers to the growth of a 'Western civic identity'; this is perhaps especially developed among elite groups. The latter refers to various 'resistance identities', emphasizing regional, ethnic or other affiliations.

State-centric scholars maintain that nationhood remains strong both in the 'community of citizens' and in the 'community of sentiment' aspect. Retreat scholars claim that the state is weakened because the link between the state and its people is diluted. The appropriate view, in my opinion, is one of nationhood undergoing a transformation so as increasingly to include supranational elements, both with respect to the 'community of sentiment' and the 'community of citizens'.

In the least developed states in the Third World, nationhood in the modern state sense is embryonic. Ethnic identities overshadow national identity. Early processes of democratization have not improved on that situation. It would appear that a broader process of successful development is necessary in order to strengthen nationhood, yet the weak states face a different situation from that confronting the old OECD countries, even if they succeed with general development. That is because they are situated in a different kind of world system where traditional nationhood as expressed in the modern state is itself under transformation.

Chapter 6

The Transformation of Sovereignty?

We have frequently referred to sovereign states in this book but what does sovereignty really mean, what is the content of that notion? And what are the consequences for sovereignty of the various ways in which the state is being transformed? Is sovereignty being transformed also? Is sovereignty alive and well or are we experiencing an 'end of sovereignty' in the context of other transformations of the state?

'Sovereignty' encapsulates the rules that define the locus of political authority and set the context for relations between states. Medieval authority was dispersed among many types of religious and secular power. Modern sovereign authority is centralized and rests with the government ruling a population within a defined territory. The institution of sovereignty thus bestows supreme political authority upon the government. That sovereignty is an institution simply means it is a set of rules that states play by (Robert Keohane defined institutions as: 'persistent and connected sets of rules, formal and informal, that prescribe behavioural roles, constrain activity, and shape expectations': 1990: 732).

For centuries, a process of institutional competition and selection took place; sovereignty competed with other forms of political organization (Spruyt 1994; Tilly 1992; see also Ferguson and Mansbach 1996). Political empires, such as the Roman Empire, had been the dominant institutions rather than a system based on sovereignty. But with the decolonization following the Second World War, the entire world became divided into sovereign states and today competing forms of political organization have all but disappeared. In that sense, a development has taken place which has significantly increased, rather than decreased, the importance of the institution of sovereignty.

What does it mean, then, that a state possesses sovereignty, that it is recognized as sovereign by other states? It means that the state in question enjoys constitutional independence. The sovereign state stands apart from all other sovereign entities, it is 'constitutionally apart' (James 1999: 461); other entities have no political authority within the state's territory. Furthermore, the sovereign state is legally equal to all other sovereign states. Irrespective of the substantial differences between sovereign states in economic, political, social and every other respect, sovereignty entails equal membership in the international society of states, with similar rights and obligations. The fact that every sovereign member state has one vote in the UN general assembly – regardless of huge differences between states in substantial power and capacities – is a concrete expression of this legal equality.

Constitutional independence is also an absolute condition. A state either has the legal title of sovereignty – meaning that international society recognizes that state's independence – or it does not have it. Legal or juridical categories are either-or; there is no in-between. It is easy to understand that point once we look at other well-known juridical categories. For example, people are either married or not married; they cannot be 70 per cent married. People are either legally recognized citizens of a particular country or they are not citizens; they cannot be 70 per cent citizens. The same with sovereignty: a country either has the legal title of sovereignty or it does not have it; there is no in-between condition.

Finally, sovereignty in the sense of constitutional independence is a unitary condition. That means that the sovereign state is of one piece; there is one supreme authority deciding over internal as well as external affairs of the state. Such is the case even in federal states or states with a high degree of political decentralization; powers may have been delegated, but there is one supreme political authority (these remarks are indebted to the analysis in James 1999).

We may look at constitutional independence as the juridical core of sovereignty; this is what the institution is about in terms of defining the place for and the distribution of political authority. But sovereignty as a legal institution is more than that; it is also a set of rules regulating how sovereign states go about playing the game of sovereignty, and how they conduct relations with each other.

It is thus helpful to look at sovereignty as a special kind of game played by a special kind of player, the sovereign state. Constitutional independence defines what the game is all about (i.e., political authority and its appropriate distribution among the players). The rules regulating the game of sovereignty, the regulative rules stipulate who gets to play and the ways in which the players treat each other once they play the game. How states go about dealing with each other in war and peace and who gets to be a member of the society of states (i.e., the rules of admission); both are examples of areas of regulative rule. Robert Jackson has identified a number of playing rules, among them 'non-intervention, making and honouring of treaties, diplomacy conducted in accordance with accepted practices, and in the broadest sense a framework of international law...the rules include every convention and practice of international life which moderate and indeed civilize the relations of states' (Jackson 1990: 35).

So, there are many different kinds of regulative rules. Not all of them will be discussed here; that is not necessary for present purposes. I will focus on two basic regulative rules, which characterize the classical game of sovereignty, played by modern states: non-intervention and reciprocity.

Non-intervention means that states have a right to choose their own path, to conduct their affairs without outside interference. States are free to decide what they want to do without meddling from others. Given that constitutional independence is in place, there is no authority above the state, no higher instance with legal power to get in its way. That also means that states are responsible for themselves; the game is one of self-help. Modern states are individually responsible for looking after their own security and welfare; the state decides for itself 'how it will cope with its internal and external problems, including whether or not to seek assistance from others... States develop their own strategies, chart their own courses, make their own decisions about how to meet whatever needs they experience and whatever desires they develop' (Waltz 1979: 96).

So 'non-intervention' is one basic rule of the modern state's sovereignty game; the other basic rule is 'reciprocity'. Reciprocity means giving and taking for mutual advantage. States make deals with each other as equal partners; no one is entitled to special benefits; there is no preferential treatment or positive discrimination. A game based on reciprocity is a symmetric game where the players enjoy equal opportunity to profit from bi- and multilateral transactions. The General Agreement on Tariffs and Trade (GATT) from 1947 is just one example of reciprocity in the sense discussed here. The basic norm of the agreement is the 'most-favoured-nation' rule which stipulates *equal treatment* in commercial relations between states, regardless of their size, power, location or any other particulars about them. In sum, the sovereignty game of modern states is conducted by the rules of non-intervention and reciprocity.

We have looked at the juridical core of sovereignty, constitutional independence; we have also identified the two major rules regulating the game of sovereignty, non-intervention and reciprocity. Both of these elements concern the legal definition of sovereign authority; they are basically about juridical rules stipulating who has political authority and how it is used. However, there is another major aspect in the debate about sovereignty which concerns the actual substance of statehood: that is, the economic, political and other major characteristics of states. In short, we might say it concerns the items discussed in the three previous chapters: the economy of the state, the political-administrative institutions of the state, and the national communities of citizens and sentiment.

This aspect of the state is *not* about formal rules of authority; it is about real, substantial characteristics of states. Therefore, it is also about real capacities for state action and control in domestic and international affairs. The difference is hugely important. In *formal, juridical* terms, sovereign states are equal: they have the same rights and obligations as members of the society of states. No state is legally more important than any other state. All states are formally equal; as noted earlier, whether large or small, every state has one vote in the UN general assembly. But in *substantial* terms, states are hugely *un*equal; some states have gigantic capacities for action and control while others are almost completely powerless. As we shall see below, some 'retreat' scholars believe that the substance of the modern state has been transformed in a way that decreases the state's capacities for action and which has negative consequences for the sovereignty of those states.

In sum, we now have an appropriate conceptual framework for addressing the debate about sovereign statehood and the transformation of sovereignty. It is set forth in Box 6.1.

Armed with this framework, we are ready to address the debate about the challenges to sovereignty and the ways in which sovereignty might or might not be in a process of transformation.

Box 6.1	*What is sovereignty? Three major aspects of sovereignty and statehood*
1 Juridical core of sovereignty	Constitutional independence
2 Regulative rules of sovereignty	Non-intervention Reciprocity
3 Actual substance of statehood	Real capacity for state action and control (based on: the economy of the state; the political-administrative institutions; the characteristics of the national community)

The debate about the end of sovereignty

Several scholars think that the substance of states has been transformed, not least because of globalization. According to these scholars, the changes mean that the state has fewer opportunities for controlling and regulating what goes on inside its borders. For that reason, so they claim, 'states can no longer be sovereign in the traditional sense of the word' (Scholte 2000: 136; see also Elkins 1995; Lapidoth 1992). What are the changes specifically? Below are some examples:

1 Computerized data transmissions, radio broadcasts, satellite remote sensing and telephone calls do not halt at customs posts. Moreover, such communications occur: (a) at speeds that make it difficult for state surveillance to detect them in advance; and (b) in quantities that a state, even with greatly enhanced capabilities, cannot comprehensively track.
2 Electronic mass media have also detracted from a state's dominion over language construction and education.
3 A state cannot exercise complete authority over transborder associations or global companies.
4 A state cannot successfully assert supreme and exclusive rule over the global financial flows that pass through its jurisdiction.
5 Transworld ecological conditions such as ozone depletion and biodiversity loss have similarly contradicted the material preconditions of sovereignty. (Scholte 2000: 136)

It is developments such as these that have convinced some observers that we are indeed moving 'beyond sovereignty' (Soroos 1986) or into 'the twilight of sovereignty' (Wriston 1992). Scholte, in a section called 'The end of sovereignty', argues that it is 'time to develop a new vocabulary of post-sovereign governance' (Scholte 2000: 138).

Note that the changes diagnosed here concern the actual substance of statehood (point 3 in Box 6.1). They have to do with the state's ability to control a variety of transborder flows and conditions. This is exactly where scholars sceptical of the notion of 'end of sovereignty' base their critique. Their argument is that the idea of 'end of sovereignty' is based on a category mistake (Ryle 1968: ch. 2). Sovereignty is a legal institution; it comprises constitutional independence and regulative rules (see points 1 and 2 in Box 6.1). So, when some scholars argue that sovereignty is ending because the opportunities for state control are being eroded, they are making the category mistake of conflating the issue of state substance (point 3) with the issue of the legal institution of sovereignty (points 1 and 2).

Robert Jackson has expressed this view in clear terms: sovereignty, he says:

> is a status, that is, a legal standing, and thus a right to participate and to engage in relations and to make agreements with other states ... the expression of 'economic sovereignty' is a conflation of two different concepts that are best kept in their separate compartments if we wish to be clear. Rather than speak of the decline or loss of economic sovereignty it would be more to the point to speak of the difficulties that independent governments face nowadays in trying to pursue nationalist economic politics in a rapidly integrating global economy. (Jackson 1999: 453)

So, those sceptical of the whole idea that sovereignty is 'ending' – or even under severe pressure – will reject the idea that changes under point 3 are at all relevant for a discussion of sovereignty, which is really about points 1 and 2.

Some of the sceptical scholars make one further argument about point 3, the actual substance of statehood. They contend that when 'end of sovereignty' scholars look at the state's actual capacities for regulation and control, these scholars tend to vastly overstate the actual degree of state control over transborder flows in earlier days. This issue was introduced in Chapter 1 of this book. Janice Thomson and Stephen Krasner maintain that there are big problems with the idea that sovereign states are being undermined by transborder flows:

> First, such arguments lack historical perspective, often tacitly assuming that states have, in some golden age in the past, been able to effortlessly control transborder movements ... or taking recent changes as indicative of long-term trends. In comparison with the past, contemporary changes in the level of international transactions do not appear particularly spectacular ... Although some ratios of international to domestic transactions have increased, others have gone down. To the extent that historical data can be obtained they do not suggest any powerful long-term trends. Second, interdependence arguments ... have focused on economic transactions and ignore military and security concern ... One of the achievements of the state over the last two centuries has been to curtail the number, activities, and kinds of non state actors in the security issue area ... Third ... the commonplace notion that there is an inherent conflict between sovereignty and economic transactions is fundamentally misplaced. The consolidation of sovereignty – that is, the establishment of a set of institutions exercising final authority over a defined territory – was

a necessary condition for more international economic transactions. (Thomson and Krasner 1989: 197–8)

In sum, the historical past is misrepresented; the state has grown stronger when it comes to military and security issues; and sovereignty is a precondition for economic globalization in the first place. This latter argument takes us back to the state–market relationship discussed in Chapter 2, so further reflections on that issue can be found there. As regards the second point about states growing stronger in other areas, those supporting 'the end of sovereignty' will retort that the sceptics are:

> conflating 'sovereignty' with state power in general, rather than focusing (following traditional usage) on the specific attribute of supreme and exclusive rule over a territorial jurisdiction ... Under contemporary conditions of globalization, no amount of institution building would allow a state to achieve absolute, comprehensive, supreme and unilateral control of the global flows that affect its realm. (Scholte 2000: 137–8)

The counterargument is that those claiming 'the end of sovereignty' are themselves guilty of such conflation when they translate the changes that have taken place into a retreat of the state.

The remarks above have focused on the substantial changes in statehood and the possible consequences for sovereignty of such changes; now let us zoom in on sovereignty as a legal institution. Have there been changes in the core content of sovereignty (point 1: constitutional independence, and point 2: the regulative rules of sovereignty), and, if so, what are the results of such changes?

Let us examine constitutional independence first. The vast majority of scholars, whether they argue for or against the 'end of sovereignty', are in agreement that sovereignty as constitutional independence remains in place. Sovereignty as constitutional independence is the one dominant principle of political organization in the international system. The persistence and continuity of sovereignty in this sense can be expressed in different ways. John Ruggie emphasizes (quoting Charles Tilly) that 'once the system of modern states was consolidated ... the process of fundamental transformation ceased: "[states] have all remained recognizably of the same species up to our time" ' (Ruggie 1998: 191). Joseph Camilleri and Jim Falk maintain that 'the trappings of legal sovereignty remain intact' (1992: 99). Robert Jackson stresses the stable core of sovereignty: it is 'constitutional independence of other states' (1990: 32).

There is thus agreement that constitutional independence remains in place. But when it comes to drawing out the implications of that situation, there is no agreement at all. Those sympathetic to the 'end of sovereignty' thesis tend to see the persistence of sovereignty as little more than an empty shell disguising the radical changes that have taken place. Camilleri and Falk put it the following way:

> If the fluctuating mix of conflict, competition and co-operation char-acteristic of the inter-state system is deeply influenced by the internal structure of states, and if these structures are effective channels for the projection of economic and military power across boundaries, then the question arises: does the concept of sovereignty shed much useful light on the system of reciprocal influence? It is doubtful, to say the least, whether the penetration by one state into another's sov-ereign domain is consistent with the coherence and independence of will and action postulated by the notion of a sovereign agent.

In other words, sovereignty is 'thus preserved but only by effectively insulating it from the content, structure and history of the political process' (quotations from Camilleri and Falk 1992: 240).

The sceptical scholars, by contrast, see in the continued dominance of sovereignty as constitutional independence the sustained viability of the institution of sovereignty. The sovereign state remains the pre-ferred form of political organization; no serious competitor has emerged. One simple way of gauging the popularity of sovereign statehood is the more than threefold increase in the number of sovereign states since 1945.

Let us turn to point 2, the regulative rules of sovereignty. In this area, there is agreement that changes have taken place but, once again, the implications of those changes are interpreted quite differently. Those contemplating an 'end of sovereignty' find that new patterns of author-ity are emerging which place regulative powers in the hands of non-state actors. In this way, the game of non-intervention that leaves all political authority in the hands of the sovereign state is gradually replaced by a different game of 'post-sovereignty' (Scholte 2000: 138) where the sources of political authority are dispersed among several different actors. The connection to a 'retreat of the state' thinking is obvious; sov-ereign states are increasingly constrained because they lose their tradi-tional monopoly on political regulation and control.

Sceptics beg to differ. They make two different arguments. First, the emergence of new sources of political authority at the supranational level (such as the EU and, in smaller measure, the WTO) is *not* seen as a loss or even as a debilitating constraint on those states that are sub-jected to it. These new sources of authority are rather seen as a way of complementing and even *strengthening* the regulative powers of the individual state. What really happens is that states bargain with their sovereignty (i.e., their territorial political authority of regulation and control) so that they allow other states to influence the regulation of their domestic affairs in return for influence on the domestic affairs of these other countries (Keohane 1995). It is such processes which lead to the creation of multilevel governance (see Chapter 4). States participate in the setting-up of multilevel governance because they perceive it as an advantage: it gives them access to regulatory powers that they would otherwise not have had.

Take the EU. During the past decade, institutions at the European level have gained considerable influence over areas that were tradition-ally considered to be prerogatives of national politics: currency, social policies, border controls, law and order. In the context of the Single Market Treaty, a majority of member states may define rules applicable to all members. A key player in this development is the European Court of Justice which has helped push supranational governance by estab-lishing the supremacy of Union law in several important areas (Caldeira *et al.* 1995).

So, the regulative rules of sovereignty are indeed changing, but this is happening in ways that have nothing to do with an 'end of sovereignty' or with a 'retreat of the state'. States do consent to comply with supranational regulation, but they do it in their own best interest because, as a collective, states are themselves the sources of that regula-tion, and seen from the single state, the new set-up allows for increased influence over fellow states. Supranational regulation gives the single state new possibilities for controlling events outside its territorial jurisdiction.

The other argument made by sceptics against the idea of an 'end of sovereignty' due to new sources of political authority is a historical one. It repeats the view presented above: challenges to the sovereign author-ity of states is nothing new at all. If we look back in history, infiltration of domestic authority structures by external actors often occurred. Stronger states imposed themselves on weaker ones; nineteenth-century moneylenders joined forces to lay their hands on state revenues; states entered into international agreements that infringed on their sovereign territorial control. 'Sovereignty has always been contested both with respect to the scope of authority exercised by states and by institutional arrangements that do not conform with exclusive territorial control' (Krasner 1993b: 238).

In Stephen Krasner's summation, there are four principal ways of deviating from the sovereign authority: conventions, contracts, coercion and imposition:

> Rulers can join international *conventions* in which they agree to abide
> by certain standards regardless of what others do. Rulers can enter
> into *contracts* in which they agree to specific policies in return for
> explicit benefits. Rulers can be subject to *coercion*, which leaves them
> worse off, although they do have some bargaining leverage. Finally
> rulers or would-be rulers can suffer *imposition*, a situation that occurs
> when the target ruler cannot effectively resist. (Krasner 1999: 26)

It should be clear from the remarks above that the debate about sovereignty is indeed complex. Scholars cannot entirely agree on which
aspect of sovereign statehood is the most relevant one for the debate.
And even if scholars agree about discussing a certain aspect, they are
certainly not of the same opinion when it comes to drawing the implications for the state of particular developments. The major viewpoints
in the debate are summarized in Box 6.2.

The real debate is not so much about change or continuity;
scholars agree that the juridical core of sovereignty – constitutional
independence – stays in place. They also agree that some changes are
taking place in the actual substance of statehood and in the regulative
rules of sovereignty. The real debate is about the appropriate interpretation of these new developments, including the extent to which they devi-
ate (or do not) from earlier historical phases of sovereign statehood. The
major views and arguments have been presented above; the evaluation of
them is up to the reader. My own view is presented in the next section.

A new sovereignty game in the making

Sovereignty in the form of constitutional independence remains the
globally dominant principle of political organization. In that sense, sovereignty contains a stable element which marks the continuity of that
institution. It is misleading to talk about 'the end of sovereignty' but, in
some parts of the world (especially in the EU areas of Europe), significant changes have taken place in the regulative rules of the classical sovereignty game. The two central rules of that game, non-intervention and
reciprocity, have undergone significant modification.

In order to understand why this has happened, it is necessary to look
at changes in the substance of statehood first. These changes do not
themselves amount to a transformation of sovereignty; to claim that
would be a category mistake. But they are important for the sovereignty
game anyway because they help us understand why states have an
incentive to change the regulative rules of sovereignty that they play by.

Box 6.2	*The debate about sovereignty: an overview*		
		Sovereignty in trouble/ 'end of sovereignty'	Sovereignty remains a strong and viable institution
1	Juridical core of sovereignty: constitutional independence	Remains in place, but is now little more than an empty shell disguising radical changes.	Remains in place. Many new sovereign states since 1945. Evidence of sovereignty's viability.
2	Regulative rules of sovereignty: non-intervention, reciprocity	In transformation. New patterns of authority constrain states; they lose their monopoly on political authority.	In transformation. Supra-national authority strengthens the state's regulatory powers. This is in the best interest of states. *History*: challenges to sovereign state authority nothing new.
3	Actual substance of statehood	In transformation. Because of globalization, states cannot control domestic and international affairs. Moving towards 'post-sovereign governance'.	Maybe in transformation. But substance of statehood not relevant for sovereignty-category mistake. *History*: interdependence nothing new; always challenges to state control; states have grown stronger in military and other respects.

The classical game of sovereignty is played by modern states. The substance of modern states was spelled out in Chapter 1. Modern state authority is centralized and rests with the government ruling a population within a defined territory. Modern states have national economies, and the major part of their economic activity takes place at home. And, finally, there is a national community, the nation: that is, a people within a territory making up a community of citizens and a community of sentiment.

Previous chapters have demonstrated how these features of modern statehood have been transformed among the advanced capitalist countries. The sharp territorial separation of sovereign states from each other has, to a large extent, been abandoned. Instead of national government there has developed – especially within the EU – multilevel governance involving supranational, international, transgovernmental and transnational relations. Instead of a national economy, major parts of the economic activity are embedded in cross-border networks. And finally, supranational elements are emerging in nationhood as well, both with respect to the community of citizens and the community of sentiment, as set out in the previous chapter. (Chapter 9 will have more to say about this transformation of statehood among the advanced countries in the triad.)

These changes in the substance of advanced statehood have spurred changes in the regulative rules of the sovereignty game. This is best seen in the context of EU cooperation. Because they are so integrated at all levels, EU member states have been compelled to modify the rule on non-intervention. The whole idea of multilevel governance is based on the creation of formal and informal channels for *legitimate outside intervention* by the EU in the affairs of member states. Modern states playing the classical game of sovereignty jealously guarded their sovereign territorial authority as spelled out in the rule of non-intervention. EU member states are doing quite the opposite: they agree to accept rules made by outsiders (i.e., fellow members) as the law in their own states, their own jurisdiction. This is anything but non-intervention; an appropriate label would be 'regulated intervention' (see Sørensen 2001: ch. 10).

As regards reciprocity, the classical game has been modified as well. In the modern game, the rule of reciprocity is basically one of equal treatment of the competing players. In the modified EU game, there is a new element of preferential treatment, or *unequal* treatment according to special needs. For example, poor regions in the EU get such special, preferential treatment. Additional economic resources are redistributed to those regions because of their special needs. They get something extra in support of their particular development needs. This might be called 'cooperative reciprocity'.

So, the modern game of sovereignty has in some measure been replaced by a new and different game. The modern game was played by the rules of non-intervention and reciprocity; the new game is played by the rules of 'regulated intervention' and 'cooperative reciprocity'. The changes from the modern to the new game are summarized in Box 6.3.

Box 6.3 *Games of sovereignty: old and new*		
	The modern game	*The new game*
1 Core of sovereignty	Constitutional independence	Constitutional independence
2 Regulative rules	Non-intervention	Regulated intervention
3 Substance of statehood	Territorially defined polity, economy and community	Multilevel governance, economic cross-border networks, supranational elements in 'national' community

This is the new sovereignty game in the context of economic globalization and multilevel governance. But even if the reader agrees that such a new game has emerged, the debate about the future of sovereignty will continue. There are two major reasons for this. First, it remains unclear to what extent EU member states have actually committed themselves to the new game. On the one hand, constitutional independence remains in place in the game. Thus, if a member state should so decide, it can opt out of the EU altogether simply because it has sovereignty (the constitutional independence) to do so.

Opting out, so the argument runs, would bring ex-members back to the modern sovereignty game. On this view, the transformation of rules identified here should be seen as policy choices made by sovereign states rather than a major transformation of the institution of sovereignty (cf. Jackson 1999). On the other hand, some scholars find that even if it may be *formally* possible, it is already 'practically' *im*possible to opt out of the EU (Christiansen 1994). Clearly, if member states have committed themselves to a point of no return, the new game is of fundamental importance.

Second, there is the question whether the EU is *sui generis* or whether the kind of cooperation it embodies is relevant for a larger group of countries. Chapter 4 argued that there is a general trend away from governance in the context of national government, towards multilevel governance in overlapping arenas. But it was also stressed that a very substantial part of global governance continues to be of a more conventional kind where states do work together and consult each other, but retain their autonomous right to implement and supervise regulations at home.

Depending on where one puts the accent, emergence of multilevel governance *or* persistence of traditional patterns of cooperation, one will also come to different evaluations of the old versus the new sovereignty game. The institution of sovereignty surely persists; there is no 'end of sovereignty'. But there is a new game in the making in some parts of the world which may be of increasing significance in the future.

The special sovereignty game of the least developed Third World countries

In substantial terms, the least developed Third World states are very weak entities; they are most often ex-colonies settled within the borders established by the colonial powers. Take most of the countries in sub-Saharan Africa; the newly independent states rarely exercised effective control over their territories. The populations are divided along ethnic, linguistic, socio-cultural and other lines. There is no developed national economy; many people are outside the formal economy, living in local subsistence economies. To the extent that a formal economy exists, it is mostly based on exports of primary products and the import of technology and consumer goods. Governments are heading weak and ineffective institutions and they are most often in the hands of small elites seeking to exploit their positions to their own advantage.

As a consequence of their weakness, it is of supreme importance for these states to have sovereignty: that is, to have received recognition of their territory and government from the international society. Weak regimes and self-seeking rulers with little legitimacy facing divided populations, a lack of functioning institutions and frail economies need all the support they can get. Sovereignty offers access to international institutions, including the UN system; it also offers access to economic, military, and other forms of aid.

Furthermore, sovereignty as constitutional independence provides a formal right of control of territory, government and citizens that is a valuable bargaining resource. On the one hand, strong states cannot merely do what they want in the weak, least developed states. Interventions in other sovereign states cannot be conducted in complete ignorance of the rules of international society, so such acts of intervention need to be justified. On the other hand, domestic rulers are empowered by sovereignty because outsiders are compelled to bargain with them. Mobutu of Zaire, for example, cooperated with the Central Intelligence Agency (CIA), but he was not merely the agency's puppet. Because of his formal control of Zaire, his possession of sovereignty, the CIA had to bargain with him over access to territory and so on. Weak state or not, sovereignty provided Mobutu with bargaining autonomy in his dealings with other countries.

For all these reasons, rulers of the weak, least developed states most strongly support the institution of sovereignty and the inviolability of borders; they embrace 'the dominant values of the Westphalian system' (Ayoob 1995: 3) to an exceptional degree. In formal terms, sovereignty leaves supreme legitimate power in domestic affairs to the government. Therefore, rulers of weak states seek to emphasize and confirm the principles and rules of sovereignty. In its charter, the Organization of African Unity (OAU) explicitly confirms its commitment to the principle of non-intervention and also emphasizes the right of the state to regulate the domestic economy. The emphasis on sovereignty by rulers of weak states amounts to a demand to be treated as *equals* in the international society of states, to enjoy recognition on a par with everybody else; to have one vote in the UN general assembly as everybody else; to have equal access to all international organizations on equal terms. In short, weak states demand *equal treatment* in the international society of states, irrespective of the fact that these states are terribly weak and able to do very little on their own.

Not even the most fertile imagination can hide the fact that the weak states are *not equal*, not on a par with more developed states, however. They are so weak that they are comprehensively incapable of taking care of themselves. In substantial terms, the weak states are highly *unequal*; from every possible angle, they are at the bottom of the international system. Rulers of the newly independent, weak states were quick to make a connection between that inferior position and what they saw as the unjust and unfair structure, both of the past system in which they had been colonies, and of the present system in which they were maltreated. As soon as the weak states got a voice in the UN system, they began complaining about the current state of affairs. In the words of one resolution:

> It has proved impossible to achieve an even and balanced development of the international community under the existing economic order. The gap between the developed and the developing countries continues to widen in a system which was established at a time when most of the developing countries did not even exist as independent states and which perpetuated inequality. (UNITAR 1976: 891)

So, the weak states now also claimed that they were *unequal*, at the losing end of the international system. And to compensate for that situation they demanded to be treated as 'unequals', to get special, favoured treatment so as to compensate for their weakness and lack of resources.

This was what the great debate on a 'New International Economic Order' which took place in the 1970s was all about (Moss and Winton 1977). The New International Economic Order comprised a large catalogue of demands made by the developing countries on the developed world. The demands concerned: favoured market access for products from developing countries; more economic aid to the developing world; control over the activities of transnational corporations; special compensation for exploitation of natural resources in developing countries; compensation for aggression, neocolonialism, and apartheid; and so forth.

In short, weak states wanted to be treated as *unequals*, and be allowed to receive extra resources from the developed world with no obligation to give back anything in return. The demand is that economic aid, for example, should be a clear international obligation for the developed countries: that is, a natural element of the international order and not something that the weak states have to courteously apply for. Economic aid is, of course, a violation of the basic rule of reciprocity, of equal treatment. Economic aid is the opposite of reciprocity, it is non-reciprocity, meaning that one party gives to the other and expects nothing or very little in return.

The weak states had optimal opportunities for extracting concessions from the developed world during the 1970s. The ideology of anti-colonialism was strong in developed countries and that created a good climate for granting economic aid. The newly independent countries had a strong voice in international organizations, especially in the UN general assembly; and they were able to play on the competition between East and West in the context of the Cold War.

So they did extract aid and concessions, but that immediately created new problems. The political and administrative systems of the weak states were not at all geared towards making effective use of economic aid; they were geared towards satisfying patrons and clients. Donors saw what was happening; economic and other forms of aid failed to bring welfare improvement, not to mention sustained processes of development. Some donors accepted the situation because they considered development aid a necessary investment for safeguarding their influence in the previous colonies. But with the end of the Cold War, demands on the weak states increased; they were exposed to economic as well as political conditionalities (Sørensen 1993). Instead of non-intervention, the basic 'golden rule' of sovereignty, donors increasingly practise some form of *intervention* in order to make sure that the resources they provide are used according to plan. The clearest cases of intervention are the so-called 'humanitarian interventions' in 'failed states' such as Somalia, Liberia and Sierra Leone. When it comes to economic and political conditionalities, the weak states can in principle reject them and not get the resources, but because of their weakness they are likely to accept them.

One further step in the direction of intervention has been triggered by the changes in US foreign policy after 11 September, 2001. The new foreign policy is primarily concerned with the threat from terrorism and 'rogue state' with weapons of mass destruction (Iraq in particular, but also North Korea and Iran). The United States now declares a readiness to make such countries targets of American force. 'In the old era, despotic regimes were to be lamented but ultimately tolerated. With the raise of terrorism and weapons of mass destruction, they are now unacceptable threats' (Ikenberry 2002: 52) This new US policy has been termed 'neoimperial' (Ikenberrry 2002) because it claims that the USA has authority, on a global basis, to conduct preventive intervention against states that harbour preceived threats from terrorism and weapons of mass destruction.

So, the rules connected with the institution of sovereignty have been twisted in new ways when it comes to the weak states. Instead of non-intervention and reciprocity, there is intervention and non-reciprocity. The special sovereignty game pertaining to the least developed, weak states is summarized in Box 6.4.

In sum, weak states have a deeply troubled relationship to the international order, and in particular to the institution of sovereignty. On the one hand, they passionately support that institution and the norms that go with it: inviolability of borders and non-intervention. They have a deep desire to be treated as *equals* in the international system, to enjoy the same rights as any other independent state, because that offers

Box 6.4 *The weak, least developed states: a special sovereignty game*	
	Weak states
1 Core of sovereignty	Constitutional independence
2 Regulative rules	'Negotiated intervention' (donor control of aid, supervision by international society). 'Non-reciprocity' (special treatment of weak states because they cannot reciprocate).
3 Substance of statehood	Weak and ineffective institutions. No national community. No national economy.

protection in an insecure world. On the other hand, they desperately want to be treated as *un*equals in the international system in order to get special treatment in terms of economic aid, humanitarian relief support, and so on. The weak states want to have their cake and eat it too.

That awkward situation must necessarily create a tension in the international order. If weak states want to have special treatment, to be treated as unequals, they have to accept massive interference in their domestic affairs because donors want to make sure that their funds are not wasted. Aid calls for supervision and intervention. If weak states want to be equals, to be on a par with more capable states and strictly enjoy non-intervention, they have to waive demands for special treatment and basically take care of themselves and solve their development problems on their own. This has been the usual procedure in the history of sovereign statehood. The institution of development aid is a very recent invention, established in force only after the Second World War.

So far, rulers of weak states are trying to play the system both ways: to retain maximum domestic autonomy and control of resources (i.e., non-intervention); and to extract as much as they can in terms of economic and other forms of aid. Donors will then have to strike a balance between the provision of economic and other resources and the level of control and supervision that will have to go with it. The system has not been a dramatic success; weak states have not, in numbers, achieved sustained socio-economic development.

Therefore, the tensions in the international system as regards the weak states are likely to remain in place; that will lead to continued debates about levels of aid, about conditions for humanitarian intervention, about the relationship between aid and supervision. Due to their weakness, these states will continue to raise problems and dilemmas with respect to international order. Sovereignty is built on the assumption that the states who have it can basically take care of themselves. Weak states fail to meet that condition; that is the core problem leading to instability in the international order. And there is no comfort to be found in the promise that aid will eventually lead to development because we do not know if that is indeed the case. We do not even know whether all countries in the world can actually become developed.

Conclusion

Sovereignty has a juridical core, constitutional independence. Furthermore, there are regulative rules shaping the concrete game of sovereignty. Basic regulative rules of the classical sovereignty game are non-intervention and reciprocity. Finally, there is the actual substance of statehood. The substance of statehood influences the game of sovereignty but the two must not be conflated.

Several scholars think that globalization and other developments have brought us 'beyond sovereignty' to a new situation of 'post-sovereign governance'. The juridical core of sovereignty (constitutional independence) remains in place, but is now little more than an empty shell disguising radical changes.

Sceptics emphasize the viability of sovereignty. Many new sovereign states have emerged since 1945. Challenges to sovereign state authority are nothing new. In several respects, states have grown stronger and more capable over time. It is helpful to look at sovereignty as a special kind of game played by a special kind of player, the sovereign state. In that way both continuities and changes in the sovereignty game can be identified.

A new sovereignty game has emerged among the advanced states, especially in the EU. The regulative rules of the new game are different from the classical game. The new game is related to (and to some extent driven forward by) changes in the substance of statehood.

The least developed Third World countries play a special sovereignty game driven by the fact that these states are very weak in substantial terms. The different sovereignty games will probably stay with us for the foreseeable future because they are based on types of state that do not change quickly, but we will probably also see new modifications of the regulative rules of sovereignty in the future.

Chapter 7

The Transformation of War?

We are living in the longest period since the end of the Roman Empire with peace between the great powers (Schroeder 1985). Between 1989 and 1998 there were only seven interstate armed conflicts (Wallensteen and Sollenberg 1999) and only two of these were wars (defined as conflicts with more than 1,000 battle-deaths in a given year). Has interstate war become obsolete, even 'subrationally unthinkable' (Mueller 1989), as some liberal scholars claim? This chapter will argue that amongst a group of advanced liberal states, largely the old OECD members, international anarchy has been replaced by a coordinated security community characterized by peaceful exchange among its members. The community rests on consolidated democracy, common institutions, economic interdependence and transnational networks. But these open, liberal societies also remain very vulnerable, as indicated by the attack on the USA on 11 September 2001. So, the advanced states will continue to have a significant role in looking after the security of their citizens.

In the very weak states, most of which are located in sub-Saharan Africa, domestic violent conflict (intrastate war) is an increasing problem. With interstate war out of the question in one part of the international system and intrastate war proliferating in another part, a transformation of war is indeed going on. Unfortunately, it appears that the overall end result is more violent conflict rather than less.

The advanced states: from great power competition to security community

The modern state was first and foremost a security arrangement. Political theory reflects the unique importance awarded to the state in this regard. Hobbes taught that security derives from the state. The state must be able to provide a sufficient level of protection from external as well as from internal threats. Without the state, there can be no protection; people will live in a 'state of nature' where anarchy will reign because egoistic humans will cut each other's throats. Law and order, not to mention welfare, are absent: life is 'solitary, nasty, brutish and short'. Under the protection of the state, by contrast, people can enjoy relative safety and thus pursue happiness and well-being: 'felicity' in Hobbes's term.

The development of the modern state was accompanied by a historical process of internal pacification. Most violent forms of punishment disappeared; the use of violence in the context of the labour contract was discontinued; and direct military participation in the domestic affairs of the state ended (Giddens 1992). It is the culmination of this process that defines the government of the modern state: domestic order; democratic rule; and state monopoly of the legitimate use of force.

In the modern state, therefore, military forces face outwards. Their role is to provide protection from external threat. That is necessary, because with domestic order in the sovereign state, anarchy – the state of nature – now exists at the international level, in the relations between states. Hobbes was very well aware of this: 'In all times, kings and persons of sovereign authority, because of their independency, are in continual jealousies, and the state and posture of gladiators; having their weapons pointing, and their eyes fixed on one another' (Hobbes 1946: 101).

The actual conduct of war between states has undergone several phases of change because it was influenced by a number of factors, not least the development of weapon technology. After the Thirty Years' War and through the eighteenth and early nineteenth century, the idea of institutionalized war was dominant. War was understood in the terms of Karl von Clausewitz, as 'the continuation of politics by other means'. Military force was an instrument of the state, to be put to use where political and diplomatic efforts failed. Battles were between well-organized troops in uniform; civilians were not meant to be involved. According to Frederick the Great's ideal of war, civilians should not even be aware that war was in progress (Holsti 1991).

This idea of limited war was replaced by the notion of 'total war' during the late nineteenth century, a development culminating with the First World War. The railway, the steamship, and the telegraph completely changed the logistical and communications basis for warfare. Industrialization also transformed every aspect of weapons production, from bullets to battle ships, introducing systems with an immensely higher capacity for destruction. 'Total war' was the idea that war could no longer be restricted to armies fighting each other; the entire population as well as the total sum of resources which the state was able to muster should be used in the war effort. The two world wars are examples of total war.

The Second World War was replaced by the Cold War confrontation between the superpowers and their allies in East and West. The Cold War was a special kind of confrontation because of the existence of large arsenals of nuclear weapons on each side. Big nuclear weapons are special due to their destructive potential. Because they entail the risk of mutual destruction, they are valuable for deterrence rather than for actual use. So, the superpowers developed a way of competing with each other that avoided the use of the ultimate weapons, although the world came close to nuclear confrontation on a few occasions, especially during the 1962 Cuban missile crisis.

Peace with the end of the Cold War

What has come after the end of the Cold War? Realist IR theorists stress the fundamental continuity of the international system of sovereign states. Anarchy remains in place and therefore the risk of interstate war remains a real one. What has changed is not this basic structure, but the distribution of power between the states in the system. The Cold War was characterized by strategic bipolarity. With the end of the Soviet Union, realists noted that 'the bipolar era draws to a close' (Waltz 1993: 45). Slowly the system is changing towards multipolarity, but that process takes time. The present system is characterized by bipolarity 'in an altered state' (ibid.: 52).

Bipolarity continues because militarily Russia can take care of itself and because no other great powers have yet emerged. The candidates for great power status in the next 10–20 years are Japan, Germany and China. Japan and Germany already possess the economic and technological means necessary for great power status. They 'only' need to make the political choice to equip themselves as great powers: that is, to acquire nuclear weapons. China has nuclear weapons and is well on the way to catching up in economic and technological terms.

Many realists are convinced that with the departure of the Soviet Union, old rivalries will re-emerge among West European powers. Britain, France and Germany will again compete more intensely and that will increase the risk of violent conflict, unless a more stable European balance of power is established (Mearsheimer 1991).

Note that the realist analysts are not particularly interested in what goes on *inside* sovereign states; their focus is on the *international system*, and the relations *between* states. The transformation of statehood diagnosed in this book is not really considered important for international security as far as realists are concerned. They stress the continuity of sovereign states in anarchy. Because of this system, conflict between states continues to be a clear and present danger, even among the advanced liberal states. That is the reasoning behind the idea of 'the same damn things over and over again'. A prominent realist, Hans Morgenthau, saw conflict and war as unavoidable among sovereign states: 'All history shows that nations active in international politics are continuously preparing for, actively involved in, or recovering from organized violence in the form of war' (Morgenthau 1966: 25).

Most liberals are much more optimistic about the prospects for peace among states after the end of the Cold War. The phrase that most succinctly captures the spirit of liberal optimism is probably Francis Fukuyama's metaphor of 'the end of history', meaning 'the end point of mankind's ideological evolution and the universalization of Western liberal democracy as the final form of human government' (Fukuyama 1989: 4). He hastens to add that it is the liberal *idea* which has emerged victorious; in the *real world*, liberal democracy is not yet dominant, but there is reason to believe it will be in the long run.

So, realists remain pessimistic, liberals profoundly optimistic, even if many liberals are less sanguine than Fukuyama. Who is right? It would appear that the liberal view is strong when it comes to the advanced liberal states. We have seen how these societies are closely integrated both economically and politically. Liberal thought argues that such integration leads to peace; they point to several different contributing factors. Commercial liberalists focus on trade and other economic exchange. The classical liberal argument is that trade leads to peace. More recent analysis by economic liberals emphasizes the move away from production based on natural resources and land. Instead of natural resources, 'the key to long-term strength is capital, labour, and information' (Rosecrance 1995: 47). In other words, advanced liberal statehood signals the rise of a world of economic integration and exchange which requires cooperation and mutual dependence, instead of a world of autonomous, economically independent states. This transformation of economic structures suggests that peaceful relations will characterize advanced liberal states.

Institutional liberals point to the beneficial effects of international institutions; they create trust and stability among states. Institutions do this by providing flows of information and opportunities for negotiation; by presenting a possibility for governments to keep an eye on each other; and by offering a forum for the resolution of conflicts (Keohane 1989: 2). In these ways, institutions 'create a climate in which expectations of stable peace develop' (Nye 1997: 39). Advanced liberal states are more than ever involved in cooperation through international institutions; that is what multilevel governance is all about.

Sociological liberals focus on the relations across borders between individuals and groups from civil society. The classical argument is that relations between people are much better for peace than relations between governments, because in the former case people develop a sense of community and a network of overlapping group memberships which prevent the emergence of a single division into antagonistic camps (Burton 1972; Rosenau 1990). Again, such relations are highly developed among the populations of advanced liberal states.

Finally, republican liberalism concentrates on the beneficial effects of liberal democracy. It is very difficult to find examples of consolidated democracies fighting one another. The theoretical reasoning behind peaceful relations among democracies goes back to Immanuel Kant (Sørensen 1998), who emphasized three factors: first, democracies have developed peaceful norms of conflict resolution domestically; second, this common moral foundation helps democracies develop bonds of mutual respect and understanding leading to peaceful ways of solving conflicts; third, these ties are strengthened through economic cooperation among democracies, creating ties of economic interdependence. Advanced liberal states are consolidated liberal democracies; therefore, the Kantian idea of a pacific union of democracies applies to them.

Liberal optimism thus appears well founded when it comes to advanced liberal states. These states have developed among them what one liberal scholar called a 'security community'. By that he meant 'a group of people which has become "integrated". By integration we mean the attainment, within a territory, of a "sense of community" and of institutions and practices strong enough and widespread enough to assure, for a "long" time, dependable expectations of "peaceful change" among its population' (Deutsch *et al.* 1957: 5). Even if the USA is supremely powerful, other consolidated liberal states do not balance her out. A recent analysis puts the matter as follows: 'No coalition has formed to counterbalance U.S. power because political liberalism constitutes a transnational movement that has penetrated most potential challenger states at least to some degree ... Liberal elites ... tend to interpret the United States as benign and devote few state resources to counterbalance it' (Owen 2001/02: 121); possible changes in this area due to the US policies after 11 September, 2001 are discussed below.

In simple terms, we can say that there is no reason whatsoever to expect violent conflict between advanced liberal states; it is entirely out of the question. In that sense, a major security problem of external threat and possible war has been removed from the agenda of these states. But even if this is the case, things are not as idyllic as they may seem. The transformation of the advanced states does not entirely lead to peace and harmony; it also contains the seeds of new problems and potential conflict. Some of these problems have been identified in earlier chapters and we need only mention them briefly here. First, as far as integration of people across borders is concerned, there is not merely the creation of transnational communities with common values; processes of fragmentation, of 'resistance identities' focused on regional, nationalistic and local movements, also exist (see Chapter 5).

Second, the advanced states are certainly consolidated liberal democracies, but the growth of multilevel governance also spells new problems for democracy concerning accountability and control (see Chapter 4). Finally, an influential sociological analysis has argued that the transformation to advanced statehood leads to the creation of a 'risk society' (Beck 1992). His analysis focuses on the environment: ecological degradation, global warming, extinction of species, pollution and so on. Other social problems and risks in an integrated community of states are not difficult to think of: disease, crime, drugs, migration and economic crisis are easily transmitted across borders.

These are indisputable problems that need to be taken seriously; but they are not likely to amount to overwhelming security threats to the physical safety of the populations of advanced liberal societies, or even to lead to violent conflict among them. It rather appears to be the case that they make up challenges which will serve to strengthen cooperation between these states. That is because the various challenges of a 'risk society', of fragmentation and of democracy, can only be fruitfully confronted through cooperative efforts. In short, these challenges are not critical threats to the security community.

New security challenge to the Western world

Yet additional security challenges to open, liberal societies of a potentially more serious nature exist. The most critical problem may be the mass-murder terrorism revealed by 11 September 2001. The world was already familiar with terrorism, of course; it was never confined to specific areas, such as the Middle East. There had been a number of other serious attacks, also in the Western world, but there was no indication that terrorists were ready to commit mass murder of innocent civilians on the scale exposed by September 11. And it came as a shock that such terrorism could be executed so relatively easy. Bring a plastic knife on board the airplane and be able to fly it straight; that is hardly a recipe for sophisticated, resource-demanding, technology-intensive operations. Furthermore, there appear to be variants of chemical or biological terror that are not too hard to initiate either.

September 11 revealed how vulnerable the open, integrated societies are to ruthless terrorism. There is a peculiar security dilemma here: how to create sufficient protection of such societies without violating their major, defining quality, namely their openness? On the one hand, sufficient protection will require surveillance, undercover intelligence, and inspection of the behaviour and movement of civilians, the citizens. Any traffic across borders of goods, services, information or people is a candidate for closer monitoring and control. On the other hand, openness requires wide-ranging possibilities for transactions, as well as individual freedom of movement, of expression and of organization (within liberal constitutional limits).

This dilemma is not entirely new, of course; it was also present during the Cold War. But it has become much more pertinent after September 11. Some commentators are rather worried that the measures needed to combat terrorism will indeed have negative consequences in other areas:

> Democracy and liberalism, both domestic and international, will be threatened by the need to combat terror within and impose Western power without. States are likely to become more authoritarian and act in violation of human rights more frequently. International political norms will decline as powerful states flout them and anti-Western forces exploit such hypocrisy for their own ends. This is not a pleasant prospect. (Hirst 2002: 341)

The worst-case scenario is a total breakdown of the underpinnings of the liberal security community, including a breakdown of liberal democracy, common institutions and liberal international norms. This is not a likely prospect under the present circumstances (more on this below), but the problems outlined here demonstrate the broader dangers of mass-murder terrorism. Furthermore, it will be argued below that the basic problems which help produce terrorism will not be solved in the short and medium term.

The dilemma concerning protection from mass-murder terror has another dimension related to the struggle against terrorism. How far are open, democratic societies allowed to go in the name of combating terrorism? Are they allowed to produce as many, or more, civilian casualties in the campaign against terrorism than the terrorists themselves murdered in the first place? Are they allowed to disregard international law in the name of fighting terrorism? The immediate answer would appear to be: no, of course not. But the events in Afghanistan and the debate about 'what to do' with Saddam Hussein and Iraq have demonstrated the acute relevance of the dilemma. The coalition led by the USA and the UK obviously felt it had good and legitimate causes for bringing down the regime of Saddam Hussein; several other states, including France, Germany and Russia, were not convinced by the arguments presented by the coalition.

Additional military actions of this kind will produce new quarrels among the great powers. There has been much debate and concern among scholars, and others, about the consequences for international order of the strong tendency for US unilateralism under the George W. Bush administration. In the words of Mohammad Ayoob:

> The United States has not merely demonstrated a lack of concern for the views of its closest allies, it has set itself up unilaterally as the arbiter of the criteria by which such high-sounding goals [i.e., international security, peace, justice, human rights, and so on] are to be served and those who violate them punished. This arrogation of moral authority and the right to make decisions about war and peace unilaterally on behalf of the society of states carries very high potential costs. It undermines the normative consensus underpinning the post-Cold War international order, thereby beginning the process of its de-legitimization ... it erodes the normative consensus underpinning that order and threatens to return the world to a more Hobbesian state. (Ayoob 2003)

At the same time, many liberal scholars believe that even if the USA is the world's only superpower, it is compelled to cooperate with others, it 'can't go it alone', as Joseph Nye explains:

> Under the influence of the information revolution and globalization, world politics is changing in a way that means Americans cannot achieve all their international goals acting alone. The United States lacks both the international and domestic prerequisites to resolve conflicts that are internal to other societies, and to monitor and control transnational transactions that threaten Americans at home. We must mobilize international coalitions to address shared threats and challenges. We will have to learn better how to share as well as lead. (Nye 2002: 40)

American unilateralism is a potential threat to strong international institutions and a stable international order. At the same time, there would appear to be much stronger limitations to US unilateralism when it comes to areas other than those directly connected to the use of military force. For example, winning the war in Iraq is one thing, but winning the peace in that country, or in the Middle East, is quite another and will require cooperation and coalition-building. As the supreme military power, the US faces hard choices: 'Should the United States choose retrenchment, isolation, selective involvement, active interventionism, or global enforcement as its strategy? Can and should the United States seek to prolong and exploit its presently unquestioned supremacy, or should it attempt to establish through cooperative approaches the best possible terms for its inevitable decline?' (Miller 2001: 27–8).

Irrespective of the US policy choices, international institutions and the international order they help promote are not dismantled overnight. Just as they took a long time to build up and mature, they will take time to tear down. The core underpinnings of the liberal security community are not yet seriously threatened. The next few years will reveal whether that will actually become the case.

The final major difficulty with 'mass-murder terrorism' is that – unlike an opponent in conventional war – it can probably never be defeated once and for all. It is, rather, an ongoing struggle where each successful campaign risks calling forth new adversaries. At the same time, there is a complex set of causal layers behind this kind of terrorism. They include: (a) traditional Muslim elites in Saudi Arabia and elsewhere unable to accommodate processes of modernization and Westernization; (b) the Middle East conflict, especially the continuing clashes between Palestinians and Israelis; (c) the existence of weak states such as Afghanistan (more on this below); and (d) socio-economic inequalities pushed by uneven economic globalization. More than one billion people exist on one US dollar a day or less; another two billion exist on two dollars or less; in all, that is roughly half of the world's population. It should be emphasized that there is no simple relationship between these underlying causes and the emergence of mass-murder terrorism; they are structural conditions, rather than triggers for the actual actors undertaking terrorism. In short, we do not really know how much terrorism these underlying factors help create, but we can also be quite sure that there are no immediate effective responses forthcoming to these underlying conditions of terrorism.

New developments in military technology constitute another security challenge to the advanced states. There is a large debate under way about the 'revolution in military affairs' (RMA) which proposes that the development of technology and communication will revolutionize modern warfare as we know it. However, this is not a short-term prospect; it may take place over the next three decades (Arquilla and Ronfeldt 1997). A more immediate possibility may be increased diffusion and use of weapons of mass destruction as they become smaller, cheaper and more readily available. Ruthless terrorists in possession of nuclear or biological weapons are a frightening prospect. At the same time, there is now public contemplation that some smaller nuclear weapons could be employed by the USA in the campaign against 'rogue states'. Should that come to pass, it will be a great change from the situation of the Cold War, where the nuclear balance of power was based on the tacit assumption that these weapons would not be put to use.

In summary, realist state-centric scholars are wrong when they posit the security situation of advanced liberal states as one of 'business as usual'. Realists focus their analysis on the international system and the continued existence of sovereign states in anarchy. They go wrong because they fail to analyze the 'domestic' changes in statehood that have taken place. Liberals are much more aware of those changes. Violent conflict between advanced liberal states is not a real issue any more; that is a dramatic change. Countries such as Britain, France and Germany have been competing for centuries and that has often resulted in war, culminating in the two world wars of the twentieth century.

Some retreat scholars see a reduced role for the state in these developments. Susan Strange, for example, says that 'the perceived need for the state as an institution necessary to defend society against violence within or beyond its territory still exists, but in many societies at a much lower level' (Strange 1996: 73). James Rosenau diagnoses an 'erosion and dispersion' of state power and argues that 'the world has become too complex to be managed through the exercise of coercive power' (Rosenau 1997: 384). It is true that the obsolescence of war among the advanced states reduces the need to focus on military defence; and compared with the deep and constant involvement of sovereign states in war-making across history, that is a significant development. But not all states are in this category so all traditional external security threats have not been eliminated. And due to mass-murder terrorism and developments in military technology, new security threats are in the making, so one cannot argue that the need for the state to provide military defence is completely redundant. Many factors are involved in the translation of new and different threats into concrete numbers in military budgets. The USA chose a historically unprecedented rise in military expenditures after September 11. West European and Japanese expenditures are on much lower absolute levels but remain significant.

In conclusion, the security situation of the advanced liberal states has been transformed. Some traditional threats of interstate war have been removed, but new security threats have emerged. In the longer term, this may spell important changes in the defence postures of these states, but there is little indication that the role of the state is being dramatically reduced as regards the provision of security; it is rather being changed in order to be able to face new threats.

The weak, least developed states: more domestic conflict

Most of the weak, least developed states are located in sub-Saharan Africa and for that reason our focus here will be on that region, although the remarks are relevant for weak states elsewhere as well. In order to understand the peculiar security situation in weak states, it is necessary briefly to describe the major features of 'personal rule', the system that replaced the colonial administrations after independence. Colonial rule in itself never came to resemble the modernizing state administrations of Europe in the nineteenth century and onwards. They were small, authoritarian undertakings, aimed at providing the necessary amount of local control, including protection of the motherland's personnel and of the export operations of raw materials and primary goods. The ethnically and culturally very diverse populations that inhabited most colonies were not actively involved in this system: they were the objects of a paternalist scheme of rule.

Some mass mobilization took place in the struggle against colonialism; nationalist parties were formed to organize popular support for independence. They were successful, even extremely so. After the Second World War, the colonial powers had lost confidence in their legitimate right to rule the colonies. In a surprisingly short period of time, the leaders of the nationalist movements were catapulted into positions of state power. But the leaders were not actively interested in the development of strong parties; they would be a potential threat to their firm grip on state power. The political parties were destroyed and the leaders focused on control of the state. To the extent that elections were held, opposition parties were not allowed access to power; they were ousted by military coups, organized by governing party leaders. 'In no state on the African mainland, from independence through to 1990, did any opposition party gain power as the result of winning a general election against an incumbent government' (Clapham 1996).

In contrast to the colonial elite, the new rulers were by no means insulated from society; they were closely connected to it via ties of clan, kinship and ethnic affiliation. The clients had great expectations of benefits from government control. This paved the way for clientelism, patronage and nepotism. The Africanization of the state took place in a context of political cultures that:

> conceived of government offices and resources in terms of possession and consumption; multiethnic societies that wanted at least their equitable share of the governmental cake, if they could not have it all; politicians who recognized that granting or denying access to

government offices and resources was a crucial modus operandi for expanding and retaining power, and, of course, the absence of, or at most the scarcity of, alternative sources of power, status, and wealth. (Jackson and Rosberg 1994: 302)

The new state elites aspired to entertain Western standards of living, irrespective of the actual poverty of the country. African officials insisted on the same level of salaries and perks that had been given to their European predecessors. At the same time, indigenization of the state administrations combined with, on the one hand, ideas about state leadership and predominance in the newly independent societies, and, on the other hand, pressure from below for access to state spoils, to produce an enormous expansion of the state administrations. Ghana's administration increased by a factor of eight between 1972 and 1980; Tanzania's tripled; Zambia's bureaucracy grew sixfold in the first decade after independence (Jackson and Rosberg 1994: 301).

The legal norms and regulations stipulating appropriate behaviour of state officials controlling public resources were left over from the colonial administrations. They were looked upon with suspicion from the beginning and were never taken seriously. Furthermore, no sense of citizenship or expectations of public accountability existed to back them up. Leaders and clients focused on the here and now; the concrete gains from access to, and control over, scarce public resources. Leaders would focus on the control of raw materials for export, on revenues from taxation of imports and exports, on incoming foreign aid; and in due course on every other possibility for quick returns. Entrenched leaders became phenomenally successful in this regard; in Zaire, for example, President Mobutu Sese Seko was reported to have accumulated personal wealth of $5 billion by 1984, much of it deposited in Western banks or invested outside the country (Young and Turner 1985: 440).

It should be clear immediately that such a system of personal rule based upon extensive chains of patronage is crisis-prone in the extreme. Economic disturbances will translate into a decline of resources available for patronage. Ethnic and other groups in the population not in favour in the established system of resource distribution will try to get into the driver's seat. External sponsors may lose their enthusiasm and start attaching harder conditions to their support.

Weak states at the end of the Cold War

Drops in the prices of primary export commodities and increasing import prices, especially in the area of energy, have plagued the weak states ever since independence, but the period around the end of the Cold War was especially serious. On the one hand, the prices of minerals, coffee and other major export items had gone down for more than a decade. Attempts to compensate via taking up loans on the international market had saddled the weak states with a huge external debt. Total outstanding public debt for the countries of sub-Saharan Africa reached $151 billion by 1991 (Clapham 1996: 167). On the other hand, the Cold War had made up a very favourable climate for extraction of resources from the two contenders in the conflict. With the dispute called off, those sources of arms delivery, political support and loans became much less available (International Committee of the Red Cross 2000: 16).

Consequently, personal rulers were under significantly increased pressure. To the extent they had legitimacy, it was based on the distribution of benefits and the accommodation of potential rivals. Threats to the patronage network meant threats to their claim to state power. They faced two principal options: either to construct a new basis for their legitimate power through political and economic reform offering the accommodation of competing elites; or retrenchment, combined with the use of violence against rivals. Rulers choosing the latter option quickly had to face violent contests with their opponents. This is the path leading to state breakdown or state failure, meaning 'a situation where the structure, authority (legitimate power), law and political order [of a state] have fallen apart' (Zartman 1995: 1).

In such a situation, evidently, the state offers no protection whatsoever to its citizens. The state is rather a major source of violent threat and ordinary people face the choice of being caught in the crossfire or lining up behind one of the contenders in the battle. In the worst cases, such as Sierra Leone, Liberia, Somalia or Zaire, domestic anarchy or complete chaos have been the result for some considerable periods of time. Ordinary people are in mortal danger; the traditional view of the system of sovereign states is turned on its head: according to conventional wisdom, order and safety exist within the state and there is anarchy between states. When it comes to failed states, anarchy and chaos exist within the state, whereas the surrounding international system displays a well-developed order: the formal survival of these states, their legitimate membership of the international society of states, is secure and guaranteed by the leading states. That guarantee of international survival must look deeply ironic to the citizens of failed states because it offers them no concrete security at all. Instead, it offers the prospect of living in mortal danger.

That is the peculiar security situation of weak states in the cases where the state's weakness of personal rule leads to state failure. It should be added that a complete, full-blown state collapse does not happen very often. Most of the time, violent domestic conflict progresses on a smaller scale. Some 30 to 40 states have experienced serious domestic conflict since 1989. Less than ten of them have suffered complete collapse. Still, the situation for the population of the other states remains one of serious domestic insecurity.

There are several possible cases to choose from for illustrating the process of state failure described above in general terms. The case of Zaire/Congo under Mobutu Sese Seko (1965–97) will suffice in the present context. Zaire is rich in natural resources: copper, zinc, cobalt and diamonds. Mobutu took private control of many of these assets, sometimes licensing them to foreign companies, sometimes leaving them to be exploited by individual strongmen in his network. He actively avoided consolidating state power, not least out of fear that bureaucracies might acquire interests and powers of their own (Reno 2000: 1). The state became what Reno calls a 'shadow state': it was maintained as a disguise for what were really private forms of wealth accumulation and political management. The state was a necessary façade because it provided access to domestic control, international support and foreign aid.

Once his control of Zaire's major resources was secure, Mobutu went about dismantling entirely the system for provision of public goods. Social services, schools, public works and even support for farmers (i.e., the majority of the population) were not necessary elements in the patronage network; they were rather liabilities to be disposed of. By 1992, the president's office controlled 95 per cent of Zaire's government expenditures (up from 28 per cent in 1972); a mere 4 per cent went to agriculture; the expenditure for social services was nil (ibid.: 4).

By 1990, Mobutu's foreign allies were increasingly disgusted with him. He was losing American, Belgian and French support and facing demands for political and economic reform. The loss of US backing was especially bad because his support for União Nacional para a Independência Total de Angola (UNITA) rebels in Angola had been an important source of patronage. Mobutu launched a programme of political liberalization, but when Etienne Thisekedi emerged as a serious rival, he opted for using violence against his opponents.

Mobutu's situation began looking better when civil war broke out in Rwanda in 1993. France wanted to assist the incumbent regime in Rwanda and needed Mobutu's services in the process. With renewed foreign support, Mobutu deftly outmanoeuvred Thisekedi, replacing him as prime minister with Kengo, a much less serious rival without any autonomous power base. But Mobutu's dealings had antagonized rulers of neighbouring states; he housed Hutu exiles from Rwanda, traded with Angolan rebels, and helped provide supplies for Rwandan insurgents. Consequently, Laurent Kabila could rely on foreign help when he emerged as a serious contender to Mobutu. When mineral-rich areas came under his control, Kabila became a commercial partner with foreign investors. He eventually prevailed in the war, toppling Mobutu in May 1997. But his attempt to expel the Rwandan and Uganda forces that had helped him to power opened a new comprehensive conflict. Kabila was assassinated in January 2001, reportedly by a child soldier. Power currently rests with his son, Joseph, but the civil war with external involvement continues. Some two million people have been displaced as a result of the fighting. Laurent Kabila's forces conducted massive killings of civilian refugees in the campaign against Mobutu. The systematic rape and maiming of women and girls has been an integral activity of all sides in the conflict (Human Rights Watch 2002).

According to UN estimates, some 15–30 per cent of all newly recruited combatants in the Democratic Republic of Congo are children under 18, many of them under 12. Here is a typical statement:

> I joined Kabila's army when I was 13 because my home had been pillaged and my parents were gone. When I found myself alone, I decided to become a soldier. Usually, I was at the front line ... I've fought a lot. It is hard. I am only a little soldier, I should return to school. (Quoted from Coalition to Stop the Use of Child Soldiers 2001)

In more general terms, the human cost of weak or failed statehood has been extremely high. The three conflicts in Sudan, Ethiopia and Mozambique each cost the lives of 500,000 to one million people (Copson 1994: 29); casualties in Angola, Somalia, Sierra Leone, Liberia and Uganda have also been very high.

Domestic conflict in weak, postcolonial states has presented the international society of states with a security problem of the utmost severity. International law is much more focused on the regulation of 'traditional' conflict *between* sovereign states, not on conflicts *within* states. During the Cold War, the bipolar confrontation between East and West severely curtailed the ability of the international society to act at all. After the end of the Cold War new possibilities for taking action have emerged; the great powers are much less divided among themselves. Humanitarian intervention – that is, measures to stop a conflict and aid civilian victims – has now become possible.

Serious problems remain, however: first, it is very difficult for international society to take pre-emptive action, to do something about domestic conflict before it occurs in earnest. In other words, humanitarian intervention is only undertaken when major groups of innocent people have already suffered the consequences of violent conflict. Second, intervention is costly, both in material and potentially also in human terms. How many material resources, and how many of 'our boys' are the capable states of the international system ready to devote to humanitarian intervention in how many weak states? American troops were quick to leave Somalia after having suffered a limited number of casualties. The states who have the capacity for intervention, the great powers, are hardly ready to accept great human and material costs. Third, major problems of a concrete, operational nature are involved in humanitarian intervention. Separating the contenders in the conflict and establishing some small amount of order is often extremely difficult, as interventions in Liberia, Sierra Leone, the Democratic Republic of Congo, Somalia and elsewhere have shown (International Committee of the Red Cross 2000; Roberts 1996). Finally, even if the intervention is a relative success, there is no guarantee of a durable, long-term solution to the underlying conflict that triggered intervention in the first place. Humanitarian intervention is rather a short-term relief operation.

If humanitarian intervention is not a durable solution, what is? The question is complicated and there is no agreement among scholars about the most promising answer. One radical proposal is to let the contenders battle it out, to 'Give War a Chance' (Luttwak 1999; see also Herbst 1996/97). Behind this idea is the hope that war will eventually bring peace 'when all belligerents become exhausted or when one wins decisively' (Luttwak 1999: 36). Furthermore, war has been a vital ingredient in state-making in Europe and elsewhere (Tilly 1992). A similar logic might unfold in the weak, postcolonial states: there is 'very little evidence that African countries, or many others in the Third World, will be able to find peaceful ways to strengthen the state and develop national identities ... war may not seem such an undesirable alternative' (Herbst 1989: 691–2).

However, the continuation of violent conflict in weak states holds little promise of paving the way for stronger states and a better future for the peoples. The major reason for this turns on the difference between earlier European state-making and the current situation of the weak states. In most of the history of European state formation, rulers had to face up to external threat. 'Any state that failed to put considerable effort into war making was likely to disappear' (Tilly 1985: 184). Many European powerholders were not successful, of course, and they were swallowed by their stronger competitors. Fundamentally, this kind of external competition was a principal driving force in European state making. The armed forces faced outwards most of the time and were busy preparing for new wars against external enemies. The preparation for war forced power holders into a series of compromises with the subject populations, which constrained their power and paved the way for early forms of citizenship rights. This meant material benefits for the population. Combined with the creation of domestic order and the promotion of capital accumulation, these processes furthered the building of bonds of loyalty and legitimacy between kings and people.

In weak, postcolonial states, by contrast, there is no deadly external threat and therefore their armies face inwards. There is frequently a great deal of violent conflict, but it is mainly domestic conflict. It is a peculiar paradox: because weak, postcolonial states are more or less completely created from the outside, in that other states collude to set them up, that act of external creation leaves domestic contenders inside the states with a free rein to do whatever they pleased to their subject populations and to each other. Weak states and their regimes are protected from outside threat by strong international norms, created in the context of decolonization and further strengthened during the Cold War. Recolonization, annexation, or any other format of strong states in the North taking over the weak states in the South is not on the agenda. Nowadays, borders are sacrosanct; the international society, for a number of reasons, is very unwilling to accept alterations of existing borders; they are considered important elements of international order (Jackson 1995). It is this situation that creates the curious context for security in weak states. They are left to the process of domestic conflict with external participation which has been a characteristic pattern since independence. With a few exceptions (Clapham 2001), such conflict has led to very little in terms of effective state-building. A certain outcome, by contrast, is incredibly high human costs.

Are there more attractive, alternative solutions? One suggestion is that the international society accepts secession and the creation of new states in a much more radical way than has been the case so far. We have seen that international society is very unwilling to change existing borders. What if that position were abandoned? Several commentators find the idea attractive; risks of secession would push predatory state elites towards getting their acts together and better accommodating ethnic and other groups. More effective states could be the result.

Yet, given the current situation in many weak states, secession could also lead to even greater problems. Especially in what used to be Yugoslavia, secession and the drawing-up of new borders have been accompanied by massive acts of so-called ethnic cleansing (Bennett 1995). In sub-Saharan Africa, the creation of many new states could lead to even higher levels of human suffering. One complicated issue concerning secession is where to stop: how far can one go in the carving up of existing states? Which groups should be allowed the creation of new states and which groups should not? In other words, the process of secession threatens 'an infinite regress of self-determination' (Zartman 1995: 268; see also Bartkus 1999).

A third possibility is international trusteeship, meaning that the international society (the United Nations) takes responsibility for the territories in trouble. East Timor and Kosovo are recent cases where the institution of international trusteeship has been revived, but several elements speak against the idea that such trusteeship is a general solution to the serious problems in weak states. First, trusteeship is highly demanding in terms of resources; there is no indication that capable UN member states are willing to provide the necessary means. Second, there is a potential element of patron–client structures in trusteeship. 'Rich' outsiders come in and are expected to serve as well as discipline 'poor' insiders. The UN operation in East Timor, for example, had great problems in fostering domestic institutions and local democracy. Indeed, the UN looked more like a colonial power, strengthening:

> the segregation between expatriates and Timorese. Two economies of scale emerged ... Timorese were turned into the servants of foreigners in their own land, since they could apply only for menial jobs. Physically, the UN's hermetic office world was increasingly disconnected from life in the streets. Floating container hotels in Dili restricted the access of Timorese, except to serve drink and food. (Chopra 2000: 33)

Finally, the 'outsiders' face the difficult task of helping forward a genuine peace and a stable reconciliation among the 'insiders' that can provide the basis for a more permanent process of effective and democratic state-building. The goals are multiparty democracy; a regulated market economy and a stable legal order; a viable infrastructure; stable currency; basic social services; and, normally, a much reduced and changed role for the military arm of the state (cf. Clapham 2000: 9). Several of these are surely long-terms tasks and, with the exception of very special cases such as West Germany and Japan after the Second World War, it is difficult to point to clearly successful cases in this area of state-making.

In conclusion, weak states in various degrees of state failure have 'retreated' to such an extent that there is virtually no substance left. Such states are little but empty shells; their existence is formally recognized by the international society, but they are of no service to their populations. On the contrary: armed branches of the state are a direct threat to the physical security and safety of large parts of the population. With the Cold War over, there is a clear willingness among capable states in international society to do something about weak and failing states. But the demands in terms of manpower, material resources and long-term commitment are so huge that capable states either cannot or will not devote themselves fully to the task. They do help, but they know very well that it is hardly enough.

Are they to blame? Sovereignty is a great value; it bestows right of self-determination and independence upon states and peoples. But it also bestows responsibility for your own fate: to succeed or to fail in state-making. Given the circumstances explained here, it is not surprising that many weak states could fail. As unreasonable as it may sound, the institution of sovereignty leaves primary responsibility for state failure resting upon the peoples of weak states themselves. It is their state; they will have to make it work. Capable states can be criticized for doing too little or for doing all the wrong things: but with sovereignty as the dominant principle of political organization, states and their peoples are ultimately responsible for their own fate.

Conclusion

Conventional wisdom stipulates that in a world of sovereign states, there is a perennial risk of interstate war. Many states are heavily armed and they may always clash; there is no world government, no supreme authority that can reconcile disputes. In some regions interstate war is a real danger: the Middle East and some parts of Asia are major examples. But there are also very significant areas where violent conflict between states is out of the question. The advanced liberal states are consolidated democracies; they make up a security community with peaceful relations. Conflicts of interest and very different views on important problems may occur, as the debate over measures against the Saddam Hussein regime in Iraq demonstrated, but there is no risk that such disagreement will lead to violent conflict among the advanced liberal states themselves.

The removal of the risk of interstate war between some of the world's major powers is a significant change from the traditional international system with its permanent risk of war, a state of affairs that led to two world wars in the twentieth century; yet security challenges to the advanced liberal states have not been completely eliminated. The mass-murder terrorism of September 11 revealed a painful security dilemma, which concerns the need to create sufficient protection of open societies without undermining openness itself. If measures against terrorism lead to the undermining of liberal democracy's basic values and institutions, the liberal security community may be in danger.

In the weak, least developed states, there is an alarming prospect of sustained domestic violent conflict. The state is a source of violent threat to ordinary people rather than a source of protection. The international society has no clear answer to this problem. Humanitarian intervention, secession and trusteeship do not appear to be appropriate long-term solutions, and there is little prospect that the domestic contenders in the weak states will solve the problem on their own.

In short, the security problem for the sovereign states of the international system has been transformed in major ways. The role of the state is not being reduced; among the advanced liberal states it is rather being changed in order to face new security challenges. Among the weak states, the emergence of 'failed states' demonstrates how important effective and capable statehood is for the creation of security, order, freedom and economic progress.

Chapter 8

The Modernizing States: Winners or Losers?

China
India
Russia
Conclusion: modernizing states and the debate
  about the state

Previous chapters have focused on the advanced capitalist states and on the least developed states in the Third World. I have tried to show how the transformation of statehood has consequences for security (i.e., the transformation of war discussed in the previous chapter); for welfare and economic growth (involving the relationship between states and markets; see Chapters 2 and 3); and for international order (Chapter 6). The picture outlined in previous chapters is incomplete because the focus was on two groups of states: the advanced states and the least developed Third World states. If the advanced and the least developed states are at different ends of a continuum, there has been little mention of the states in-between. These 'in-betweens', which I shall term 'modernizing states', are the subject of this chapter.

Most modernizing states are found in Asia, Latin America, the Middle East, and in Eastern Europe. I have decided to focus on three very significant states – China, India and Russia – because they are of particular consequence in the development of sovereign statehood in the twenty-first century. They also help shed additional light on the debate between state-centric and retreat scholars.

The chapter will discuss how the three modernizing states confront the basic values of security, welfare and economic growth, and international order. Each of the three states contains a unique mixture of the different major types of statehood discussed earlier in this book. The economic characteristics of weak states (i.e., incoherent amalgamations of traditional agriculture, an informal petty urban sector, and some fragments of modern industry) are appropriate for many parts of India, but the country also has major elements of a modern structure. It even has some sprinklings of an advanced capitalist economy in that it now seeks active integration in cross-border networks via direct investment

142

and much more involvement in economic globalization. A similar mixture can be found in China, but this country is already a much more active participant in economic globalization; at the same time, China has had more success in economic modernization, moving people out of the agricultural sector. Russia has modernized even more, but its relationship to the global economy remains more like a member of OPEC, the Organization of Petroleum Exporting Countries, as it is an exporter of energy and raw materials and an importer of more sophisticated products.

As far as the political level is concerned, a similar mixture of different types of state exists. All three countries contain elements of the weak state characteristics (i.e., inefficient and corrupt administrative and institutional structures; rule based on coercion rather than the rule of law; and no established monopoly on the legitimate use of violence). Each of them also contains elements of the modern, effective state. Democracy came to India first; it has a foothold in Russia, and is merely embryonic in China. But not even India is a fully consolidated democracy. Finally, some elements of multilevel governance are also beginning to emerge in these states as they slowly become more integrated into international society.

In short, modernizing states are by definition in-betweens. They are undertaking a process of transition from one type of statehood towards another. The process is anything but smooth and straight; it contains problems and setbacks, and unsurprisingly a country can get stuck in various ways along the road, as has India. So, the peculiar combination of characteristics from different types of state is nothing out of the ordinary for modernizing states; it is a general feature that they share as states in a process of modernization.

The purpose in the following sections is thus to demonstrate how three modernizing states face the problems of security, of welfare and economic growth, and of international order. This complements the picture of the transformation of statehood drawn in earlier chapters by highlighting some of the peculiar features of major modernizing states. A full analysis of statehood today would have to include at least the major states in Latin America, the Middle East and Eastern Europe. That will not be possible in the present context, but the three states discussed here are considered sufficient to give an idea about the special circumstances that the modernizing states face and the way in which these states contribute to the debate on sovereign statehood.

China

China is a giant: 1.3 billion people and an economy worth $5.5 trillion. An ancient civilization, the Chinese empire lasted more than two thousand years: the Han Dynasty was established in 206 BC; the republican revolution took place in 1911. China had the potential for an industrial revolution long before it occurred in the West, but it also had a social structure which 'guaranteed continued stagnation' (Riskin 1987: 19). Political, economic, and social power was concentrated in the gentry (landowners, state bureaucrats, and intelligentsia); domestic challengers were held down. Imperial China had no rivals in East Asia and the rulers took no interest in Western goods and ideas.

By the mid-nineteenth century, foreign powers were strong enough to impose themselves on the empire. After the Opium War (1839–42), Britain, followed by other European powers and the USA, established trading ports in China, took control of the access of goods and people to the country, and legalized the import of opium. The 1911 revolution replaced imperial rule with famine, civil war and economic crisis. Amidst political chaos and the dominance of China by foreign powers, the Chinese Communist Party (CCP) was founded in 1921.

Japan occupied the northeast provinces of Manchuria from 1931; a large-scale Japanese invasion took place in 1937. The Japanese forces killed as many people in Nanking by 'conventional' means as did the Americans in the nuclear bombings of Hiroshima and Nagasaki eight years later. It was this context of civil war against the Gūomindang and profound humiliation by foreigners that shaped the Communist perception of security after its victory in 1949.

Security for the people in China

When the Communists came to power, China had several characteristics of the weak, less developed state described in previous chapters. The economy was undeveloped and fragmented; the political system was authoritarian and not highly institutionalized; and the population was divided after many years of civil war. In 1949, more than 85 per cent of the population lived in the countryside, engaged in various forms of traditional agriculture. Of modern industry, there was very little: it accounted for less than 5 per cent of the economy (ibid.: 17). Manufacturing consisted of handicraft production in small-scale enterprises. People at the bottom led miserable lives; it has been estimated that 4.5 per cent of each generation died in famines (ibid.: 25). No less than 80 per cent of the population had to get by on a very low level of subsistence.

Communist rule was centralized and non-democratic. The civil war had imposed a hierarchical, military structure on the Communists, characterized by discipline, secrecy and a top–down command structure. The CCP took over the traditional Chinese (imperial) view, according to which all power should reside in a central authority. Their vision was one of a 'people's democratic dictatorship' (Nathan 1986: 6). The word 'democratic' has nothing to do with the openness of the system to popular influence. It rests on the conviction that the regime serves the higher, and most fundamental, interests of the masses, the people. It was a system based on the personal rule of Mao Zedong more than on formal procedures and institutions. Personal relations and patron–client relationships meant more than legal-rational authority.

In sum, there were personal rule, a weak agrarian economy, and a divided population. In the days of civil war, some responsiveness to ordinary people had been a condition of survival in an otherwise hostile environment. With Communist victory:

> the masses must rely on the party and its cadres, but the party and its cadres are no longer in a position of direct, reciprocal dependence and vulnerability. The remaining clout of the masses is reduced to their discretion as producers, consumers, and risk-taking resisters. The masses have become the fish and the party controls the water. (Womack 1987: 498)

A powerless people exposed to the whims of authoritarian government: it sounds like the familiar story from weak states described in Chapter 7. Why, then, did China not sink into the chaos, misery and turmoil characterizing many weak, less developed states? For two major reasons: on the one hand, the CCP was a highly organized and disciplined force based on a strong ideology of development for and by the people. Even if it was centralized and authoritarian, the CCP also allowed an interplay between leadership and people (Mao called this 'the mass line'). It took several concrete forms (Blecher 1986: 26): grassroots and country-level leaders were given a high degree of latitude in ensuring that higher-level instructions were in accordance with local needs; cadres were sent to the villages to work and live alongside the peasants, sharing their circumstances, in order to learn from rural life; some limited forms of political expression were encouraged; and finally, the armed forces were to take part in civilian affairs under rules which required subordination to civil authority.

On the other hand, the external threat was of great importance. China was subjected to a containment policy by the USA and the leadership had reason to believe that both state and regime were in severe danger. The external threat was felt even more intensely by the Chinese when the Sino–Soviet alliance broke up in the early 1960s. Under Khrushchev, the Soviet Union initiated a policy of 'peaceful coexistence' with the USA. The Soviets discontinued their assistance to the Chinese nuclear programme, criticized mainland aggression towards Taiwan, and did not support China in its border conflict with India. Until the early 1970s, China had every reason to think that its international environment was hostile and threatening.

So, external threat and domestic discipline made the CCP push for real – and fast – socio-economic development and popular legitimacy. Within a brief period of reconstruction (1949–52), the regime was able to get inflation under control, restore the infrastructure, and stimulate production in industry and agriculture. Redistribution of land and swift efforts in health and education meant real progress and much improved security for the people, including the large masses of very poor. But at the same time, the regime made grave mistakes which meant periods of enormous suffering and loss of life. Ironically, such problems were most acute when the leadership tried to push even faster ahead with economic and social development. During the so-called 'Great Leap Forward' (1958–61) grain production dropped, first by 15, then by 25, and then again by another 25 per cent. These were disastrous years with widespread famine, killing perhaps as many as 30 million people (Ashton *et al.* 1984). The 'Cultural Revolution' in the late 1960s uprooted millions of people and created political turmoil with factional infighting bordering on civil war (Thurston 1984–5).

Since the late 1970s, economic reforms and decentralization of political decision-making in many areas have led to sustained improvements for the population. But the regime also upholds policies of strict control of its people and non-tolerance of dissidence. Freedom of movement is limited and freedoms of organization, speech and the press are severely restricted. Particularly harsh repression is used against people suspected of nationalist or religious activities. The minority areas, Tibet and Xinjiang, are especially exposed in this regard.

In sum, the security situation for the Chinese people is indeed peculiar. People have benefited from great improvements in nutrition, health, education and material well-being. An authoritarian socialist regime has led the way, undertaking swift reforms on a large scale. But the power to do good has been matched by the power to be very wrong, to commit horrible mistakes and even persevere in failed policies after they have been proved wrong. In either case, the population is, to a very high degree, at the complete mercy of its leaders (Sørensen 1991). This situation is slowly changing because socio-economic changes also create new social groups, including a stronger civil society (Brook and Frolic 1997). Yet the tension between economic freedom and political control is likely to remain in place for some time.

Welfare and growth in China

After the first, very successful, phase of reconstruction, China adopted the Soviet model of development: a planned economy emphasizing the leading role of heavy industry and capital goods; and a system of collectivized agriculture where the surplus should finance industrialization. All was under the control of a centralized bureaucracy and a central five-year plan. The model delivered respectable growth rates, especially in heavy industry, and even if a huge surplus was transferred out of agriculture, there was room for some improvement for the peasants as well because agrarian reforms increased the overall output.

However, Mao was not happy with the model. Unemployment remained a serious problem. The gap between the cities and the villages was growing; 'experts' were taking the lead instead of 'reds'. In the context of the split with the Soviet Union, Mao embarked on the experiments of the 'Great Leap Forward' and later the 'Cultural Revolution'. As mentioned above, they resulted in severe economic setbacks, although there was a phase of readjustment and consolidation between the two initiatives (i.e., between 1962 and 1966).

The struggle among factions of the Chinese leadership about the appropriate economic strategy was not settled until Mao died in 1976. Under the headship of Deng Xiaoping, a fresh quest for economic growth and modernization emerged. Beginning with agriculture, reforms were implemented in several stages; there was not an overall blueprint from the start. The CCP summed up the core content of the reforms in 1997: 'the market, controlled at the macro level by the state, will serve as the basic means for the allocation of resources' (quoted from Andreassen 1999: 17).

Agriculture was reformed first. A system of household farming replaced the collectives. Private farm markets reopened in cities and rural areas; peasants could claim much higher prices for their products and they were allowed to set up small-scale undertakings in industry and service. In the industrial sector, a system of decentralization and less state control was combined with the introduction of private enterprise. An 'open door policy' was launched as early as 1980 with the aim of expanding foreign trade and welcoming foreign investment in the country. The major part of the economy's output is now traded at free market prices; the financial sector has introduced a stock exchange and a competitive banking system has replaced the old structure of one dominant state bank.

Some neoliberal scholars applaud the Chinese case as a model victory for a 'free market economy': market forces have been allowed to operate and that has led to rapid economic growth. It is certainly true that the mechanism of demand and supply is much more in use now than in earlier days of state control. But even after the reforms, the Chinese economic arrangement is quite some way from being a neoliberal 'free market' system. Price liberalization began in earnest only in the early 1990s, and many production inputs remain subject to regulation. Many large, unproductive state-owned enterprises have been kept afloat by the government although serious efforts are being made at reform. The labour market is not free: most people still need formal permission to move, especially when they want to go to the big cities. Land is, at least in formal terms, publicly owned and citizens cannot buy or sell land as they choose.

So, instead of a neoliberal 'free market' model, the state–market matrix in China is rather a 'market economy with special Chinese characteristics'. The model is based on two specific preconditions: first, the development achievements (and problems) during the period of Maoist rule; second, the Chinese political-economic culture which includes an entrepreneurial work ethic focused on the well-being of the family (Harrell 1985), a risk-taking, pragmatic and flexible approach to business and market opportunities; and a strong outward orientation, ready to develop transactions across borders. These cultural elements were present under Mao as well, of course; but they needed the conducive context of the Deng reforms to unfold their potential.

In some ways, it has been a startling economic success. Gross national income per capita stood at PPP $4,260 in 2001, which is more than seven times the income level of the mid-1970s. Exports and imports amounted to 44 per cent of GDP in 2001; behind the figure is the fastest growing rate of international trade ever experienced by any country over a sustained period of 25 years. Some 85 per cent of value added comes from industry (52 per cent) and services (33 per cent); a mere 15 per cent comes from agriculture. Yet poverty has not been eradicated; 19 per cent of the population has below $1 a day; 52 per cent has below $2 a day (all figures from World Bank 2003). Inequality has increased dramatically (the income distribution is now more unequal than in India), and corruption remains a major problem in Chinese society.

In sum, China has a market economy with a set of special twists reflecting the Chinese experience. One can point to 'state failures' (such as corruption) as well as 'market failures' (including inequality and unemployment) in the present system, but it has also produced unparalleled rates of economic change and growth.

China and the international order

China greatly emphasizes sovereignty and the norm of non-intervention. The history of foreign dominance is an important reason for this view. The official Chinese historical memory is about 'one hundred years of sufferings and humiliations' at the hands of Japan and Western powers. China's international isolation during the Cold War, especially after the separation from the Soviet Union, further strengthened the idea of a hostile and extremely competitive international environment.

China's economic opening to the world in the context of domestic reforms initiated a new period of Chinese participation in international society. Post-Mao China has joined a very large number of international regimes and organizations, some of which were previously criticized as parts of American hegemony. Most recently, China became a member of the World Trade Organization. In November 2000, President Jiang Zemin declared that a nation's participation in economic globalization is an 'objective requirement' for economic development. He went on to argue that globalization has a beneficial impact on international relations, in that 'closer economic and technological ties between nations and regions' make up 'a positive factor to promote world peace and stability' (quoted from B. Garrett 2001: 409).

The rapid change in China's relationship with the outside world creates a tension in its approach to international society and international order. On the one hand, China has increasingly adopted a more liberal view, according to which continued participation in economic globalization and further integration into the institutions of international society is the appropriate course for the country. On the other hand, a strict realist view, according to which international politics is essentially a struggle for power and relative advantage, continues to influence and perhaps even dominate among Chinese decision-makers. They 'continue to view the world as essentially conflict-prone, interstate relations as zero-sum power struggles, [and] violence as by no means a less common solution' (Deng 1998: 316).

Against this background, what kind of participant is China going to be in terms of international society and international order? We cannot know for sure; China is certainly joining the world but only reluctantly, and it remains a highly egoistic player. Despite some hardline nationalist opposition to globalization, there is every reason to believe that China will continue its policy of economic openness and political participation in international institutions, but China will surely also continue to be an unenthusiastic member of international society for some considerable time. It is possible that the forthcoming Olympic Games may have a positive effect, as they did in Korea. China will maintain a low profile in international institutions, with a narrow focus on its national interests. In the foreseeable future, the country will not become a member of the liberal community of states devoted to close cooperation.

India

Next to China, India is the only other country in the world with more than one billion people. The Indian subcontinent came under British rule in the eighteenth century and it therefore developed some of the typical traits of colonial economy: for instance, industrial development was held down because Lancashire producers dominated the Indian textile market. But British rule also brought a certain measure of law and order, and the construction of railways provided a basis for economic integration of the subcontinent. Especially during the world wars, when ties to Britain were severed, some industrial development could get under way. Yet it remained an overwhelmingly agrarian economy; at independence it was one of the poorest countries in the world, both in terms of per capita income and in terms of the number of people who could be considered poor, which came to close to half of the 360 million population.

Third World countries with socio-economic structures comparable to India's would almost always be subjected to authoritarian rule at independence, but British promotion of modern education and the rule of law had fostered an Indian stratum of liberal professionals. They were also the backbone of the independence movement, led by the Indian National Congress (INC). Mahatma Gandhi forged links between the INC and the masses of peasants in the countryside. They were mobilized for a strategy of 'non-violent non-cooperation' with the British. So, the peasant masses who made up the bulk of the people could count on some support from a government based on the rule of law. But other factors were in play, including ethnic conflict and abject poverty, which help to explain why people had reasons to feel insecure.

Security for the people in India

Hindus and Muslims could not agree to stay together. When British rule ended in 1947 power was transferred not to one but to two states: India and Pakistan. The partition was not orderly: there were perhaps as many as one million killings and ten million refugees in a two-way flow. Indo–Pakistani relations from then on made up the core security problem on the subcontinent. The legacy of partition was a bitter one, building great resentment on both sides. The conflict over Kashmir continues to this day, now in a context where both contenders are equipped with nuclear weapons; many Kashmiris have reached a point where they would rather be on their own than with either one of the parties.

The troubled relationship with Pakistan has been a decisive factor in India's relations with the great powers. Pakistan turned to the USA for help from the beginning. India emphasized non-alignment, but when armed border conflict broke out with China in the early 1960s, it began close cooperation with the Soviet Union. After the end of the Cold War, China focused on its own development; Russia is much less of a player in South Asia than was the USSR, and the USA concentrates on the terrorist threat and 'rogue states'. The conflict with Pakistan is again the central external security concern of India. But the relationship with China is also important; India senses it has to push economic growth in order to avoid getting too far behind China.

Partition left a large Muslim minority in India (over one hundred million people today), yet Nehru was determined to seek a secular state that should not discriminate against any minority. Indira Gandhi and her son, Rajiv, were much more ready to manipulate religious factions in their political games. In 1984, the army attacked the Golden Temple in Amritsar where Sikh radicals had set up headquarters. More than 500 were killed; the conflict led to the assassination of Indira Gandhi by Sikh bodyguards in the same year. Serious communal violence broke out again in 1992 when Hindu extremists demolished the Babra Mosque in Ayodhya (Manor 2001). Since then, Hindu nationalism has grown a great deal stronger, led by the Bharatiya Janata Party (BJP) and several other, more extremist organizations (Basu 2001). The Congress Party is a much weaker force for national unity than it used to be, and that has led to a new trend towards political decentralization, threatening a significantly more fragmented polity (Sandy 1997).

Yet religious and ethnic strife in India has never led to the extremes experienced in 'failed states'. The political system of pluralist politics remains resilient; it is able to promote accommodation and compromise. The BJP has followed a less extremist course in recent years; so has the political representation of Muslim forces. Furthermore, due to its political system, India has never been exposed to radical, experimental reforms of the kind inflicted upon the Chinese people. Most of the time, basic civil and human rights have, by and large, been protected. Policy excesses have been avoided; so have human disasters such as large-scale famines. But Indian democracy has also maintained a highly unequal social structure, headed by a dominant elite that resists structural change benefiting the poor. Raising the income levels of the rural poor has been a major objective of the nation's development policy for many years and yet, when it comes to practical implementation of the programmes, there has been very limited success, if any at all.

The ruling classes are able – within the democratic structure – to resist real change in this area. Thus, the lack of progress on the welfare dimension in India has led to human suffering and loss of life, not through spectacular disasters and catastrophes as in China, but through the quiet, continuous suffering of the absolute poor (more than one-third of the population). Democracy protects the people from extremist policies; it does not protect the people from elite dominance and lack of policies of basic reform (Sørensen 1991).

Welfare and growth in India

Congress leaders were not in agreement about the appropriate economic policies after independence. Gandhi had special ideas about self-reliance focused on agriculture and the villages. Patel and Nehru had different plans. Nehru eventually prevailed, emerging as the undisputed leader by 1951. His vision of economic development and the state–market relationship was much inspired by the planned economies. Emphasis was to be on the expansion of industry, especially heavy industry, in a context of five year plans with a substantial role for public enterprise. The development of the public sector was seen as a step on the road towards establishment of a 'socialistic pattern of society' (see Rudra 1985). Yet none of this was terrifying to the large industrial enterprises in the private sector; they were pleased with the development of a public sector because it provided cheap inputs of raw materials and energy (Martinussen 1980).

In agriculture, the Congress Party consolidated its political position through an alliance with landowners and caste-leaders. This meant that any radical plan for agrarian reform through redistribution of land was abandoned. Instead, a 'Green Revolution' strategy was adopted, aimed at increasing agricultural output through the use of fertilizers, irrigation, pesticides and new crop varieties. This was a policy of betting on the strong; it helped strengthen a *kulak* layer of rich farmers.

Overall, then, behind the socialist rhetoric and the five-year plans there was a model of development that built on the industrial bourgeoisie, the rich landowners and the bureaucracy: that is, the professionals and white-collar staff of the public sector (Bardhan 1984, 2001). Private industrialists enjoyed a protected domestic market and cheap inputs; landowners received price support for farm products, a wide range of subsidized inputs, and absurdly low levels of taxation. The bureaucracy retained the rights to grant licences and subsidies, and juggled with a wide range of regulatory controls of the private sector. This peculiar state/market matrix produced reasonable rates of economic growth, but the economy did less well in terms of being innovative, competitive and cost-effective. Widespread poverty, external debt and public deficits were other major problems connected with the model.

A significant shift in economic strategy took place in 1991, at the suggestion of the IMF and the World Bank, but also backed by local business elites. External trade was liberalized, import restrictions relaxed, the duty barriers reduced, foreign investment was encouraged, the rupee was devalued and made partially convertible, and a policy of privatization of public sector undertakings was initiated. This is usually seen as the starting signal for India's participation in economic globalization.

Some even speculate that the 'caged tiger' has now finally been let loose and that India is ready to follow the lead of other successful globalizers, not least China.

The truth is somewhat less romantic. Foreign investment is coming in, but in small amounts compared to China: by the mid-1990s, India received a mere 5 per cent of what came to China (Smitu 1997). The Indian infrastructure (roads, ports, energy) is not geared up to receive large amounts of foreign investment. Investors remain doubtful about the government's intentions. The spin-offs in terms of employment have been meagre because the traditional sectors are being squeezed while the modern sector provides only a limited increase in the workforce. Poverty remains widespread: 44 per cent of the population have less than $1 a day, and a staggering 86 per cent have less than $2 a day (World Bank 2003).

Some measures of liberalization have certainly been realized, but a huge number of subsidies remain in place; so do the fiscal deficit and an enormous public debt with interest payments claiming 5 per cent of GDP. In short:

> the changes are as yet not substantial and purposive enough to break the political logjam in the macroeconomy ... very little has been achieved in actually breaking the grip of the network of subsidies catering to the dominant interest groups ... or restructuring the management of public-sector companies and installing truly independent regulatory authorities (which involves seriously challenging the dominance of much of the obstructive bureaucracy and the pervasiveness of the nexus with the criminal underworld in pilfering public-sector-produced inputs at all levels of the enterprise hierarchy, or kickbacks from supply contracts or underinvoicing to buyer clients). (Bardhan 2001: 232)

India presently suffers from a particularly vicious combination of 'state failures' and 'market failures'. As regards the state, liberalization has not done away with bureaucracy, patronage, the proliferation of government handouts at all levels, or even a polity where, at state level, 'a significant number of elected politicians ... are crime bosses or their accomplices' (ibid.: 237). As regards the market, new private investment is not coming in to compensate for the public sector cutbacks, and new jobs are not being created in sufficient number. There are some benefits for the poor in this system because some of the government's handouts go to them; but it remains a hugely inefficient system which does not provide a solid, long-term basis for sustained economic growth and welfare improvement.

India and the international order

Far more than global issues, regional and domestic concerns have shaped India's external relations. In economic affairs, Nehru preferred self-reliance combined with regional cooperation. In foreign affairs, the relationship to Pakistan has overshadowed all other concerns. As regards the larger international order, India most strongly endorsed its membership of the Non-Aligned-Movement. Nehru took this stance in 1946: 'We propose, as far as possible, to keep away from the power politics of groups, aligned against one another' (quoted from Bradnock 1990: 16).

Non-alignment proved hard in the context of the Cold War. The USA strengthened its ties with Pakistan; India instead moved closer to the Soviet Union. The Sino–Soviet split coincided with the border conflict between India and China; that paved the way for the Indo–Soviet Treaty of Friendship signed in 1971. Western support for Pakistan's position on Kashmir in the UN further reinforced the rapport between India and the USSR.

With the end of the Cold War and of the Soviet Union, India would appear to be in a wholly new situation, but that is only partly the case. Regional concerns, including the relationship to Pakistan, continue, now as before, to be the defining axis of India's approach to international order, yet the context is a different one. In the Cold War days, India stressed fundamental principles of international order as the basis for its external relations: mutual respect for territorial integrity and sovereignty, mutual non-aggression, mutual non-interference in internal affairs, equality and mutual benefit, and peaceful coexistence. At the same time, in the regional context, India has always been ready for direct involvement in its neighbours' affairs and willing to apply force when it was considered necessary to protect the national interest, so in regional terms the lofty principles of international order have always been little more than self-righteous hypocrisy.

With a more fluid international situation after the Cold War, India will have to decide whether hard-nosed realism or liberal norms of mutual respect should be the guiding principles of its stance in foreign affairs. Early indications indicate support for the former. In early 2001, for example, India sought closer cooperation with the USA. India was one of a few major countries that approved of the Bush administration's declaration that it would continue its national missile defence (NMD) programme. '[W]hen set against the almost uniform condemnation that the Bush administration's announcement received from Moscow, Beijing, and most European capitals, the Indian reaction was widely, and probably accurately, viewed as a cynical endorsement undertaken in the hopes of obtaining concessions in other areas, most notably the lifting of sanctions' (Swamy 2002: 171).

Nonetheless, India will remain a primarily regional player for some considerable time. The country will be ready to resort to force to protect core national interests. Democracy has a long history in India, but a liberal, democratic peace in the region is nowhere in sight.

Russia

Russia (with a population of 146 million) emerged from the Soviet Union in 1991. The Soviet Union had been a large experiment in authoritarian socialism combined with a planned economy. This was not the original intention; Lenin and Trotsky saw Moscow as a temporary headquarters for socialism, hoping that revolutions would take place in Germany and elsewhere in the West. That did not happen, and Soviet attempts at economic cooperation with the leading capitalist countries were turned down. It was against this background that Stalin launched a strategy of 'socialism in one country', combining forced industrialization emphasizing heavy industry with a collectivized agriculture. The political system became an autocracy with all power vested in the Communist Party, and party power concentrated in one person, Josef Stalin. Nevertheless, the system was not a complete failure. It produced high rates of industrial growth and full employment. And the Soviet Union was, after all, capable of defeating Germany in the Second World War.

Yet it was clear after Stalin's death in 1953 that there were immense problems because the system lacked flexibility and capacity for innovation. Khrushchev, and leaders after him, were convinced that the command economy was fundamentally sound; what it needed was reforms in select areas. Gorbachev's reforms began from a similar premise: socialism was the superior system, it merely had to go through *perestroika* and *glasnost*. His own reform measures unleashed forces way beyond his control. Russia did not emerge from the Soviet Union according to a reform plan; it emerged because reformers did not have clear ideas about what should be put in place instead of the system they were dismantling (Hobsbawm 1994: 482).

Security for the people in Russia

The Soviet Union faced a hostile international environment from the beginning. The USA did not even diplomatically recognize the USSR until 1933. Still, the external threat was not severe during most of the interwar period; the capitalist countries were in economic crisis and preoccupied with their own problems. Stalin focused on what he saw as the domestic threat. He introduced a rule of repression, coercion and terror, and was responsible for the extermination of millions of people, and of a whole generation of political leaders.

In Stalin's Soviet Union, therefore, the security situation for ordinary people was indeed peculiar. On the one hand, the system delivered work, basic education and health, and thus, the satisfaction of human needs on a low level, at least for most of the people part of the time (collectivization of agriculture also produced famines and human disasters). On the other hand, people – and even members of the elite – were permanently in mortal danger of falling into disfavour. Stalin sent millions of people to the labour camps and purged the party several times.

Khrushchev emptied the gulags and wanted to increase the living standards of workers and peasants. As in the case of China, external threat was an incentive for the political elite to keep its house in order and ensure domestic support for the regime. But the terror balance based on nuclear weapons provided a special twist to the external threat: both Cold War contenders were actively interested in avoiding an all-destructive nuclear confrontation. So external threat was muted: the nuclear balance provided a shield behind which developmental experiments could take place. There was no pressure for immediate success.

At the same time, attempts to reform the system were always constrained by a basic premise: any reform must not threaten the power and position of the socio-political elite which had monopolized political, economic and social power: the *nomenklatura*. We now know that it proved impossible to revitalize the system under those conditions.

The new conditions – a Russia in transition towards some form of market economy and some form of a more open political system – have fundamentally changed the security equation for ordinary people. On the one hand, the days of stable employment and a predictable life within a social structure characterized by a high level of equality (if the fundamental gap between masses and elite is discounted) are gone. New opportunities for wealth and upward mobility have appeared, but so have unemployment, marginalization, and social and economic crisis. Within a very short period (1989–94), life expectancy for Russian men dropped from 64 to 57 years (Aslund 2001). Opinion polls reveal the deep sense of longing in many people, for the predictability and the safety of the old system (Saunders 2001).

On the other hand, the days of living in mortal danger, of risking the labour camps, are gone. This does not mean that present-day Russia safeguards human rights in every respect. One group monitoring the human rights situation in Russia recently stated that 'there is not a single region in Russia where the observance of human rights would meet international requirements' (quoted from Mendelson 2002: 49). The worst problems are connected with the second war in Chechnya that reportedly involves indiscriminate use of force against both Chechens and Russians. On another level, there are the individuals who have been 'investigated, intimidated, interrogated, jailed, accused of treason, or beaten by federal authorities. In addition to journalists, they include environmentalists, human rights activists, students and academics' (Mendelson 2002: 47–8).

For most people, the situation has surely improved in the sense that they live under a much less repressive system than before; but, in contrast to China, the transformation has not yet delivered substantial improvement in the socio-economic conditions of daily life.

Welfare and growth in Russia

The planned economy developed under Stalin was an autarkic system, even more so than its leaders had wanted, because of the Western embargo of the USSR. The embargo was eased in 1954, leading to increased economic exchange with the West. The desire to open up to the world market was re-emphasized by Brezhnev in the 1970s, but neither this nor other reform measures of the planned economy were capable of overcoming the problems of decreasing productivity and lack of economic efficiency in general.

Russia attempted a rapid transition to a market economy through 'shock therapy', supported by the international financial institutions. On 1 January, 1992, price controls of most goods were eliminated; liberalization of trade policies, privatization and currency convertibility quickly followed. The transformation was accompanied by a substantial inflow of foreign capital in terms of loans and aid.

Many observers find that there was too much 'shock' and too little 'therapy' in the Russian transition to a market economy. Russia averaged a negative growth rate of minus 0.2 per cent between 1990 and 2001 (World Bank 2003). This average figure conceals great variations, including huge setbacks up to 1998 and more than 5 per cent growth rates since 1999. The dramatic downturn was due to the fact that Russia did not have the appropriate institutions for a market economy in place. It takes time to prepare an orderly privatization, a legal framework for market competition and contracts, and so on.

Therefore privatization took place in a way that handed the nation's treasures on a plate – that is, the natural resources, especially the oil and gas industry – to a small group of speculators, the oligarchs. That has created problems for the entire transition to a market economy. The oligarchs have:

> impeded significant and transparent economic reform. Successive economic policies have been characterized by varying degrees of political commitment to reform, including often contradictory measures. Ongoing problems include inadequately developed legal and financial systems, wage arrears, a seriously flawed banking system, widespread corruption throughout virtually all sectors of the economy, and a large informal economy. Interior Ministry officials maintain that in Moscow markets alone, illegal turnover, none of which is taxed, amounts to $5.6 billion a year and employs some 245,000 people. (Karatnycky 2002: 331)

Capital flight out of Russia is estimated at $20–25 billion for 2001, due to the poor climate for investment. About one-third of the population is below the national poverty line (World Bank 2003). Some commentators see light at the end of the tunnel for Russia because economic growth has picked up in the last two to three years (Aslund 2001); others remain very sceptical (Karatnycky 2002; Saunders 2001). There is no doubt that very serious problems continue to plague Russia. Democracy has deteriorated recently because Vladimir Putin is attempting to concentrate power in the executive branch and does not have links to a political party. The two other major groups in Russian society today are the oligarchs and the regional political elites. It is most certainly a misunderstanding to imply that Putin has declared war on the oligarchy: on the contrary, he has allowed it to retain the fortunes made from the privatization deals. The ambition is to make the oligarchs pay more tax and to reduce their meddling in the government. That is the reasoning behind the pressure applied to selected tycoons, such as Boris Berezovsky and Vladimir Gusinsky. Eventually, the hope is that the oligarchs will start behaving like responsible capitalists and emphasize long-term productive investment instead of capital export and asset-stripping (Karatnycky 2002: 333).

In addition to the oligarchs, there are the problems of a large informal economy and an unreformed industrial sector with enterprises that take away more value than they add: that is, they do not merely lag in productivity, they are actually counterproductive. This sector makes up a 'virtual economy' with business conducted at non-market, or 'virtual', prices. It persists because it provides jobs and pensions, but it is no basis for sustained economic progress (Gaddy and Ickes 1998).

In sum, the current state–market matrix in Russia is both peculiar and problematic. It is peculiar because what is supposed to be a market economy is rather a mixture of an informal sector, unreformed industry and oligarch dominance. It is problematic because at the moment Russia has the worst of both worlds: not enough state and not enough market. The state has not, in a very short time, been able to set up the institutions and implement the rules of the game needed for a market to function appropriately. The market thus covers only part of the economy and what market there is remains overly directed towards short-term financial gain rather than long-term capital accumulation.

Russia and the international order

During the Cold War, the Soviet Union was a global player, projecting its interests to all areas of the globe in the competition with the USA. The attempt to play an active global role stretched Soviet resources far beyond its limits; eventually it contributed to the demise of the USSR. It is abundantly clear that Russia does not have the capacity to play a global role (Bluth 1998: 324). Russia has dismantled its activities in the Third World and it no longer seeks continued dominance of Eastern Europe. Its focus is on domestic problems including the conflict in Chechnya and on the near abroad: Russia still needs full settlement of its borders with China, Japan and the Baltic republics. In addition, the Caspian Sea borders involving Azerbaijan, Iran, Kazakhstan and Turkmenistan are not yet determined.

A contradiction exists between continued Russian great power ambitions and the reality of its more modest current circumstances. Russia's stressing of its great power role is encouraged by the way in which the great powers in the Group of 7 (G7) have invited Russian participation in an enlarged Group of 8 (G8). Russia's more assertive stance is especially emphasized by democratic forces' loss of influence within Russia. As indicated earlier, major factions of the old regime in Russia continue to exert immense power today. They include 'the armed forces, the military-industrial complex, the gas and oil industries, the agricultural sector and the security service (the successors to the KGB [the state security organization])' (ibid.: 325).

With little domestic change in the direction of more support for democratic forces and institutions, the currently dominant groups in Russia have reached a consensus that Russia remains a great power. 'This means that while Russia seeks a cooperative relationship with the West, it does so on equal terms and it will not toe the Western line in international organizations. [Furthermore], Russia claims the right to a dominant position in the former Soviet space, which remains its special sphere of influence' (ibid.).

As in the cases of China and India, Russia is no enthusiastic member of the international society. It is strictly focused on its national interests and jealously guards its special role in the former Soviet space, the Commonwealth of Independent States. Russia may be a G8 member, but it is not at all closely related to the liberal community of states.

Conclusion: modernizing states and the debate about the state

The debate between retreat and state-centric scholars fails to capture what really goes on in modernizing states. These states certainly contain weak elements, as we have seen, but it is highly misleading to say that modernizing states are in retreat. They are in a process of transformation to states in a market economy. That process demands that the state is growing stronger in a number of respects: it needs the relevant institutions, rules and regulations, and instruments of supervision for making the market economy work smoothly. It also needs a more efficient bureaucratic apparatus, an increased ability to collect taxes, and so on. At the same time, there are areas of state activity previously dominated by state enterprises, by central plans, by bureaucrats, that are now reduced or completely dismantled: that is an integrated part of the transition to a market economy. This whole transition is complicated by the fact that powerful social groups are not necessarily interested in creating a new system. In all three countries, some groups profit from bureaucracy and patronage; they actively work against a successful transition. In both India and Russia, and even to some extent in China, these groups have had considerable success.

The point in the present context is that this complex process of transition cannot be grasped with any simple notion of 'retreat', and neither can it be grasped with a similarly simple notion of state-centrism. Specifically, we have seen how the problems of security for the people of modernizing states play out in ways not foreseen in the standard notion of modern statehood. At the same time, the modernizing states' approach to the international order is profoundly shaped by the twists and turns of their own transitions. Neither the peculiar security problem nor the special elements in relation to international order can be grasped through the lens of the 'state-centric' approach.

Instead of either the retreat or the state-centric approach, the modernizing states must be understood as what they really are: as systems in a complex and contradictory process of transformation, profoundly changing states from what they were but not subjecting them to a simple process of becoming either 'weaker' or 'stronger'.

Chapter 9

Transformation to What? And Why? Sovereign Statehood in a New Millennium

Our starting point in this book was the debate on what is happening to the sovereign state. This chapter sets forth my own view about how the state has been transformed. I formulate that view in terms of different ideal types of state, the idea being to avoid unnecessary empirical detail and focus on the major aspects of state transformation.

Chapter 1 emphasized that we need some notion of what the state looked like earlier – a baseline – in order to assess the extent to which change has taken place. The typical features of the modern, Westphalian state as it had developed mainly in Western Europe and North America around 1950 represent such a baseline (see Box 1.1, p. 14). Chapters 2–4 analysed each of these features (i.e., economy, government and nationhood) in order to find out about the changes in statehood which have taken place. Taken together, these changes indicate a transformation of the modern state. What has taken its place?

The postmodern state – and a few words about what caused it

It was emphasized in Chapter 1 that state transformation is the rule and not the exception: states have always undergone development and change. The modern, Westphalian state of the mid-twentieth century has been transformed. We cannot be entirely sure about what has taken its place because the changes are still in progress. Major developments are easier to identify after the event; the development of the modern

161

state, for example, was under way for many decades, even hundreds of years. We now know, in retrospect, that the modern state came to full maturity by the mid-twentieth century, but we are much less sure where the current process of state change will take us because that process has only lasted a few decades and is still unfolding. That is why I suggest the label of 'the postmodern state' as a way of summarizing those changes still under way. As already pointed out, the 'post-' prefix is a way of emphasizing that we are not quite clear on what shape and form the postmodern state will eventually take but, at the same time, we are quite certain that it is different from the modern state. The reader should be warned that the label 'postmodern' is being used in several different ways by scholars, some of which do not correspond at all to the way it is used here.

Our present situation can be compared with the situation in which the observers of the modern state found themselves during the first part of the nineteenth century; they knew that big political, economic and other changes were taking place, but they were not quite sure where they were going to lead in the end because the modern state came to full maturity only many years later. We also know today that big political, economic and other changes are still taking place, but we are not quite sure where they are going to lead. Nevertheless, we want to make sense of what is going on. The ideal type of the postmodern state is an attempt to do just that, and Box 9.1 sets out its key features in a format allowing direct comparison with the ideal type modern state set out in Box 1.1.

Other chapters have discussed what this transformation means for the role of the state and especially for the ways in which the state can or cannot uphold the basic social values we have come to expect from it: security, welfare and growth, and international order. But what about

Box 9.1	*The postmodern state*
Government	Multilevel governance in several interlocked arenas overlapping each other. Governance in context of supranational, international, transgovernmental and transnational relations.
Nationhood	Supranational elements in nationhood, both with respect to the 'community of citizens' and the 'community of sentiment'. Collective loyalties increasingly projected away from the state.
Economy	'Deep integration': major part of economic activity is embedded in cross-border networks. The 'national' economy is much less self-sustained than it used to be.

the causes of this change from the modern to the postmodern state: how and why has it taken place? This is a big question, as are most of the interesting questions in social science, so the answer is bound to be complex. We can surely not expect any single factor – whether economic, political, social, cultural or other – to be completely responsible for this comprehensive transformation, so we are looking for a broader set of different factors.

What kind of broader set are we looking for? In the social world, everything is, in the final analysis, connected with everything else. So, in the widest sense, every action – historical or contemporary – undertaken by groups or by individuals is, in principle, relevant for inclusion in the set of factors that we are looking for. It ought to be obvious that the facts alone will not offer us an explanation of the transition from modern to postmodern statehood; they simply point in too many different directions, and they do not offer us a way of distinguishing between more and less promising explanatory roads to take. For that undertaking, we need theory. The primary task of theory is to discriminate between what is more important and what is less important; theory offers a way to organize all the bewildering empirical facts because it is an analytical tool that directs our attention towards certain facts and leaves others in the dark. Theory makes sense of the world by focusing on selected parts of it and by suggesting a certain ordering of those parts into patterns that help us understand what is going on. No explanation is possible without some theory, or at least some fragments of theory.

Theory is necessary; so far so good. But there are many different theories to choose from, as we are painfully aware. How to pick the right one? Facts may help; we know, for example, that economic globalization is an important factor in state transformation, a subject analysed in Chapter 2. That points us in the direction of theories emphasizing economic globalization, but there are still many theories to choose from. Just as facts alone do not offer an explanation of what is going on, facts alone cannot guide us all the way in the selection of theories.

This is where values come in. Our values point us in certain directions; they make us more interested in some subjects and less interested in others; and within given subjects, they influence the way in which we approach them. Values are an integrated part of any research undertaking; they cannot and should not be left out completely. But values must never dominate the enterprise because when that is the case, they determine our entire view of the world: fact and theory become irrelevant. The radical Muslim or the radical Christian or the radical Communist will have a certain view of the world irrespective of facts and theories. Such a pure value view can never be the belief of a social scientist; it is rather the view of a priest or a disciple of a certain faith.

The social scientist, by contrast, must respect the importance of facts and theories even if he or she is guided by certain convictions or values. Social science cannot and must not be based purely on personal faith and convictions, or what amounts to purely subjective valuations. The social scientist must produce what is called 'intersubjectively transmissible knowledge' (Brecht 1965: 113–16; Rasmussen 1971: 14–19). That means, quite simply, that it is possible to check every part of the analysis, including the theoretical approach and its meta-theoretical foundation as well as the empirical data.

The social science 'research triangle' (cf. Galtung 1977), then, is made up of the three elements shown in Figure 9.1. Good research within social science needs all three corners of the triangle, even if they can be present in combinations of different relative importance depending on the task at hand. This is really a long story (see, e.g., Galtung 1977). The important point here is the need for all three elements to be present and to be aware of the dangers of retreating to one of the corners, neglecting the others. Relying purely on data is akin to descriptive journalism, merely reporting about events. Relying purely on theory is akin to philosophy, withdrawing into abstract thinking, not analysing the real world. Relying purely on values is akin to preaching, merely emphasizing certain values.

So, how can the research triangle be of help in the present analysis? Let us see what we have in terms of the triangle. In the data corner, we have the transformation from modern to postmodern state; in the value corner, we are motivated by a desire to discover what is happening to the state: in that broad sense we are 'truth seekers' and we do not have any particular ideological or other 'value axes' to grind. Given that starting point, how do we approach the selection of theory in the

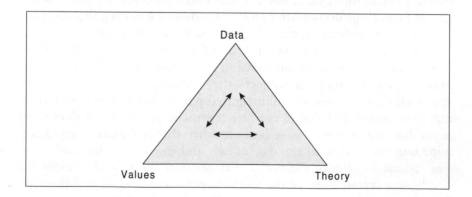

Figure 9.1 *The social science triangle*

theory corner? Simply by finding 'the current version of the theoretical truth' as the scholarly community of social scientists working in our area see it. That is to say, we want to identify the dominant theories addressing our research question as they are to be found in the current scholarly debate about it. Our own ambition is to drive the scholarly debate a further step forward, to refine and nuance the current version of 'the truth'. At the end of the day, that is what social science research is all about.

The only difficulty is that there are a great number of different theories to choose from. 'The current version of the theoretical truth' is certainly no objective entity so, even if we are guided by an ambition to find the truth, our theoretical choices can never be objective. Any selection of theory, including the one below, can always be questioned and criticized. But this is not a problem; criticism of this kind is what much of the scholarly debate is about anyway. As long as we are open and clear about what we do, as long as we strive to produce intersubjectively transmissible knowledge, we are on the right track. The ambition is not to end the scholarly debate by discovering some sort of 'final truth' because there is no such final truth. The activity in the research triangle never stops. Fresh data in the data corner, a different ordering of values in the value corner, and new theories in the theory corner will see to it that the debate goes on. The ambition can never be to end the debate, therefore, but merely to submit a contribution to it.

How to explain the transformation from modern to postmodern statehood

Recall the question that sparked the above remarks: what causes the change from modern to postmodern statehood? No single factor can be responsible for this; we are looking for clusters of factors. Such clusters come in the form of major theories addressing the research question. In my opinion, there are three major theories to choose from: one theory comes out of the realist tradition. It stresses the role of states: that is, of governments and state leaders. Another theory is based on the liberal tradition. It stresses the role of international institutions and of individuals and groups in society. The final theory comes out of the critical tradition. It stresses the interplay between states and markets in the general development of a capitalist system. The reader will recall these theories from the introduction of them in Chapter 1, where they were presented as 'three main ways of looking at states and power'. In the present context, they are employed in order to understand the transition from modern to postmodern statehood. The theories do not focus specifically on the issue of why postmodern states emerge, but we may infer their answers to this question from their general analyses.

Realism

Realism casts the states as the principal and most powerful actors. They are the principals because they set the rules for everyone else; other actors (organizations, companies, groups, individuals) have to play by the rules created by states. They are the most powerful because they control the means of violence and a host of other power resources. Governments and state leaders are highly autonomous in relation to their societies, providing them with a lot of room for manoeuvre.

Against this background, realists suggest that the transformation from modern to postmodern statehood has basically happened because states (i.e., leaders and governments) – and especially the most powerful states – wanted it to happen. Western states, led by the USA, deemed it in their own self-interest to pursue a much closer cooperation after the Second World War, in the context of the East–West confrontation. Furthermore, the USA and her wartime Western allies wanted to create a framework of cooperative linkages and national structures which ensured that Germany and Japan would not again emerge as belligerent powers. The close cooperation initiated by the leading states opened the path to the multilevel governance and globalized economies of postmodern states.

Starting from the idea of strong states deciding what they want to do, realist analysis can move in different directions, all of which cannot be treated in detail here. The dominant variant of realist thinking about close cooperation between states is called 'hegemonic stability theory'. It posits that a hegemon, a dominant military and economic power, is necessary for the creation and full development of a cooperative, liberal world market economy (Gilpin 1987; Kindleberger 1973). A hegemon is needed, so the theory goes, because the goods it provides are collective goods that can benefit everybody, such as a currency system for international payments or the chance to trade in a free market. To supply such goods requires resources that only strong countries possess. Furthermore, a strong state is needed in order to discipline or punish possible free riders: that is, states making use of collective goods without contributing anything to the system.

The dominant state needs a number of different power resources to perform the role of a hegemon (Keohane 1984: 32). In addition to military power, it requires control over four sets of major economic resources: raw materials; sources of capital; markets; and a competitive advantage in the production of goods that can command a high price. Tangible power resources alone are not enough. The dominant state must also be willing to take on the responsibility for creating a cooperative, liberal world order. The USA had the power to lead the creation of such an order in the 1930s but she became willing to do so only after the Second World War.

So, after the Second World War the USA took the lead in setting up the institutional framework of a liberal world order. The Bretton Woods institutions were the backbone of that order: the IMF, the World Bank and the GATT (now the WTO). In Europe, the USA pushed for close cooperation between her West European allies. The reconstruction of Japan and the country's integration in the Western camp was also masterminded by the USA.

One possible critique of this realist theory concerns the all-pervasive role of the hegemon. Can it really be true that the entire postwar development in the triad of Western Europe, North America and Japan was, in the main, directed by the leaders of the dominant power? Two objections suggest themselves. One is that other states were very much involved, even if the USA took the lead. European cooperation, for example, has been dominated by the European participants in the process, not by the USA. Another objection concerns the role of non-state actors, including organizations, companies, groups and individuals. Are they not the true drivers of cooperation and, therefore, the real forces behind the transition from modern to postmodern statehood? That is the liberal view which will be discussed shortly. As to the first objection, about the role of other states, that will not make most realists uncomfortable because even if it points away from the hegemon, it confirms that states are indeed the masters of their own fate and the driving forces behind state transformation.

Still, there is an additional way of challenging the realist view about the leading role of states which concerns the assumption realists make about states as unitary and coherent actors. The assumption contends that the state is one single actor expressing one single national interest. But we know many different actors claim to represent the state, and that 'the national interest' is really an amalgamation of a number of different views and demands, competing with each other. In short, even if states play an important role in their transition from modern to postmodern statehood, the entire process is somewhat more complex than many realists appear ready to admit.

Liberals

Liberals, as we saw in Chapter 1, are sceptical of the realist idea about states as unitary and coherent actors. According to them, relations between states are much more complex and take place on many different levels. International relations increasingly look like domestic politics with a composite array of issues and coalitions. One major reason for this is that states represent societies that are themselves complex, with many different groups and varieties of interests. The transition from modern to postmodern statehood, on this view, is driven much more by groups, individuals and organizations in society than it is driven by states. The practice of 'citizenship without moorings', mentioned in Chapter 5, is another indicator of how people are leading the way in connecting societies across borders. Commercial exchange for the benefit of all is yet another driving force in the process.

Another strand of liberal thinking focuses more on the role of international regimes and institutions as drivers of the transition from modern to postmodern statehood. International institutions are more than mere handmaidens of strong states. They are of independent importance and they can promote cooperation between states. International institutions provide information and opportunities for negotiation; they improve the abilities of governments to monitor mutual compliance, and they serve to strengthen the solidity and trustworthiness of international agreements (Keohane 1989). The institutions of the European Union, for example, have played a significant role in the process of European integration. Both the Commission and the European Court have led the way towards a much closer relationship between member states in several areas.

Finally, liberals feel vindicated by the emergence of multilevel governance in the context of postmodern statehood. The fact that governance now takes place in a framework of supranational, transgovernmental and transnational relations is highly consistent with liberal expectations. In sum, for liberals a primary force in the transition from modern to postmodern statehood is the efforts of people, groups and organizations from society as well as international institutions. States do play a role, but that role is not nearly as significant as implied by realists.

Critical theorists

Critical theory, the third and final approach to be taken up here, contains a variety of theories about the relationship between politics and economics. In the present context, it is relevant to focus on theories about the relationship between states and markets. Even within this category, there are several contributions to choose from (e.g., Cox 1994; Gill 1994; Hoogvelt 2001; Stopford and Strange 1993) but, in broad terms, they share a common argument. This argument posits that global markets – and the major actors in those markets, the transnational corporations in production, distribution and finance – are the major driving forces in the current process of transformation. Once states have helped set up deregulated economies and open markets, they unleash economic forces over which they have no firm control. These forces push for further economic globalization and tend to force a process of adaptation on states.

For present purposes, let me focus on the contribution by Robert Cox. He argues that the present phase of capitalist development is related to the crisis of the Bretton Woods system set up after the Second World War. The system fell into crisis in the early 1970s:

> During this period, the balanced compromise of Bretton Woods shifted toward subordination of domestic economies to the perceived exigencies of a global economy. States willy-nilly became more effectively accountable to a *nébuleuse* [observity] personified as the global economy ... The crisis of the post-war order has expanded the breadth and the depth of a global economy that exists alongside and incrementally supersedes the classical international economy. (Cox 1994: 46, 48)

At the same time, the financial sector has become increasingly important. On the one hand, governments need to borrow, so they 'have to care about their international credit ratings' (ibid.: 47). On the other hand, manufacturing industrial corporations are also dependent on financial manipulators. 'Finance has become decoupled from production to become an independent power, an autocrat over the real economy' (ibid.: 48).

In Cox's view, then, states are being transformed in a process of economic globalization which they themselves have helped initiate; now, however, the new realities of a globalized economy put new constraints on states:

> The state becomes a transmission belt from the global to the national economy, where heretofore it had acted as the bulwark defending domestic welfare from external disturbances. Power within the state becomes concentrated in those agencies in closest touch with the global economy – the offices of presidents and prime ministers, treasuries, central banks. The agencies more closely identified with domestic clients – ministries of industry, labour ministries, etc. – become subordinated ... Out of the crisis of the post-war order, a new global political structure is emerging. The old Westphalian concept of a system of sovereign states is no longer an adequate way of conceptualizing world politics. Sovereignty is an ever looser concept. The old legal definitions conjuring up visions of ultimate and fully autonomous power are no longer meaningful. (Cox 1994: 49, 52)

Summary

We have looked at three different ways of explaining the transformation from modern to postmodern statehood. Realists focus on the states themselves; the transformation took place because states (governments), especially the leading states, wanted it to happen. Liberals focus on the role of groups and individuals in society or on international institutions as the major players in the transformation. And finally, critical theorists focus on the dynamics of global capitalist development.

Who is right? One possibility is that all are wrong because they missed something important. A possible candidate here is the role of technology. Without innovations in transport technology, communication technology and the ability to split up complicated production processes into segments which are then scattered worldwide, the transformation to postmodern statehood could not take place. But it is hardly the presence of technology by itself that explains what is going on. Technology has to be put to use by actors; left alone it plays no role, present or not. It is more instructive to look at technology as an *enabling condition* for the transformation (for an emphasis on the role of technology, see Dror 2001). It is needed as part of the process but does not in itself explain it.

So, we return to the three explanations. Each one sounds plausible on its own terms. It also appears that each is open in the sense that it is ready to accept some insights from the others. That leads us towards a combination of the three. Realists make a valid point when they emphasize the role of leading states, especially the USA, in setting up a new international order after the Second World War. Strong states did lead the way in constructing the international framework within which cooperation and all kinds of increased interdependence between countries could unfold. We may quarrel about the relative preponderance of the USA compared to other states and about the degree to which states are really unitary and coherent actors, but none of that invalidates the main point about the crucial role of states.

Once states have established the appropriate conditions, groups, individuals and organizations from society can step in. So can the players in the marketplace. They are the real drivers of transformation; they do the legwork. But states are never far away: they supervise the entire process and they become very visible in periods of crisis where it is necessary to re-establish or re-organize the existing conditions.

This may sound as a vindication of the realist view, yet there is an additional aspect which realists have not taken into account: states do affect societies and markets, but societies and markets also affect states. Economic globalization created by the market players, and much intensified interdependence created by groups and individuals in societies, compel states to change. They are driven to demand more international cooperation, and they become more dependent on world markets. More international cooperation means an increased role for international institutions, as foreseen by liberals. Dependence on world markets makes states more attentive to the demands of market players. It is a two-way street and it is exactly this interaction between states on the one hand and societies/markets on the other which – in the broadest terms – explains the transformation from modern to postmodern statehood. Figure 9.2 summarizes this view.

The states behind the new postwar order were modern states. By setting up a new international order, they took a first step towards their own transformation. Actors from society and markets stepped in and created a world of interdependent societies and global markets. That whole process pushed states in a new direction, towards multilevel governance. The result is the postmodern state. The process of change has not stopped; that is why we cannot be sure about what shape and form the postmodern state will eventually take (if indeed it does end up in some stable state).

The general controversy between retreat and state-centric scholars lurks immediately behind the different ways of explaining the transition from modern to postmodern statehood. State-centric scholars will be comfortable with the view that this is all engineered and masterminded by states, while retreat scholars will emphasize how the changes have made states dependent on the market and actors from society, and how markets and societies affect states. Figure 9.2 contains both views, so in that sense both are correct. States dominate certain phases of the

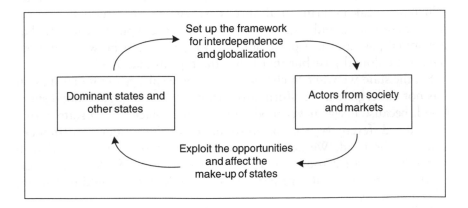

Figure 9.2   *From modern to postmodern statehood*

process of transformation; societies and markets dominate other phases. Note also that the accent here is on 'transformation' rather than on states 'losing' or 'winning'. Quite possibly, postmodern states have grown stronger in some respects and weaker in others compared to modern states. A calculation of the net result is extremely difficult because a precise assessment of state capacities must always be tied to specific issues or arenas.

The weak postcolonial state – and a few words about what caused it

The transformation from modern to postmodern statehood discussed above concerns the advanced states in the triad. It does not accurately portray the states in the Third World, in particular the weakest states, primarily concentrated in sub-Saharan Africa. At the same time, the analysis in the preceding chapters has made it quite clear that the weakest states are qualitatively different from the modern states. So, how do we characterize these weak states and what are the causes behind their emergence?

Before answering this question, a few words about terminology. I have used the term 'weak' states above, meaning the least developed countries in the Third World. 'Weak' is not the ideal term because many will think of states that are weak with regard to military power and that is not the meaning here. Sometimes the term 'weak' is used in another way, to designate states that have 'strong' societies and 'weak' state institutions (such as the USA) in contrast to states that have 'weak' societies and 'strong' state institutions (such as France), but that is not what is meant here either. In this book, the term is used to designate states which are weak in terms of all three core aspects of statehood: government, nationhood and economy. In this sense, the typical weak state has a colonial past and is a postcolonial state (states can be weak without having a colonial past but that is not the typical pattern).

So, the state we want to characterize is the weak, postcolonial state. It has not undergone a transformation from modern to postcolonial statehood, because it was never modern in the first place. It is a state with a radically different type of background from the modern/postmodern states of the triad. We need to study it because there are several such states in the world today. If we focused merely on modern and postmodern states, a significant part of the world's states would be left out of our analysis.

Pulling together the conclusions of Chapters 2 to 4, the weak, postcolonial state can be characterized in ideal typical terms as in Box 9.2.

Box 9.2	*The weak postcolonial state*
Government	Inefficient and corrupt administrative and institutional structures. Rule based on coercion rather than the rule of law. Monopoly on the legitimate use of violence not established.
Nationhood	Predominance of local/ethnic community. Neither the 'community of citizens' nor the 'community of sentiment' has developed to become the primary bond between people. Low level of state legitimacy.
Economy	Incoherent amalgamations of traditional agriculture, an informal petty urban sector, and some fragments of modern industry. Significant dependence on the world market and on external economic interest.

A more detailed analysis of the weak, postcolonial state has been offered in previous chapters. Presently, it is relevant to ask how this type of state emerged in the first place. What are the major causes behind the weak, postcolonial state? We return to the three theories discussed above and infer the answers from their general analyses. The realist tradition focuses on the role of leading states. In an earlier phase, these states played the role of colonisers. It was noted in Chapter 5 that the colonial period frequently had too little to offer the colonies in terms of overall development; they remained backward. Decolonization after the Second World War took place in a new international order which was dominated by the USA and the Soviet Union. Both countries pushed for an end of colonial empires; the old colonial powers, Britain and France, were much more hesitant but they now held second rank in the international system.

The leading states in the postwar international system pressed for decolonization, meaning the independence of existing colonial territories, no matter how weak they were politically, economically, or in any other way. The UN general assembly declaration (Resolution 1514) stated that 'all peoples have the right to self-determination'. The formulation did not mean that individuals and groups were to decide about which communities they wanted to belong to. The 'nations' that were entitled to self-determination were not nations in any community sense, but were the people living within given colonial borders. In effect, the right of 'peoples' meant the right of existing colonies to independence. Furthermore, it did not matter that the colonies were weak states politically, economically, and in terms of national cohesion. Declaration 1514 explicitly declared that 'inadequacy of political, economic, social or educational preparedness should never serve as a pretext for delaying independence' (quoted from Jackson 1990: 77).

Weak, postcolonial states have a certified life insurance, deposited with the UN and backed by the leading states of the system. That life insurance guarantees the absence of external mortal danger, no matter how bad things may look in the domestic realm. That is to say, international society, led by the dominant states, has decided to accept the existence of weak, postcolonial states. In earlier days, such weak entities would have been gulped up by stronger states, as has happened many times in the history of European state-making. The situation today is different. The weak entities persist because the international society of states wants it that way (Jackson 1990).

Liberals take a different view of the weak, postcolonial state. Development experiences in the Third World show great variation. Not all states with a colonial background have become weak and underdeveloped; some have done better. Liberals focus on social forces in society in order to explain the difference. In general, Third World countries can be expected to follow the same path of development as that taken earlier by the developed countries in the West: a progressive transition from a traditional, pre-industrial, agrarian society towards a modern, industrial society. Development means overcoming the barriers of pre-industrial production, backward institutions and parochial value systems which impede the process of growth and modernization (see, e.g., Rostow 1960, 1978). But in some countries the traditional forces in society (landowners, moneylenders, farmers, and so on) remain strong. In alliance with political elites, they can halt the process of modernization and economic progress. The liberal explanation, then, stresses the role of groups in society that resist modernization.

Critical theory has a number of different contributions to choose from. Most relevant in the present context is neo-Marxist analysis of Third World economic dependency. Radical dependency theorists (Amin 1976, 1990; Frank 1969) argue that underdevelopment is caused by factors external to the poor countries. It is due to domination by foreign economic interests originating in the developed West. These forces cripple and distort societal structures inside Third World countries. Third World dependency and underdevelopment, therefore, is the result of a global process of uneven capitalist development. The radical dependency explanation thus emphasizes the negative role of foreign economic interests as the primary factor in understanding weak, postcolonial statehood.

All three explanations appear to contain relevant insights. The role of leading states is undeniable. They were the major players, both as holders of colonial empire and, in a later phase, as leaders in the process of decolonization. The weak, postcolonial states would hardly be able to exist if international society had not set up a framework within which weak states can disintegrate in the extreme (e.g., Somalia, Sierra Leone, Liberia and the Congo), but still retain formal membership of the international society of states and be officially recognized as independent, sovereign entities.

Yet liberals are perfectly right in underlining the fact that the experiences of Third World states vary. A colonial past and a process of decolonization do not inevitably lead to underdevelopment and misery. Some countries with a colonial past have done very well, such as Taiwan or South Korea. It takes the active effort of social forces in society in alliance with state elites to create development and prosperity; but it takes an equally active effort of those forces to create underdevelopment and misery, as liberals point out.

Radical dependency theorists have a point when they call attention to the possibly negative effects of foreign economic interests. But these theorists tend to downplay overly an aspect analysed in Chapter 2: foreign economic interests do not create underdevelopment – or development – on their own. The effects of their presence are always connected to the environment in which they function, especially to the economic and political capacities of host countries. It is true that weak, postcolonial states are poorly equipped to benefit from foreign investment, but foreign investment does not always and everywhere produce underdevelopment.

In sum, we need insights from all three approaches in order fully to explain the emergence of weak, postcolonial states. I have implied that my own ordering of the approaches in terms of relative explanatory value corresponds to the order in which they have been presented above. The reader is invited to contest this ranking and to suggest alternative explanations.

Conclusion

States never stand still; they continue to change. The modern, Westphalian state as it had emerged mainly in Western Europe and in North America around 1950 took a very long time to mature; but once it had, a new process of transformation immediately began. I have diagnosed that transformation as a transition from modern to postmodern statehood.

The causes behind this transformation are many. In order to make systematic sense of them, it is necessary to consult the relevant major theories. There are three of those: one from the realist tradition, stressing the role of states themselves; one from the liberal tradition, emphasizing the role of international institutions and of individuals and groups in society; and one from the critical tradition, underlining the interplay of states and markets. It turns out that explanations from the three traditions can be combined, as demonstrated above.

The transformation from modern to postmodern statehood concerns the advanced states. Weak, postcolonial states are qualitatively different; they were never modern in the first place. They emerged from a process of colonization and decolonization. Leading states carry major responsibility for this entire process, but the insights from liberals and dependency theorists are also relevant for explaining the emergence of the weak, postcolonial state.

The ideal types of the 'postmodern' and the 'weak, postcolonial' state do not exhaustively describe all states in the world today: they are basically relevant for the advanced states on the one hand and for the least developed states on the other. A large group of states fits neither the one nor the other description. In ideal type terms, that large group rather displays a mixture of modern, postmodern and weak postcolonial qualities. So, instead of fitting an ideal type of its own, these states combine elements from the three ideal types I have identified in various patterns; they are the 'modernizing states' discussed in Chapter 8.

Chapter 10

Theoretical Perspectives and New Debates

Realism
Liberalism
The critical view
Issues of state transformation
Conclusion

We began with the debate between retreat and state-centric scholars about what was happening to the sovereign state. It was demonstrated how scholars from the two camps tended to paint rather misleading pictures of states either 'losing' or 'winning' in their contests with other actors. I argued that the idea of 'state transformation' was a better analytical starting point. That gets us away from the zero-sum view of states either 'winning' or 'losing' and opens up the idea that both of these processes can take place at the same time, in complex combinations.

Many observers are ready to speak about state transformation, but there are rather few attempts to specify in detail just *how* the state has changed and what the *consequences* are for the state's provision of basic social values: security, welfare and growth, and international order. This book has made an attempt to fill that gap by analyzing the changes and their consequences.

It is clear that the debate about state transformation is fixed upon the advanced states: what is really being discussed, in the terminology of this book, is the transformation from modern to postmodern statehood. But other types of statehood in the present international system also merit attention. This book has identified and analyzed the weak, postcolonial states. The investigation underscored the fundamental differences between modern and postmodern states on the one hand, and weak, postcolonial states on the other. Furthermore, 'modernizing' states were discussed in Chapter 8. They are a mixture of ideal types, containing weak, modern and some postmodern elements.

It is appropriate to end this survey of state transformation with a return to theory. What are the theoretical implications of the analysis? Stated differently, what are the theoretical consequences of the insights for the major existing theories on states and power? Chapter 1 identified three theoretical approaches to the subject, one based on realism, one on liberalism, and one – the critical view – on sociology and political economy. Let us look at each of them in turn.

Realism

To realists, the sovereign state is the basic unit of the international system; other actors are 'a manifestation of the preferences and capabilities of states' (Krasner 1994: 14). Sovereign states are not difficult to identify; they are made up of a defined territory, a population, and a government. Realists are not very interested in what goes on inside states. To repeat from Chapter 1, the realist view is a systemic one; it looks at sovereign states from the outside, from the perspective of the international system. Seen from that perspective, states are unitary and coherent actors. They are unitary in the sense that state leaders speak and act on behalf of their respective states; they are coherent in the sense that the power of the government and the power of the state as a territorial unit with population and resources are seen as one and the same.

According to most realists, it is entirely legitimate to downplay what goes on inside states. That is because sovereign states are all alike in their domestic make-up: they are all 'like units'. All states are required to have governments, to have defence ministries and other state institutions, to have education and health systems, to collect taxes, and so on. States are similar because they compete with each other and socialize each other (Waltz 1979). They are different only in one basic respect: their capabilities (i.e., their power resources). There are great powers and small powers, and the great powers matter most for what goes on in international relations. But it is not necessary to look inside states in order to understand that; it is sufficient to focus on the development of the balance of power in the international system.

There is a plain core of truth in the realist theory. States really *are* the basic units of the international system. The international society and its organizations – most importantly the UN system – are made up of states. Individuals, people, citizens matter, of course, but the rights and duties of people are defined through their membership of states. The entire world (with the exception of Antarctica) is divided into sovereign states. The state continues to be the single most important organization for people's lives; being a citizen of a well-functioning postmodern state is, indeed, very different from living in a weak, 'failed' state. And being without a state – stateless – is not an attractive situation at all. In short, realists have a point: states are the basic units of the international system.

The next fundamental assumption made by realists is that all other actors are secondary; in Krasner's words above, they are 'a manifestation of the preferences and capabilities of states'. This is the hard core of the state-centric position; it says that other actors matter only to the extent that states allow them to matter. States set the rules for corporations, for markets, for groups in civil society, for international organizations, for the development of economic globalization, and so on. This assumption makes realism impregnable against any claim about the state being in retreat because markets, or firms, or any other non-state actors, allegedly grow stronger. Realist state-centric scholars are predestined to reject all such claims because they violate an essential realist assumption.

This, then, is where realist state-centric scholars go too far. They tend to forget that the assumption about the primary role of the state and the secondary role of everybody else is merely that: an assumption. It is *not* an accurate description of the *real world* out there. The real world can change so that it becomes less in line with the realist assumption. Previous chapters in this book have demonstrated that this is indeed what has happened. The transformation from modern to postmodern statehood implies a more prominent role for non-state actors than was the case under the conditions of modern statehood. Realist state-centric scholars must be ready to admit as much. They cannot continue to hide behind a misleading assumption while the world changes in front of their eyes. Realists assume too much and analyze too little.

That being said, it is important not to go to the other extreme and reject the special importance of the state. The analyses in previous chapters have also demonstrated that realist state-centric scholars do have a valid point when they say that states make the rules other actors play by. That fact makes states actors of a special kind. What is needed is not a rejection of the idea that states are exceptional actors with special powers; it is a *relaxation* of the realist assumption about states controlling everybody else. States do set the rules for others, but they are themselves influenced by these 'others', be it companies, civil society groups, or international institutions. Relaxing the assumption about the state opens up the study of a complex interplay between states and non-state actors, instead of a prejudiced view of the state being by definition dominant and thus always 'winning'. But note also that this more open view wants to avoid the opposite extreme: that the state is necessarily 'losing' (there will be more on this in the next section).

Previous chapters of this book have attempted to uncover the most important aspects of the complex interplay between states and non-state actors and to discover how it has affected states. A central element in this analysis has been the claim about a transition from modern towards postmodern statehood; this development is most pronounced in the EU, but some similar developments also take place in other triad states (i.e., in North America and Japan/East Asia). As set out in detail in earlier chapters, the transition fundamentally affects the structure and content of government, of the economy, and of nationhood in these states.

Note that the relaxation of the realist assumption, innocent as it may seem, has far-reaching implications. When it can no longer simply be assumed that states control everybody else, it becomes necessary to look *inside* states in order to discover the interplay between states and non-state actors. This interplay can lead in different directions; it is also affected by what goes on in the international system, of course. In short, states are not all alike. States do compete with each other and socialize each other, but that does not turn them into 'like units' (cf. Sørensen 2001). This book has identified three ideal types of state: the modern, the postmodern, and the weak, postcolonial state. It has also identified a hybrid type, the modernizing state. Realists must be more ready to look inside states because the development of different types of state has implications, not only for the retreat versus state-centric debate, but also for what goes on in the relationship between states in the international system.

Furthermore, the transformation from modern to postmodern statehood undermines realist assumptions about states as unitary and coherent actors. It was emphasized in Chapter 4 that multilevel governance is a transnational activity that includes governments and international institutions, but also NGOs and other non-state actors. It is governance in the context of supranational, international, transgovernmental and transnational relations.

As a consequence of all this, other major realist claims will need revision as well. Realists focus on anarchy and the constant risk of violent conflict; they also focus on military power as the most important power resource. But it was demonstrated in Chapter 7 that there is no reason whatsoever to expect violent conflict between postmodern states. They make up a security community, and in that sense the major security problem of external threat and possible war has been removed from the agenda of postmodern states. Not all violent threats are gone, but the consolidated peace between postmodern states would appear sufficient to warrant a revision of realist views.

A further result of these developments must be a downgrading of the emphasis realists put on military power. If violent conflict between postmodern states is removed from the agenda, the saliency of other non-military power resources must be expected to increase. As we saw in Chapter 1, liberals speak of the increased importance of 'soft power'.

Finally, realist state-centric scholars support a traditional view of national community, according to which nationhood has not been replaced, or even severely weakened, by new developments. Chapter 5 argued that the content of nationhood is being transformed so as to include supranational elements, both with respect to the 'community of sentiment' and the 'community of citizens' aspect. Realists need to take note of new developments in this area as well.

In sum, realism needs some revision, away from the stark assumptions of the state as the superior actor compared to all other actors, towards a view of the state as an actor of special importance which is influenced by non-state actors; away from an assumption of states as 'like units', towards a view of different main types of state in the present international system; away from an assumption of states as unitary and coherent actors, towards a view of (postmodern) states involved in complex forms of multilevel governance; and away from a singleminded focus on war and military power, towards a view of (postmodern) states in a security community leading to increased salience of non-military power resources.

Realists are not going to like this kind of advice. They will claim that the assumptions they make are necessary for the analytical undertaking that they want to pursue. Realists want to focus on the international system; they want to know about the dynamics of the balance of power between leading states in the system. In order to pursue this analysis, they need *simplifying assumptions* about states as 'like units', as unitary and coherent actors. Realists know very well that these assumptions will not always be empirically accurate, but according to them that is not the point. The assumptions are *analytically necessary* in order to be able to study the power play between states in an anarchic international system (cf. Waltz 1986). If we do not simplify in this manner, so the realists claim, we cannot focus on the 'big and important things' in the international system. Instead, our view will be clouded by many less important things.

As seen from the debate between retreat and state-centric scholars on the transformation of the state, the answer to this objection is simple: realist assumptions may well be needed for the analytical undertaking that they proclaim, but they are not at all adequate for the analysis of state development and transformation. In other words, if realists want to make serious contribution to the debate about what happens to the state, it is necessary that they modify some of their core assumptions. If they do not, they will remain painted into a corner where the realist state-centric position is always vindicated, irrespective of what happens in the real world, because the unassailable power of the state is built into the realist assumptions about the world. This reduces the realist state-centric view to a mere matter of faith and the debate with retreat scholars is turned into a 'religious' shouting competition instead of an analytical endeavour to find out what is actually happening. Nobody really benefits from that in the long run, neither realists nor anybody else.

Liberalism

Liberals begin with individuals rather than with states. States are nothing but amalgamations of individuals anyway; they are the caretakers of the rule of law and the right of citizens to life, liberty and property. Focus is on the liberal, democratic state. The state is derived from the people, the individuals. Without them, the state would have no power and no legitimacy. What always matters most are individuals and groups in civil society.

This theoretical position is well suited for analyzing the transformation from modern to postmodern statehood. Liberals emphasize how economic globalization and a host of other relations across borders – including the movements and connections of individuals and groups – continue to develop. They diagnose the change from national towards multilevel governance in a context of transnational, transgovernmental and supranational relations. Liberals also underscore the significant role of international institutions in the promotion of integration and cooperation across borders. They point to the increasing importance of soft power and the declining importance of military power in a more peaceful world of relations between postmodern states that are consolidated democracies. In short, liberal analysts are much more ready than realists to appreciate the emergence of postmodern states.

The simple core of truth in liberal theory is the emphasis on the importance of individuals. At the end of the day, states *are* nothing but amalgamations of individuals. And individuals, groups, companies and organizations from civil society help determine what states do in international and domestic affairs; they are also important for international relations in their own right (i.e., they create transnational relations, shape the patterns of globalization, and so on).

However, many liberals tend to take this simple core of truth too far and transform it into a general claim about an overall retreat of the state. The problems with a narrow retreat view have been discussed many times in previous chapters. What must be emphasized in the present context is how the theoretical assumption made by liberals compels them to adopt a too radical view of 'states in retreat'. Liberals assume that individuals and groups in civil society are important; so far, so good. But, from there, liberals tend to go one step further and argue that individuals and groups are *all that matters* and that states, consequently, are not important in their own right. The state is a guarantor of rights in the liberal view, so liberals do not deem it irrelevant; yet individuals come first. As liberals will say: what are states anyway, other than institutions derived from individuals, from the people?

In this way, liberals go too far in their emphasis on individuals. Where realists adopt a 'states-are-all-that-matter' view, many liberals commit a similar mistake by adopting an 'individuals-are-all-that-matter' view. This liberal assumption is the hard core of the retreat position. States and other institutions matter to the extent that individuals (and groups) allow them to matter. If individuals decide to pursue globalization, to develop transnational relations across borders, and so on, there is little states can do about it. States are bound to be in retreat. In this way, the retreat position is built into the liberal assumption about the all-inclusive importance of individuals.

The liberal assumption about states being derived from individuals goes wrong when it is used to deprive states of any autonomous power whatsoever. States are derived from individuals, yes; but states are not the mere handmaidens or slaves of individuals in civil society. Governments, bureaucracies and state institutions (in sum, state apparatuses) have autonomous powers of their own. Individuals not only have rights with regard to states: they also have obligations and duties. They pay taxes, obey laws, and they play by the rules states set up. Individuals do elect politicians on election day, but that does not leave them in full control of the state and that certainly does not leave the state powerless in relation to individuals, a fact we are all aware of in our daily lives as citizens.

So, liberals need to relax the assumption about the all-inclusive importance of individuals and leave some room for the autonomous power of states. That theoretical starting point is much better suited for a discussion of state development and change because it avoids giving the game away by assuming from the start that individuals (and, by implication, the retreat position) must always prevail. The previous section noted how realists painted themselves into a corner where the state-centric position was always vindicated. Liberals are in a similar situation, albeit in the opposite corner: their assumption about the all-encompassing importance of individuals ensures that the retreat position is always vindicated, but that merely takes us back to the shouting competition. What we need are more open assumptions to help us get the analytical undertaking under way.

In their focus on individuals, liberals are basically optimistic: they have great faith in human reason and rationality. People can and will cooperate for their mutual benefit and that will tend to bring about progress: that is, change for the better. This liberal road to progress goes via the application of liberal principles: when individuals are set free, and when liberal democracy and a market economy are introduced, progressive change will take place. In the real world, this may very well be the case, but then again it may not, as the analyses in previous chapters have demonstrated. Progress has not taken place in weak, postcolonial states in accordance with high liberal expectations. Personal rulers and their clients have resisted the introduction of liberal principles; where they have been introduced, progress has frequently been very slow or entirely absent. In modernizing states, progress is often gradual, hesitant, and replete with both 'state failures' and 'market failures'. Even in the advanced states, the change from modern to postmodern statehood has brought not only progress but also new problems, of democratic governance, of violent reactions from some groups, of an unstable state–market matrix.

Liberals may have some answers to these problems; a major claim made by liberals is that they are due to either insufficient strength of liberal principles (i.e., liberal democracy and a liberal market economy are not yet in place) or to policy failures that have little to do with the validity of the general liberal principles (i.e., better democratic governance and stable state–market relations can be set up in postmodern states if decision-makers get their act together). But even if liberals are right in making such claims, it is clear that liberal analysis is less strong when it comes to *lack of progress* or even to veritable *decline*.

This leads us to the normative implications of liberal analysis. With their belief in rational individuals and the idea of progress, liberals tend to imply that the 'retreat of the state' is a good thing because it means that individuals – who are good, rational and cooperative – will come to matter more and that can only be for the better. But insofar as it takes place, the 'retreat of the state' may not be an entirely good thing, either in weak, postcolonial states, or in modernizing (or even postmodern) states. In sum, liberals need to adjust their view so that rational cooperation among individuals and general progress becomes a *possibility* rather than an assumed fact of life. This more open assumption will make possible a more balanced analysis of what goes on in the real world.

The critical view

The critical view is less sharply defined than realism and liberalism. Coming mainly from IPE, it focuses on studying the dynamic interplay between states and markets. Some IPE scholars overly emphasize the importance of markets and the ways in which they are able to discipline states (e.g., Friedman 1999; Strange 1996). Others overly emphasize the importance of states and their ability to control markets (e.g., Gilpin 1999); in that sense, IPE has scholars who are basically aligned with the liberal and the realist positions respectively. The focus here is not on them; it is on those scholars who perceive the state–market connection as an evolving relationship of mutual dependence. We have seen in previous chapters that the critical view, with its concentration on state–market dynamics, is well suited for understanding major aspects of state transformation and for avoiding both the retreat and the state-centric extremes. That gives the critical view an advantage over both realism and liberalism.

Given the more open approach, theorists within the critical view are not in full agreement about the fate of the state. One major analysis criticizes the retreat view on the grounds that it leads to 'The Myth of the Powerless State' (Weiss 1998). Linda Weiss singles out three weaknesses of the retreat view. First, it 'tends to exaggerate state powers in the past in order to claim feebleness in the present ... there is little compelling evidence that the state once had the sorts of power that it is now deemed to have surrendered' (ibid.: 190). The state was always subject to a variety of pressures which might entail restructuring of tax systems and the reduction of tax burdens. Present problems 'would seem to have more to do with *internal* fiscal difficulties caused by recession than with "globalization"' (ibid.: 191).

Second, the retreat scholars are overstating the uniformity of state response when it comes to evaluating the various responses states make to problems concerning welfare, industrial restructuring and employment. The emergence of a global financial market 'has not exerted the uniformly debilitating effects on public policy so often claimed for it' (ibid.: 192). Finally, retreat scholars have also 'overgeneralized' the degree of state powerlessness; they do not take state variety and different dynamics of adaptation into account. Weiss agrees that changes in state power have indeed taken place:

> [but] these changes have to do not with diminution but with reconstitution of power around the consolidation of domestic and international linkages. As macro-economic tools appear to lose their efficacy, as external pressures for homogenization of trade regimes increase, and as cross-border flows of people and finance threaten the domestic base, a growing number of states are seeking to increase their control over the external environment. State responses to these pressures have not been uniform. They have varied according to politico-institutional differences. (Weiss 1998: 209)

Another major analysis emphasizes a transformation from a 'Keynesian Welfare National State' to a 'Schumpeterian Competition State' and, more specifically, a 'Schumpeterian Workfare Postnational Regime' (SWPR: see Jessop 2002). Several parts of Jessop's analysis overlap with the points made by Weiss. Jessop, too, stresses the variation in state responses. He does so by discussing different variants of the SWPR (labelled 'neoliberalism', 'neocorporatism', 'neostatism' and 'neocommunitarianism' respectively). At the same time, however, Jessop is more ready to accept that the new conditions for state manoeuvring are characterized by an increased world market involvement and subjection to global norms and standards (cf. Chapter 2 in this book). So, most critical theorists concur with the general view suggested in this book – namely, that states are in a complex process of transformation rather than one of 'winning' or 'losing' – but they stress different aspects of the transformation and they have different views on the importance of world market integration in the context of economic globalization.

One potential weakness of the critical view is that it remains fixated on the state–market relationship and thus it may be less suited to discovering and analyzing the larger aspects of state transformation which concern identities, governance and democracy, sovereignty, security and conflict, international order, and so on. In this sense, the critical view is a more one-sided or narrow approach than either realism or liberalism. That is a problem when we want to study *all the relevant aspects* involved in the transformation of the state.

Furthermore, most critical scholars are engaged in the study of the advanced states or the modernizing states. They are less interested in the peculiar problems of weak and failed states, so the critical view is not really developed with respect to the whole range of different types of state in the present international system.

However, it is entirely possible to expand the critical analysis to incorporate more aspects as well as different types of state. Historical sociologists have shown how this is possible. A recent analysis by Michael Mann (1998) demonstrates such a broader approach. He looks more closely at the development dynamics of the EU (which he refers to as 'Euro') from a very open starting point: 'Human societies have always consisted of multiple, overlapping, intersecting networks of interaction each with differing boundaries and rhythms of development ... I investigate the degree of internal coherence and external closure of European social networks' (Mann 1998: 185). The analysis covers three broad areas: 'ideological power networks' which have to do with identity, culture and community; 'economic power networks' covering trade, multinational corporate organization, and finance; and 'political power networks' involving political processes at the national and the 'Euro' level (i.e., Brussels/Strasbourg).

Mann's conclusion is that even if a complex process of state transformation is taking place, a society called 'Euro' is not in the making:

Euro seems especially to lack overall internal cohesion and external closure. Doubtless, it will gain both in the foreseeable future. Perhaps it will eventually attain the moderate degree of cohesion and closure attained by nation-states during the relatively transnational phases of modern development – in the period after 1815, for example, or around 1900. My own guess is that Euro will be less than this, less salient as a network of interaction than networks constituted both by the North as a whole and by the more successful nation-states of the world. (Mann 1998: 205)

In sum, the critical view, as employed in different variants by international political economists, historical sociologists and other scholars, emerges as a desirable starting point for the study of complex processes of state transformation. With some exceptions, this cluster of approaches avoids giving the game away by making misleading assumptions where either the state-centric view (i.e., realism) or the retreat view (i.e., liberalism) is always vindicated. Instead, it adopts an open attitude according to which several different types of change can take place simultaneously. That opens up the possibility of including relevant insights from state-centric as well as retreat scholars. And even if it is sometimes overly fixed on the state–market relationship, it can be extended to incorporate other major aspects of changes in statehood.

Issues of state transformation

Democracy in a new context

The sections above examined three major theories in the light of the analyses in previous chapters. The next sections take a different path; they outline the substantial challenges to analysis that emerge from a system of different types of state undertaking various processes of transformation. Let us begin with the issue of democracy. A standard textbook introduction to politics (e.g., Heywood 1997: 66) identifies three basic questions in the scholarly debate on democracy.

1   Who are the people?
2   In what sense should the people rule?
3   How far should popular rule extend?

The first question is answered by discussing which groups are given political influence: in Greek city-states, it was only male citizens over 20, thus excluding women, slaves and foreigners. The current definition of 'the people' includes all adult citizens. The second question is answered by discussing forms of political participation, emphasizing the distinction between direct democracy and representative democracy. The third question is answered by discussing the relationship between the public and the private realm in order to determine what the people should decide and what should be left to individual citizens.

The point in the present context is that these questions are all raised and asked as if the democratic process always takes place *within the context of a sovereign state*. Furthermore, the questions are often asked as if we may assume that the sovereign state functions properly and is capable of instituting democratic rule: that is, the state is believed to be much like the modern, Westphalian state introduced in Chapter 1.

But this book has made clear that such a premise for the study of democracy is no longer valid. Multilevel governance in the context of postmodern statehood raises a number of new problems and makes the response to the three classical questions asked by political scientists much more complicated. Some major elements of these issues were discussed in Chapter 4. One recent analysis argues that these developments must open the way to a project of cosmopolitan social democracy that:

> can be conceived as a basis for uniting around the promotion of the impartial administration of law at the international level; greater transparency, accountability and democracy in global governance; a deeper commitment to social justice in the pursuit of a more equitable distribution of the world's resources and human security; the protection of community at diverse levels (from the local to the global); and the regulation of the global economy through the public management of global financial and trade flows, the provision of global public goods and the engagement of leading stakeholders in corporate governance. (Held and McGrew 2002: 131)

One important element in this vision is the strengthening of 'regional governance infrastructures and capacities' (ibid.: 132; see also Held 1993: 40). The most advanced example of regional governance is the EU, yet other observers are highly sceptical about the democratic potential of the EU. Christopher Patten recently stated that the EU 'has to accept that there is no European "demos" in the sense of a population which feels itself to be one. The problem of legitimacy and democracy is therefore especially difficult. And it is especially acute, because the European Union is so powerful' (quoted from Lee and Rivkin 2001: 46). A recent analysis points to the 'alarmingly undemocratic drift of the European Union' (Lee and Rivkin 2001) and claims that the 'citizenry has been transformed from the ultimate source of legitimate authority ... into one of several stakeholders in the process of government' (ibid.: 47).

This debate on democracy in the EU confirms how any assessment of democratic theory and practice today will have to begin from the premise that the relevant political context is *not* the sovereign state but a larger regional (or even global) realm. The discussion about the possibilities for democratic government in the new situation has barely begun. As we have seen, it is plagued by vast disagreement both about prospective developments and about the actual current state of affairs (e.g., in the EU). Classical democratic theory will only be of limited help because it is based on the framework of the sovereign state.

Other challenges to democratic thinking emerge from the weak states and from some of the modernizing states. One pertinent question is whether democracy is possible at all under the adverse conditions that characterize most weak or failed states. Some level of order, of minimally decent conditions for human existence, of education and information, would appear to be necessary preconditions for a democratic system worthy of the name; or is it possible to devise democratic models for such states that somehow circumvent these serious problems? Answers to questions such as these are hard to find in the literature on democracy.

Finally, democracy has gained foothold in modernizing countries such as India, but to many poor people it does not really seem to be worthwhile: for several hundred million poor Indians, democracy has not paved the way for improvements in spheres of life other than those narrowly connected with some measure of political freedom. The percentage of the population living in absolute poverty (at a minimum level of subsistence or below) is as high as 40 per cent in India, and it has remained basically unchanged since independence. With a population increase from 360 million at independence to more than one billion today, the absolute number of poor people has, of course, increased dramatically. Again, mainstream democratic theory has had too little to say about that problem.

In sum, the processes of state transformation traced in this book, and the existence in the world today of different major types of states, are a dramatic challenge to political theory about democracy and the 'good life'.

Sovereignty in a new context

In the traditional view, sovereignty is closely connected with the 'golden rule' of non-intervention (cf. Jackson 1990). To be sovereign means that states have a right to set their own course and to conduct their affairs free of external interference. But we saw in Chapter 6 that the institution of sovereignty changes in the context of postmodern statehood. Multilevel governance is quite the opposite of non-intervention: it is rather systematic *intervention* in national affairs by international or supranational institutions. It was argued that the EU was the clearest example of that new practice. Why do states do that? Why would they not prefer complete freedom from outside interference? The answer is because they get something in return: a measure of influence on the *domestic affairs of other states*; and they want that because what goes on there has significant consequences for their own situation. In short, the institution of sovereignty is changing in basic ways. What it means to be sovereign is very different under conditions of multilevel governance compared with under traditional conditions of national government. The discipline of IR has begun to take note of that fact, but there is much more to do. Many realists continue to look upon sovereignty and the sovereign state as a fixed and basically unchanging entity.

Students of comparative politics are also challenged by the changes in sovereignty: with economic and political integration between countries, with multilevel governance, countries can no longer be treated as separate entities for the purpose of comparative analysis. The study of comparative politics must prepare for a new situation where 'domestic' affairs and the 'international' context of any one country are no longer easily separated. That calls for new ways of conducting comparative analysis of political systems.

In weak states, sovereignty has changed as well. Sovereignty entails international equality: equal rights and duties of member states in the international system. But weak states are highly *unequal* so they need help from the developed world. Aid leads to intervention, to external supervision of what comes in. A number of weak states in the world are unable to take care of themselves, but sovereignty – which they have – assumes that they can. This tension leads to speculation about what will happen to weak states that do not succeed in developing. Should such countries come under the trusteeship of the international society, as we have seen in East Timor and elsewhere? The debate about these issues is only in its early stages. Better answers are needed to the question about the appropriate treatment of weak states that possess sovereignty without being able to meet the requirements of sovereignty.

State power in a new context

Let us turn to the issue of state power. There are three major ways of looking at state power; they were briefly presented in Chapter 1. Realists focus on a number of material power resources; the most important one is military power which, like economic power (money), is highly fungible. Liberals emphasize non-material, intangible sources of power and especially point to the increasing importance of 'soft power'. Power is seen as much less fungible, and does not travel easily from one issue area to another. Finally, critical theorists focus on state power as the capacity for economic development and often use the concept of 'embedded autonomy' or 'infrastructural power' to underline the importance of state–society relations in that context.

So what does it mean to be a powerful state today? The transformation of statehood makes the question more complicated than earlier. Postmodern states would appear to support the liberal view of power because violent conflict between postmodern states is out of the question and 'soft power' is clearly of increasing importance. A recent liberal analysis by Joseph Nye (2002) emphasizes 'the paradox of American power', arguing that 'the world's only superpower can't go it alone'. Power today means the ability to get other countries on board, to be able to make them understand that it is in their interest to support your point of view. But since September 11, the USA has increasingly acted unilaterally and wielded its military power on a global scale in whatever ways President Bush and his advisers have seen fit (Waltz 2002). That is much more in line with a realist view of power. What is state power today, and who has it?

The question is also relevant for the weak states because their 'power portfolio' is indeed peculiar. On the one hand, they are unable to survive on their own; an important power asset for them is thus the sovereignty they have been granted by international society in the context of decolonization. The possession of sovereignty gives access to negotiations with outsiders, the right to participate in international organizations and to be qualified for aid and other resources. On the other hand, the countries are usually desperately poor, yet personal rulers – strongmen – have been able to command state power, often for decades, combining violent repression with a patron–client system of incentives. And in several cases, they have been able to amass huge personal fortunes in the process. In what ways is it relevant, if it is relevant at all, to talk about state power in such a context?

Security in a new context

Let us move on to security. The traditional view of the security for a sovereign state was set out in Chapter 6; it concerns protection from the external threat posed by other states in an anarchical international system. That view is clearly outdated when it comes to postmodern states, but what does it really mean for a postmodern state to be secure when that same state is deeply integrated economically, politically and otherwise with other states? Security cannot simply mean defence of the territorial realm, because the substantial components of the state stretch far beyond that realm: that goes both for the economic basis and for the political institutions. When security is no longer purely national, what is it? Is it regional, or is it global? And insofar as it can be territorially demarcated, what is the actual substance of security? It is hardly merely protection from violent threat of other countries; but should the concept be stretched to cover environmental threats, threats to social welfare, to identities, and so on? The debate on these issues has only just begun and there are no clear answers.

In weak states, the major security threat to people most often comes from their own government. Personal rulers have taken control of the state apparatus; they support a group of clients, although the majority of the population not only expect no services from the state, but they see it – and rightly so – as a source of great danger to themselves. How is security for the people created under such conditions? The conventional view of security for sovereign states has no answer to that question. An appropriate response is surely related to the larger issue about socio-economic development and the creation of more responsive and capable states in the Third World, but there are no obvious solutions.

Economic globalization, growth and welfare

Economic globalization has brought substantial improvements in standards of living to many people; but progress has been unevenly distributed. The poorest 20 per cent of the world's population receive 1.4 per cent of world income; the richest 20 per cent receive 82.7 per cent (Wade 2001). Behind these overall figures, a growing gap can be found between rich and poor countries, as well as between wealthy groups and poor groups within countries. According to a recent analysis, 'the general pace of globalization in the 1980s and 1990s ... has increased inequality and risk ... at the intrastate and the interstate level' (Thomas 2000: 23, 26; for additional statistics, including accounts that point to decreasing inequality, see Held and McGrew 2002: 77–87).

Chapter 2 analyzed how economic growth and improved welfare can go hand in hand with economic globalization; but it was also shown how weak states are not at all equipped to benefit from economic globalization. Much continues to depend on how national economic and political systems are prepared or not prepared to reap benefits from economic globalization.

It is clear, however, that in an increasingly globalized world, purely national measures are not sufficient. A much better global governance is needed, as indicated by the call for 'cosmopolitan social democracy' mentioned above. The market alone cannot create a global order where everybody has minimally decent living conditions. Governance, especially global governance, is needed.

How can that be brought about? The short answer is that we simply do not know, but it is possible to identify some of the elements that have to be in place if an ambitious project of global governance is to succeed (cf. Cox 1996). There are three major requirements: the first is power to lead the way; the second is appropriate ideas about the right policies; the third is the proper international institutions (see Figure 10.1).

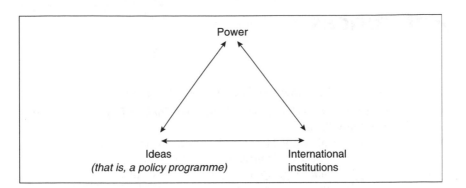

Figure 10.1 *Preconditions for global governance*

Great powers must take the lead if global governance is to succeed; that is the reasoning behind the 'power' requirement. But the USA is certainly not interested in doing so at the moment; and the EU does not appear ready for the task either. 'The ideas' are not in place. We saw the call for cosmopolitan social democracy above, but there is certainly no global or even regional consensus on the major elements of a programme for global governance of globalization. Finally, it would also appear that better and more powerful global institutions are required. Some scholars want to reform the UN Security Council and create a second UN chamber with the long-term aim of creating a global Parliament. This would go hand in hand with a new human rights court and regional as well as global agencies for economic coordination (Held 1995: 279).

The point here is that none of the three preconditions for global governance is in place and there is no indication that they will be in a foreseeable future. Therefore, better global governance is not likely to be forthcoming. What, then, should be done? Once again, there are no clear answers.

Conclusion

The transformation of statehood presents scholars with a large new menu of analytical and substantial challenges. The traditional theoretical approaches need to be further developed in order to confront the new situation. There are many big questions that call for better answers than scholars (and policy-makers) have been able to come up with so far. We do live in turbulent times, but we also have quite clear ideas about what is going on and how the sovereign state is changing. That is not a bad starting point for further analysis – and action.

References

Dates in square brackets show the date of first publication.

Albrow, M. (1996) *The Global Age. State and Society Beyond Modernity*, Cambridge: Polity Press.

Altvater, E. and B. Mahnkopf (1997) 'The World Market Unbound', *Review of International Political Economy*, 4:3, pp. 448–71.

Amin, S. (1976) *Unequal Development*, New York: Monthly Review Press.

Amin, S. (1990) *Delinking: Towards a Polycentric World*, London: Zed.

Anderson, B. (1991) *Imagined Communities: Reflections on the Origin and Spread of Nationalism*, rev. edn, London: Verso.

Andreassen, K.R. (1999) 'China's Engine of Growth: State, Market, or Culture?', MA thesis, Aarhus: Dept of Political Science.

Arquilla, J. and D. Ronfeldt (eds) (1997) *In Athena's Camp: Preparing for Conflict in the Information Age*, Santa Monica, CA: RAND.

Ashton, B., K. Hill, A. Pigaaq, R. Aeita (1984) 'Famine in China', *Population and Development Review*, 10:4, pp. 613–45.

Aslund, A. (2001) 'Russia', *Foreign Policy*, 125, pp. 20–6.

Ayoob, M. (1995) *The Third World Security Predicament*, Boulder, CO: Lynne Rienner.

Ayoob, M. (2003) 'The War Against Iraq: Normative and Strategic Implications', *Middle East Policy*, 10:2, pp. 27–39.

Baeg-Im, H. (1987) 'The Rise of Bureaucratic Authoritarianism in South Korea', *World Politics*, xxxix:2, pp. 231–57.

Bardhan, P. (1984) *The Political Economy of Development in India*, Oxford: Basil Blackwell.

Bardhan, P. (2001) 'Sharing the spoils: group equity, development, and democracy', in A. Kohli (ed.), *The Success of India's Democracy*, Cambridge: Cambridge University Press, pp. 226–42.

Bartkus, V.O. (1999) *The Dynamic of Secession*, Cambridge: Cambridge University Press.

Barya, J.-J.B. (1992) 'The New Political Conditionalities of Aid: An Independent View From Africa', paper for the European Association of Development Institute (EADI) Conference, Vienna, 23–24 April.

Basu, A. (2001) 'The Dialectics of Hindu Nationalism', in A. Kohli (ed.), *The Success of India's Democracy*, Cambridge: Cambridge University Press, pp. 163–91.

Bates, R. (1981) *Markets and States in Tropical Africa: The Political Basis of Agricultural Policies*, Berkeley, CA: University of California Press.

Beck, U. (1992) *Risk Society*, London: Sage, trans. by Mark Ritter.

Beck, U. (2000) 'What is Globalization?', in D. Held and A. McGrew (eds), *The Global Transformations Reader*, Cambridge: Polity Press, pp. 99–105.

Beisheim, M., S. Dreher, G. Walter, B. Zangl and M. Zürn (1999) *Im Zeitalter der Globalisierung? Thesen zur gesellschaftlichen und politischen*

Denationalisierung [In the Age of Globalization? Theses on societal and political denationalization], Baden-Baden: Nomos Verlagsgesellschaft.

Bennett, C. (1995) *Yugoslavia's Bloody Collapse – Causes, Course and Consequences*, London: Hurst.

Bhagwati, J. (2000) 'Globalization: A Moral Imperative', *UNESCO Courier*, September, pp. 19–20.

Bienen, H. and J. Herbst (1996) 'The Relationship between Political and Economic Reform in Africa', *Comparative Politics*, 29:1, pp. 23–42.

Blecher, M. (1986) *China. Politics, Economics and Society*, London: Pinter.

Bluth, C. (1998) 'The post-Soviet Space and Europe', in R. Allison and C. Bluth (eds), *Security Dilemmas in Russia and Eurasia*, London: Royal Institute of International Affairs, pp. 323–42.

Boyer, R. and D. Drache (eds) (1996) *States Against Markets*, London: Routledge.

Bradnock, R.W. (1990) *India's Foreign Policy since 1971*, London: Pinter.

Brecht, A. (1965) *The Theory and Method of Political Analysis*, Homewood, IL: Richard Irwin.

Brenner, N., B. Jessop, M. Jones and G. Macleod (eds) (2003) *State/Space. A Reader*, Oxford: Basil Blackwell.

Brook, T. and B.M. Frolic (eds) (1997) *Civil Society in China*, London: M.E. Sharpe.

Bull, H. (1995 [1977]) *The Anarchical Society. A Study of Order in World Politics*, London: Macmillan.

Burton, J. (1972) *World Society*, Cambridge: Cambridge University Press.

Caldeira, G.A., J.L. Gothson and D.J. Klein (1995) 'The Visibility of the Court of Justice in the European Union', paper for the 1995 American Political Science Association (APSA) Meeting, Chicago.

Callaghy, T. (1991) 'Africa and the World Economy: Caught Between a Rock and a Hard Place', in J. Harbeson and D. Rotschild (eds), *Africa in World Politics*, Boulder, CO: Westview, pp. 39–69.

Camilleri, J.A. and J. Falk (1992) *The End of Sovereignty?*, Aldershot: Edward Elgar.

Cardoso, F.H. and E. Faletto (1979) *Dependency and Development in Latin America*, Berkeley, CA: University of California Press.

Carroll, B.W. and T. Carroll (1997) 'State and Ethnicity in Botswana and Mauritius: A Democratic Route to Development?', *The Journal of Development Studies*, 33:4, pp. 464–86.

Castells, M. (1998) *The Power of Identity*, Oxford: Basil Blackwell.

Cerny, P.G. (1990) *The Changing Architecture of Politics: Structure, Agency and the Future of the State*, London: Sage.

Cerny, P.G. (2000) 'Restructuring the Political Arena: Globalization and the Paradoxes of the Competition State', in R.D. Germain (ed.), *Globalization and its Critics*, London: Macmillan.

Chopra, J. (2000) 'The UN's Kingdom of East Timor', *Survival*, 42:3, pp. 27–39.

Christiansen, T. (1994) 'European Integration Between Political Science and International Relations Theory: The End of Sovereignty', *European*

University Institute Working Paper RSC 94/4, Florence: European University Institute.

Clapham, C. (1996) *Africa and the International System. The Politics of State Survival*, Cambridge: Cambridge University Press.

Clapham, C. (2000) 'Putting State Collapse in Context: History, Politics and the Genealogy of a Concept', paper for International Committe of the Red Cross/Population and Social Integration Section Conference, Geneva, 7–9 December.

Clapham, C. (2001) 'War and State Formation in Ethiopia and Eritrea', paper for Failed States Conference, Florence, 10–14 April.

Clark, I. (1999) *Globalization and International Relations Theory*, Oxford: Oxford University Press.

Coalition to Stop the Use of Child Soldiers (2001) www.child-soldiers.org/ report 2001.

Coates, D. (1999) 'Models of Capitalism in the New World Order: the UK Case', *Political Studies*, 47:4, pp. 643–60.

Coates, D. (2000) *Models of Capitalism*, Cambridge: Polity Press.

Copson, R.W. (1994) *Africa's Wars and Prospects for Peace*, Armonk, NY: M.E. Sharpe.

Cox, R.W. (1987) *Production, Power and World Order: Social Forces in the Making of History*, New York: Columbia University Press.

Cox, R.W. (1994) 'Global Restructuring: Making Sense of the Changing International Political Economy', in R. Stubbs and G.R.D. Underhill, *Political Economy and the Changing Global Order*, London: Macmillan, pp. 45–60.

Cox, R.W. (1996) 'Civilisations in World Political Economy', *New Political Economy*, 1:2, pp. 141–56.

Czempiel, E.-O. (1989) 'Internationalizing Politics: Some Answers to the Question of Who Does What to Whom', in E.-O. Czempiel and J.N. Rosenau (eds), *Global Changes and Theoretical Challenges. Approaches to World Politics for the 1990s*, Lexington, MA: Lexington Books, pp. 117–35.

Dahl, R.A. (1999) 'Can international organizations be democratic? A sceptic's view', in I. Shapiro and C. Hacker-Cordón (eds), *Democracy's Edges*, Cambridge: Cambridge University Press, pp. 19–37.

Deng, Y. (1998) 'The Chinese Conception of National Interests in International Relations', *The China Quarterly*, 154, pp. 308–29.

Deudney, D. and G.J. Ikenberry (1999). 'The Nature and Sources of Liberal International Order', *Review of International Studies*, 25:2, pp. 179–96.

Deutsch, K.W., S.W. Burrell, R.W. Kann, M. Lee Jr, M. Lichterman, R.E. Lindgren, F.L. Loewenheim and R.W. van Wagenen (1957) *Political Community and the North Atlantic Area*, Princeton, NJ: Princeton University Press.

Diamond, J. (1998) *Guns, Germs, and Steel*, New York: Vintage.

Diamond, L., J. Linz and S.M. Lipset (eds) (1988, 1989) *Democracy in Developing Countries*. Vol. 1: *Persistence, Failure, and Renewal*. Vol. 2: *Africa*. Vol. 3: *Asia*. Vol. 4: *Latin America*, Boulder, CO: Lynne Rienner.

Dicken, P. (1998) *Global Shift. Transforming the World Economy*, London: Paul Chapman.

Dror, Y. (2001) *The Capacity to Govern: A Report to the Club of Rome*, London: Frank Cass.

Dunning, J. (2000) 'The New Geography of Foreign Direct Investment', in Ngaire Woods (ed.), *The Political Economy of Globalization*, London: Macmillan, pp. 20–54.

Eberlei, W. and C. Weller (2001) 'Deutsche Ministerien als Akteure von Global Governance' 'German Ministries–Actors For Global Governance', INEF (Das Institut für Entwicklung und Frieden: Institute for Development and Peace) Report 51, Duisburg: Gerhard Mercator Universität.

Economist, The (1995) 'A Survey of the World Economy: Who's in the driving seat?', 7 October, special section.

Economist, The (2001) 'Poverty and Property Rights. No Title', 31 March, pp. 19–22.

Elkins, D.J. (1995) *Beyond Sovereignty. Territorial and Political Economy in the Twenty-First Century*, Toronto: University of Toronto Press.

Elklit, J. (1994) 'Is the Degree of Electoral Democracy Measurable?', in D. Beetham (ed.), *Defining and Measuring Democracy*, London: Sage, pp. 89–111.

Esping-Andersen, G. (1990) *The Three Worlds of Welfare Capitalism*, Princeton, NJ: Princeton University Press.

Esping-Andersen, G. (1999) *Social Foundations of Postindustrial Economies*, Oxford: Oxford University Press.

Evans, P. (1995) *Embedded Autonomy. States and Industrial Transformation*, Princeton, NJ: Princeton University Press.

Ferguson, Y. and R. Mansbach (1996) *Polities: Authority, Identities, and Change*, Columbia, SC: University of South Carolina Press.

Frank A.G. (1969) *Capitalism and Underdevelopment in Latin America: Historical Studies of Chile and Brazil*, New York: Monthly Review Press.

Friedman, T. (1999) *The Lexus and the Olive Tree*, London: HarperCollins.

Fukuyama, F. (1989) 'The End of History?' *The National Interest*, 16, pp. 3–18.

Gaddy, C. and B. Ickes (1998) 'Russia's Virtual Economy', *Foreign Affairs*, 77:5, pp. 53–67.

Galtung, J. (1977) *Methodology and Ideology. Theory and Methods of Social Research*, vol. 1, Copenhagen: Chr. Ejlers Forlag.

Garrett, B. (2001) 'China Faces, Debates, the Contradictions of Globalization', *Asian Survey*, 41:3, pp. 409–27.

Garrett, G. (1998) 'Global Markets and National Policies: Collision Course or Virtuous Circle?', *International Organization*, 52:4, pp. 787–824.

Garrett, G. (2001) 'Globalization and Government Spending around the World', *Studies in Comparative International Development*, 35:4, pp. 3–29.

Gereffi, G. (1994) 'The organization of buyer-driven global commodity chains: how US retailers shape overseas production networks', in G. Gereffi and M. Korzeniewicz (eds), *Commodity Chains and Global Capitalism*, Westport, CT: Praeger, ch. 5.

Giddens, A. (1990) *The Consequences of Modernity*, Cambridge: Polity Press.

Giddens, A. (1991) *Modernity and Self-Identity. Self and Society in the Late Modern Age*, Stanford, CA: Stanford University Press.

Giddens, A. (1992) *The Nation-State and Violence*, Cambridge: Polity Press.

Giddens, A. (1994) *Beyond Left and Right. The Future of Radical Politics*, Stanford, CA: Stanford University Press.

Gill, G. (2003) *The Nature and Development of the Modern State*, Basingstoke: Palgrave.

Gill, S. (1994) 'Knowledge, Politics, and Neo-Liberal Political Economy', in R. Stubbs and G.R.D. Underhill (eds), *Political Economy and the Changing Global Order*, London: Macmillan.

Gilpin, R. (1987) *The Political Economy of International Relations*, Princeton, NJ: Princeton University Press.

Gilpin, R. (1999) 'No One Loves a Political Realist', in R.J. Art and R. Jervis (eds), *International Politics: Enduring Concepts and Contemporary Issues*, 5th edn, New York: Longman, pp. 348–62.

Gold, T.B. (1986) *State and Society in the Taiwan Miracle*, New York: M.E. Sharpe.

Gray, J. (1998) *False Dawn: the Delusions of Global Capitalism*, London: Granta.

Greenberg, E.S. (1990) 'State Change: Approaches and Concepts', in E.S. Greenberg and T.F. Meyer (eds), *Changes in the State: Causes and Consequences*, Newbury Park, MA: Sage, pp. 11–41.

Greider, W. (1997) *One World, Ready or Not. The Manic Logic of Global Capitalism*, Harmondsworth: Penguin.

Grindle, M. (1996) *Challenging the State: Crisis and Innovation in Latin America and Africa*, Cambridge: Cambridge University Press.

Gruner, W. (1992) 'Germany in Europe: the German question as burden and as opportunity', in J. Breuilly (ed.), *The State of Germany*, London: Longman, pp. 201–23.

Guehenno, J.-M. (1995) *The End of the Nation State*, Minneapolis, MN: University of Minnesota Press.

Gurr, T.R. (ed.) (1993) *Minorities at Risk. A Global View of Ethnopolitical Conflicts*, Washington, DC: United States Institute of Peace Press.

Habermas, J. (1975) *Legitimation Crisis*, Boston, MA: Beacon Press.

Habermas, J. (1999) 'The European Nation-State and the Pressures of Globalization', *New Left Review*, 235, pp. 46–59.

Hall, J.A. and G.J. Ikenberry (1989) *The State*, Milton Keynes: Open University Press.

Hamilton, C. (1987) 'Can the Rest of Asia Emulate the NICs?', *Third World Quarterly*, 9:4, pp. 1,128–46.

Harrell, S. (1985) 'Why Do the Chinese Work So Hard?', *Modern China*, 11:2, pp. 203–26.

Held, D. (1993) 'Democracy: From City-states to a Cosmopolitan Order?', in D. Held (ed.), *Prospects for Democracy*, Cambridge: Polity Press, pp. 13–53.

Held, D. (1995) *Democracy and the Global Order*, Cambridge: Polity Press.

Held, D. and A. McGrew (2002) *Globalization/Anti-Globalization*, Cambridge: Polity Press.

Held, D. and A. McGrew (eds) (2003) *The Global Transformations Reader*, Cambridge: Polity Press.

Held, D., A. McGrew, D. Goldblatt and J. Perraton (1999) *Global Transformations: Politics, Economics and Culture*, Cambridge: Cambridge University Press.

Herbst, J. (1989) 'The Creation and Maintenance of National Boundaries in Africa', *International Organization*, 43:4, pp. 673–92.

Herbst, J. (1996/97) 'Responding to State Failure in Africa', *International Security*, 21:3, pp. 120–44.

Hettne, B. (1997) 'The Double Movement: global market versus regionalism', in R.W. Cox (ed.), *The New Realism*, Tokyo: United Nations University Press, pp. 223–42.

Heywood, A. (1997) *Politics*, London: Macmillan.

Hirst, P. (2002) 'Another Century of Conflict? War and the International System in the 21st Century', *International Relations*, 16:3, December, pp. 327–43.

Hirst, P. and G. Thompson (2000) *Globalization in Question*, 2nd edn, Cambridge: Polity Press.

Hobbes, T. (1946) *Leviathan*, Oxford: Basil Blackwell.

Hobsbawm, E.J. (1993) *Nations and Nationalism Since 1780*, Cambridge: Cambridge University Press.

Hobsbawm, E.J. (1994) *Age of Extremes. The Short Twentieth Century 1914–1991*, London: Michael Joseph.

Hobsbawm, E.J. (1996) 'The Future of the State', *Development and Change*, 27, pp. 267–78.

Holm, H.-H. and G. Sørensen (1995) 'Introduction', in H.-H. Holm and G. Sørensen (eds), *Whose World Order? Uneven Globalization and the End of the Cold War*, Boulder, CO: Westview, pp. 1–19.

Holsti, K.J. (1991) *Peace and War: Armed Conflicts and International Order, 1649–1989*, Cambridge: Cambridge University Press.

Hooghe, L. (ed.) (1996) *Cohesion Policy and European Integration: Building Multi-Level Governance*, Oxford: Oxford University Press.

Hooghe, L. and G. Marks (2001) 'Types of Multi-Level Governance', *European Integration online Papers (EIoP)*, 5:11, www.eiop.or.at/eiop/texte/2001–011a.htm

Hoogvelt, A. (2001) *Globalisation and the Postcolonial World*, Basingstoke: Palgrave Macmillan.

Horsman, M. and A. Marshall (1994) *After the Nation-State. Citizens, Tribalism and the New World Disorder*, London: HarperCollins.

Human Rights Watch (2002) *Sexual Violence Against Women and Girls in Eastern Congo*, New York: Human Rights Watch.

H-world (1998) Website debate on 'the rise of the West', at: www2.h-net.msu.edu/~world.

Hydén, G. (1983) *No Shortcuts to Progress. African Development Management in Perspective*, London: Heinemann.

Hymer, S.H. (1976) *The International Operations of National Firms: A Study of Direct Foreign Investment*, Cambridge, MA: MIT Press.

Ikenberry, G.J. (2002) 'America's Imperial Ambition', *Foreign Affairs*, 81:5, pp. 49–60.

Ingram, D. (1995) 'NGOs Keep the Pressure Up on Bureaucrats', *Bangkok Post*, 21 July, p. 5.

International Committee of the Red Cross (2000) *State Collapse and Reconstruction. Lessons and Strategies*, Geneva: International Committee of the Red Cross.

Jackson, R. (1990) *Quasi-States: Sovereignty, International Relations and the Third World*, Cambridge: Cambridge University Press.

Jackson, R. (1995) 'International Community Beyond the Cold War', in G.M. Lyons and M. Mastanduno (eds), *Beyond Westphalia? State Sovereignty and International Intervention*, Baltimore, MD: Johns Hopkins University Press, pp. 59–87.

Jackson, R. (1999) 'Sovereignty in World Politics: A Glance at the Conceptual and Historical Landscape', *Political Studies*, 47:3, pp. 431–57.

Jackson, R. and C.G. Rosberg (1982) *Personal Rule in Black Africa: Prince, Autocrat, Prophet, Tyrant*, Berkeley, CA: University of California Press.

Jackson, R. and C.G. Rosberg (1994) 'The Political Economy of African Personal Rule', in D.E. Apter and C.G. Rosberg (eds), *Political Development and the New Realism in Sub-Saharan Africa*, Charlottesville, VA: University Press of Virginia, pp. 291–325.

Jackson, R. and G. Sørensen (2003) *Introduction to International Relations*, Oxford: Oxford University Press.

James, A. (1999) 'The Practice of Sovereign Statehood in Contemporary International Society', *Political Studies*, 47:3, special issue, pp. 457–74.

Jessop, B. (1990) *State Theory: Putting the Capitalist State in its Place*, Cambridge: Polity Press.

Jessop, B. (1997) 'Capitalism and its future: remarks on regulation, government and governance', *Review of International Political Economy*, 4:3, pp. 561–81.

Jessop, B. (2002) *The Future of the Capitalist State*, Cambridge: Polity Press.

Johnson, C. (1987) 'Political Institutions and Economic Performance: the Government Business Relationship in Japan, South Korea, and Taiwan', in F.C. Deyo (ed.), *The Political Economy of New Asian Industrialism*, Ithaca, NY: Cornell University Press, pp. 135–65.

Jørgensen, K.E. (1997) 'PoCo: The Diplomatic Republic of Europe', in K.E. Jørgensen (ed.), *Reflective Approaches to European Governance*, London: Macmillan.

Julius, D. (1997) 'Globalization and Stakeholder Conflicts: A Corporate Perspective', *International Affairs*, 73:3, pp. 453–69.

Kapstein, E.B. (1994) *Governing the Global Economy: International Finance and the State*, Cambridge, MA: Harvard University Press.

Karatnycky, A. (2002) *Nations in Transit 2002: A Mixed Picture of Change*, Somerset: Transaction.

Katzenstein, P. (1985) *Small States in World Markets*, Ithaca, NY: Cornell University Press.

Keohane, R.O. (1984) *After Hegemony: Cooperation and Discord in the World Political Economy*, Princeton, NJ: Princeton University Press.

Keohane, R.O. (1989) *International Institutions and State Power: Essays in International Relations Theory*, Boulder, CO: Westview Press.

Keohane, R.O. (1990) 'Multilateralism: an agenda for research', *International Journal*, 45.

Keohane, R.O. (1995) 'Hobbes's Dilemma and Institutional Change in World Politics: Sovereignty in International Society', in H.-H. Holm and G. Sørensen (eds), *Whose World Order? Uneven Globalization and the End of the Cold War*, Boulder, CO: Westview Press, pp. 165–87.

Keohane, R.O. and J.S. Nye Jr (1977) *Power and Interdependence: World Politics in Transition*, Boston, MA: Little, Brown.

Keohane, R.O. and J.S. Nye Jr (2001) *Power and Interdependence*, 3rd edn, New York: Longman.

Keynes, J.M. (1933) 'National Self-Sufficiency', *Yale Review*, Summer, and *New Statesman and Nation*, 8 and 15 July 1933. Also in *Collected Writings of John Maynard Keynes*, vol. XXI [1933] Activities 1931–39, edited by Donald Moggeridge. London: Macmillan and Cambridge University Press, 1982 (p. 237).

Kindleberger, C. (1973) *The World in Depression, 1929–1939*, Berkeley, CA: University of California Press.

Kjær, M. (2004) *Governance*. Cambridge: Polity Press (forthcoming).

Krasner, S.D. (1992) 'Realism, Imperialism, and Democracy. A Response to Gilbert', *Political Theory*, 20:1, pp. 38–52.

Krasner, S.D. (1993a) 'Economic Interdependence and Independent Statehood', in R.H. Jackson and A. James (eds), *States in a Changing World: A Contemporary Analysis*, Oxford: Clarendon, pp. 301–21.

Krasner, S.D. (1993b) 'Westphalia and All That', in J. Goldstein and R.O. Keohane (eds), *Ideas and Foreign Policy*, Ithaca, NY: Cornell University Press, pp. 235–65.

Krasner, S.D. (1994) 'International political economy: abiding discord', *Review of International Political Economy*, 1:1, pp. 13–31.

Krasner, S.D. (1999) *Sovereignty. Organized Hypocrisy*, Princeton, NJ: Princeton University Press.

Krugman, P. (1995) *Development, Geography and Economic Theory*, Cambridge, MA: MIT Press.

Kymlicka, W. (1999) 'Citizenship in an era of globalization', in I. Shapiro and C. Hacker-Cordón (eds), *Democracy's Edges*, Cambridge: Cambridge University Press, pp. 112–27.

Lapidoth, R. (1992) 'Sovereignty in Transition', *Journal of International Affairs*, 45, pp. 1–25.

Lee, C. and D.B. Rivkin (2001) 'Europe in the Balance', *Policy Review*, 107, pp. 41–54.

Linklater, A. (1998) *The Transformation of Political Community*, Cambridge: Polity Press.

Luttwak, E. (1999) 'Give War a Chance', *Foreign Affairs*, 78:4, pp. 36–44.

Mann, M. (1993) *The Sources of Social Power, vol. II*, Cambridge: Cambridge University Press.

Mann, M. (1997) 'Has globalization ended the rise of the nation-state?', *Review of International Political Economy*, 4:3, pp. 472–96.

Mann, M. (1998) 'Is There a Society Called Euro?', in R. Axtmann (ed.), *Globalization and Europe*, London: Pinter, pp. 184–207.

Manor, J. (2001) 'Center–State Relations', in A. Kohli (ed.), *The Success of India's Democracy*, Cambridge: Cambridge University Press, pp. 78–102.

Marks, G., L. Hooghe and K. Blank (1996) 'European Integration from the 1980s: State-Centric v. Multi-level Governance', *Journal of Common Market Studies*, 34:3, pp. 341–78.

Marshall, T.H. (1950) *Citizenship and Social Class and Other Essays*, Cambridge: Cambridge University Press.

Martin, D.A. and T.A. Aleinikoff (2002) 'Double Ties. Why nations should learn to love dual nationality', *Foreign Policy*, November–December, pp. 80–2.

Martinussen, J. (1980) *The Public Industrial Sector in India*, Aarhus: Dept of Political Science.

McGrew, T. (2000) 'From Global Governance to Good Governance: Theories and Prospects of Democratizing the Global Polity', Copenhagen: Workshop on The Global Polity.

Mearsheimer, J. (1991) 'Back to the Future: Instability in Europe After the Cold War', in S. Lynn-Jones (ed.), *The Cold War and After: Prospects for Peace*, Cambridge, MA: MIT Press, pp. 141–92.

Mendelson, S.E. (2002) 'Russians' Rights Imperilled: Has Anybody Noticed?', *International Security*, 26:4, pp. 39–70.

Miller, J.D.B. (1981) *The World of States. Connected Essays*, New York: St Martin's Press.

Miller, S. (2001) '*International Security* at Twenty-five', *International Security*, 26:1, pp. 5–39.

Morgenthau, H. (1966) *Politics Among Nations: The Struggle for Power and Peace*, New York: Alfred Knopf.

Moss, A.G. and H.N.M. Winton (1977) *A New International Economic Order. Selected Documents 1945–75*, 2 vols, New York: UNITAR.

Mueller, J. (1989) *Retreat from Doomsday: The Obsolescence of Major War*, New York: Basic Books.

Naisbitt, J. (1994) *The Global Paradox*, New York: Avon.

Nathan, A.J. (1986) *Chinese Democracy*, London: Tauris.

Ndegwa, S.N. (1997) 'Citizenship and Ethnicity: An Examination of Two Transition Moments in Kenyan Politics', *American Political Science Review*, 91:3, pp. 599–617.

North, D.C. (1990) *Institutions, Institutional Change and Economic Performance*, Cambridge: Cambridge University Press.

Nye, J.S. (1990) *Bound to Lead: The Changing Nature of American Power*, New York: Basic Books.

Nye, J.S. (1997) *Understanding International Conflicts*, New York: Longman.

Nye, J.S. (2001) 'Globalization's Democratic Deficit', *Foreign Affairs*, July–August, 80:4, pp. 2–6.

Nye, J.S. (2002) *The Paradox of American Power*, Oxford: Oxford University Press.

Nye, J.S. and J.D. Donahue (eds) (2000) *Governance in a Globalizing World*, Washington, DC: Brookings.

Ohmae, K. (1996) *The End of the Nation State: The Rise of Regional Economics*, London: HarperCollins.

Ostrom, V. and E. Ostrom (1999) 'Public Goods and Public Choices', in M. McGinnis (ed.), *Polycentricity and Local Public Economies. Reading from the Workshop in Political Theory and Policy Analysis*, Ann Arbor, MI: University of Michigan Press, pp. 75–105.

Ottaway, M. (1995) 'Democratization in Collapsed States', in W.I. Zartman (ed.), *Collapsed States. The Disintegration and Restoration of Legitimate Authority*, Boulder, CO: Lynne Rienner, pp. 235–51.

Ougaard, M. and R. Higgott (2002) 'Introduction', in M. Ougaard and R. Higgott (eds), *Towards a Global Polity*, London: Routledge, pp. 1–20.

Owen, J.M. (2001/02) 'Transnational Liberalism and U.S. Primacy', *International Security*, 26:3, pp. 117–53.

Polanyi, K. (1957 [1944]) *The Great Transformation: The Political and Economic Origins of Our Time*, Boston, MA: Beacon Books.

Porter, B.D. (1994) *War and Rise of the State. The Military Foundations of Modern Politics*, New York: The Free Press.

Radice, H. (1984) 'The National Economy – A Keynesian Myth?', *Capital and Class*, 22, pp. 111–40.

Radice, H. (1999) 'Taking globalisation seriously', in L. Panitch and C. Leys (eds), *The Socialist Register 1999: Global Capitalism versus Democracy*, Woodbridge: Merlin Press.

Rasmussen, E. (1971) *Komparativ politik 1* [Comparative Politics], Copenhagen: Gyldendal.

Reinicke, W.H. (2000) 'The Other World Wide Web: Global Public Policy Networks', *Foreign Policy*, 117 (Winter), pp. 44–57.

Reno, W. (2000) 'Sovereignty and Personal Rule in Zaire', http://web.africa.ufl.edu/asq/v1/3/4.htm

Rieger, E. and S. Leibfried (1998) 'Welfare state limits to globalization', *Politics & Society*, 26:3, pp. 363–90.

Riskin, C. (1987) *China's Political Economy. The Quest for Development since 1949*, Oxford: Oxford University Press.

Roberts, A. (1996) 'Humanitarian Action in War', *Adelphi Paper 305*, London: International Institute for Strategic Studies.

Rodrik, D. (1997) *Has Globalization Gone Too Far?*, Washington, DC: Institute of International Economics.

Rodrik, D. (1998) 'Why Do More Open Economies Have Bigger Government?', *Journal of Political Economy*, 106, pp. 997–1,032.

Rosecrance, R. (1995) 'The Obsolescence of Territory', *New Perspectives Quarterly*, 12:1, pp. 44–50.

Rosecrance, R. (1999) *The Rise of the Virtual State*, New York: Basic Books.

Rosenau, J.N. (1990) *Turbulence in World Politics. A Theory of Change and Continuity*, Princeton, NJ: Princeton University Press.

Rosenau, J.N. (1993) 'Citizenship in a Changing Global Order', in J.N. Rosenau, and E.-O. Czempiel (eds), *Governance without Government: Order and*

Change in World Politics, Cambridge: Cambridge University Press, pp. 272–95.

Rosenau, J.N. (1997) *Along the Domestic–Foreign Frontier. Exploring Governance in a Turbulent World*, Cambridge: Cambridge University Press.

Rosenau, J.N. and E.-O. Czempiel (eds) (1993). *Governance without Government: Order and Change in World Politics*, Cambridge: Cambridge University Press.

Rostow, W.W. (1960) *The Stages of Economic Growth: A Non-Communist Manifesto*, Cambridge: Cambridge University Press.

Rostow, W.W. (1978) *The World Economy: History and Prospect*, Austin, TX: University of Texas Press.

Royal Institute of International Affairs (1968) 'The rise of National Feeling in Western Europe', in Reinhard Bendix (ed.), *State and Society*, Berkeley, CA: University of California Press, pp. 215–30.

Rudra, A. (1985) 'Planning in India: An Evaluation in Terms of its Models', *Economic and Political Weekly*, xx:17, pp. 758–65.

Ruggie, J.G. (1982) 'International regimes, transactions, and change: embedded liberalism in the postwar economic order', *International Organization*, 36:2, pp. 195–231.

Ruggie, J.G. (1997) 'Globalization and the Embedded Liberalism Compromise: The End of an Era?', working paper 97/1, Frankfurt: Max Planck Institute for the Study of Societies.

Ruggie, J.G. (1998) *Constructing the World Polity*, London: Routledge.

Rustow, D.A. (1970) 'Transitions to Democracy', *Comparative Politics*, 2:3, pp. 337–65.

Ryle, G. (1968) *The Concept of Mind*, Harmondsworth: Penguin.

Sandbrook, R. (2000) *Closing the Circle. Democratization and Development in Africa*, London: Zed Books.

Sandy, G. (1997) 'Globalization and Economic Reform in India', *Australian Journal of International Affairs*, 51:1, pp. 73–91.

Sassen, S. (1997) *Losing Control? Sovereignty in an Age of Globalization*, New York: Columbia University Press.

Saunders, P.J. (2001) 'Why "Globalization" didn't Rescue Russia', *Policy Review*, 105, pp. 27–40.

Scharpf, F.W. (1991) *Crisis and Choice in European Social Democracy*, trans. by R. Crowley and F. Thompson, Ithaca, NY: Cornell University Press.

Scharpf, F.W. (1997) 'Introduction: the problem solving capacity of multi-level governance', *Journal of European Public Policy*, 4:4, pp. 520–38.

Schmitter, P. (1999) 'The Future of Democracy: Could it be a Matter of Scale?', *Social Research*, 66:3, pp. 933–58.

Scholte, J.A. (1997) 'Global Capitalism and the State', *International Affairs*, 73:3, pp. 427–52.

Scholte, J.A. (2000) *Globalization – A Critical Introduction*, London: Macmillan.

Schroeder, P. (1985) 'Does Murphy's Law Apply to History?', *The Wilson Quarterly*, 9:1, pp. 82–93.

Schwartz, H. (2000) *States versus Markets. The Emergence of a Global Economy*, London: Macmillan.

Senghaas, D. (1985) *The European Experience. A Historical Critique of Development Theory*, Leamington Spa: Berg.

Skocpol, T. (1979) *States and Social Revolutions*, Cambridge, MA: Cambridge University Press.

Slaughter, A.-M. (1997) 'The Real New World Order', *Foreign Affairs*, 76:5, October, pp. 183–98.

Smith, A.D. (1992) 'National Identity and the Idea of European Unity', *International Affairs*, 68, pp. 55–76.

Smith, A.D. (1995) *Nations and Nationalism in a Global Era*, Cambridge: Polity Press.

Smitu, K. (1997) 'Whose Independence? The Social Impact of Economic Reform in India', *Journal of International Affairs*, 51:1, pp. 85–117.

Snyder, F. (1999) 'Global Economic Networks and Global Legal Pluralism', papers from European University Institute, Law No. 99/6.

Soederberg, S. (2001) 'Deconstructing the IMF's recent bid for transparency', *Third World Quarterly*, 22:5, pp. 849–64.

Sørensen, G. (1983) *Transnationale selskaber og udviklingsprocessen i perifere samfund*, [Transnational Corporations and the Development Process in Peripheral Societies], Aalborg: Aalborg University Press.

Sørensen, G. (1991) *Democracy, Dictatorship and Development. Economic Development in Selected Regimes of the Third World*, London: Macmillan.

Sørensen, G. (1993) 'Democracy, Authoritarianism and State Strength', in G. Sørensen (ed.), *Political Conditionality*, London: Frank Cass, pp. 5–35.

Sørensen, G. (1998) *Democracy and Democratization. Processes and Prospects in a Changing World*, 2nd edn, Boulder, CO: Westview.

Sørensen, G. (1999) 'Sovereignty: Change and Continuity in a Fundamental Institution', *Political Studies*, 47:3, pp. 590–604.

Sørensen, G. (2001) *Changes in Statehood. The Transformation of International Relations*, Basingstoke: Palgrave.

Soroos, M.J. (1986) *Beyond Sovereignty: The Challenge of Global Policy*, Columbia, SC: University of South Carolina Press.

Soto, H. de (2001) *The Mystery of Capital: Why Capitalism Triumphs in the West and Fails Everywhere Else*, New York: Basic Books.

Soysal, Y.N. (1994) *Limits of Citizenship. Migrants and Postnational Membership in Europe*, Chicago, IL: University of Chicago Press.

Spruyt, H. (1994) *The Sovereign State and its Competitors*, Princeton, NJ: Princeton University Press.

Steinmo, S. (1993) *Taxation and Democracy*, New Haven, CT: Yale University Press.

Stelzer, I. (1999) 'The Welfare State Lives On (Alas)', *New Statesman*, 128:4,418, pp. 29–30.

Stone, D. (2002) 'Knowledge networks and policy expertise in the global polity', in M. Ougaard and R. Higgott (eds), *Towards a Global Polity*, London: Routledge, pp. 125–44.

Stopford, J. and S. Strange with J.S. Henley (1993) *Rival States, Rival Firms. Competition for World Market Shares*, Cambridge: Cambridge University Press.

Strange, S. (1996) *The Retreat of the State. The Diffusion of Power in the World Economy*, Cambridge: Cambridge University Press.

Sunkel, O. and E.F. Fuenzalida (1979) 'Transnationalization and its National Consequences', in J.J. Villamil (ed.), *Transnational Capitalism and National Development*, Hassocks: Harvester Press, pp. 67–95.

Swamy, A.R. (2002) 'India in 2001. A Year of Living Dangerously', *Asian Survey*, 42:1, pp. 165–76.

Swank, D. (2001) 'Social Democratic Welfare States in a Global Economy: Scandinavia in Comparative Perspective', in R. Geyer, C. Ingebritsen and J. Moses (eds), *Globalization, Europeanization, and the End of Scandinavian Social Democracy?*, New York: St Martin's Press, pp. 85–138.

Swank, D. (2002) *Global Capital, Political Institutions, and Policy Change in Developed Welfare States*, Cambridge: Cambridge University Press.

Taylor, L. (1997) 'The Revival of the Liberal Creed – the IMF and the World Bank in a Globalized Economy', *World Development*, 25:2, pp. 145–52.

Thomas, C. (2000) *Global Governance, Development, and Human Security*, London: Pluto Press.

Thomson, J.E. and S.D. Krasner (1989) 'Global Transactions and the Consolidation of Sovereignty', in E.-O. Czempiel and J.N. Rosenau (eds), *Global Changes and Theoretical Challenges. Approaches to World Politics for the 1990s*, Lexington, MA: Lexington Books, pp. 195–220.

Thurston, A.F. (1984/5) 'Victims of China's Cultural Revolution: The Invisible Wounds', *Pacific Affairs*, 57:4, pp. 599–620.

Tilly, C. (1985) 'War Making and State Making as Organized Crime', in P. Evans, D. Rueschemeyer and T. Skocpol (eds), *Bringing the State Back In*, Cambridge: Cambridge University Press, pp. 169–91.

Tilly, C. (1992) *Coercion, Capital, and European States, AD 990–1990*, Oxford: Basil Blackwell.

UNITAR (United Nations Institute for Training and Research) (1976) 'Resolution 3201', proceedings from the Non-Aligned Movement, New York: UNITAR Document Service, vol. II.

United Nations (1997) *World Investment Report 1997*, New York: UN.

United Nations Conference on Trade and Development (1993) *World Investment Report 1993: Transnational Corporations and Integrated International Production*, New York: UN.

Vogel, S.K. (1996) *Freer Markets, More Rules. Regulatory Reform in Advanced Industrial Countries*, Ithaca, NY: Cornell University Press.

Wade, R. (2001) 'Winners and Losers', *The Economist*, 28 April, pp. 93–97.

Waever, O. (1998) 'Explaining Europe by Decoding Discourses', in A. Wivel (ed.), *Explaining European Integration*, Copenhagen: Copenhagen Political Studies Press, pp. 100–46.

Wallensteen, P. and M. Sollenberg (1999) 'Armed Conflict 1988–1998', *Journal of Peace Research*, 36:5, pp. 593–607.

Wallerstein, I. (1974) *The Modern World System*, New York: Academic Press.

Waltz, K.N. (1979) *Theory of International Politics*, Reading, MA: Addison-Wesley.

Waltz, K.N. (1986) 'Reflections on *Theory of International Politics*: A Response to My Critics', in R.O. Keohane (ed.), *Neorealism and its Critics*, New York: Columbia University Press, pp. 322–47.

Waltz, K.N. (1993) 'The Emerging Structure of International Politics', *International Security*, 18:2, pp. 44–79.

Waltz, K.N. (2002) 'The Continuity of International Politics', in K. Booth and T. Dunne (eds), *Worlds in Collision*, Basingstoke: Palgrave, pp. 348–55.

Weiss, L. (1998) *The Myth of the Powerless State: Governing the Economy in a Global Era*, Cambridge: Polity Press.

Weiss, L. (ed.) (2003) *States in the Global Economy: Bringing Domestic Institutions Back In*, Cambridge: Cambridge University Press.

Welsh, J. (1993) 'A People's Europe? European Citizenship and European Identity', working paper 93/2, Florence: European University Institute.

Wendt, A. (1999) *Social Theory of International Politics*, Cambridge: Cambridge University Press.

Williamson, J. (1990) 'What Washington Means by Policy Reform', in J. Williamson (ed.), *Latin American Adjustment: How Much has Happened?*, Washington, DC: Institute for International Economics, ch. 2.

Womack, B. (1987) 'The Party and the People: Revolutionary and Postrevolutionary Politics in China and Vietnam', *World Politics*, 29:4, pp. 479–507.

World Bank (1994) *Adjustment in Africa: Reforms, Results, and the Road Ahead*, New York: Oxford University Press.

World Bank (1997) *World Development Report 1997*, New York: Oxford University Press.

World Bank (2000) *Entering the 21st Century. World Development Report 1999/2000*, New York: Oxford University Press.

World Bank (2002) *World Development Report 2002*, New York: Oxford University Press.

World Bank (2003) *World Development Report 2003*, New York: Oxford University Press.

Wriston, W.B. (1992) *The Twilight of Sovereignty: How the Information Revolution is Transforming Our World*, New York: Charles Scribner's Sons.

Young, C. and T. Turner (1985) *The Rise and Decline of the Zairian State*, Madison, WI: University of Wisconsin Press.

Zacher, M.V. (1992) 'The decaying pillars of the Westphalian temple: implications for international order and governance', in J.N. Rosenau and E.-O. Czempiel (eds), *Governance without Government: Order and Change in World Politics*, Cambridge: Cambridge University Press, pp. 58–102.

Zartman, W.I. (1995) 'Introduction: Posing the Problem of State Collapse' and ch. 17 ('Putting Things Back Together'), in W.I. Zartman (ed.), *Collapsed States. The Disintegration and Restoration of Legitimate Authority*, Boulder, CO: Lynne Rienner, pp. 1–15; 267–73.

Zürn, M. (1998) *Regieren jenseits des Nationaalstaates. Globalisierung und Denationalisierung als Chance* [Government/Governance beyond the

Nation-State: Globalization and Denationalization as Opportunity], Frankfurt am Main: Suhrkamp.

Zürn, M. (1999) 'The State in the Post-National Constellation – Societal Denationalization and Multilevel Governance', working paper, University of Bremen.

Zürn, M. (2000) 'Democratic Governance Beyond the Nation-State: The EU and Other International Institutions', *European Journal of International Relations*, 6:2, pp. 183–221.

Index